WITHDRAWN
L. R. COLLEGE LIBRARY

W9-AEV-983

832.6
Sch3w

91321

DATE DUE			

WITHDRAWN
L. R. COLLEGE LIBRARY

WALLENSTEIN

A Dramatic Poem

FRIEDRICH von SCHILLER

WALLENSTEIN

*A Historical Drama
in Three Parts*

WALLENSTEIN'S CAMP

THE PICCOLOMINIS

THE DEATH OF WALLENSTEIN

Translated by
CHARLES E. PASSAGE
*Assistant Professor of World Literature
Brooklyn College*

Revised Edition

FREDERICK UNGAR PUBLISHING CO.
NEW YORK

CARL A. RUDISILL LIBRARY
LENOIR RHYNE COLLEGE
HICKORY, N. C. 28601

832.6
Sch3w
91321
Jan. 1975

Third Printing, 1963

Copyright 1958, 1960 by Frederick Ungar Publishing Co.

Printed in the United States of America

Library of Congress Catalog Card No. 60-15799

INTRODUCTION

In 1618, one hundred and one years after the beginning of the Protestant Reformation, the smouldering fire of religious conflict burst into raging flame. At first it seemed as though the fire might be different neither in kind nor in degree from the four civil wars that had seared the history of France during that century, or from the intermittent disorders in England, in the Netherlands, or in German territory itself through the same period. Indeed, toward the year 1600 it looked as if Europe had, district by district, settled itself into fixed compartments according to the options of rulers and people either for the old Catholicism or for one of the new faiths. There were even signs, such as King Henry IV's Edict of Nantes in France, to suggest the grudging concession to coexistence of different faiths within a single dominion. The depth of latent fires, especially in central Europe, was underestimated. In 1618 such a conflagration developed as no one could control or stop, and it was to rage for thirty years.

It began in the German principalities, those three hundred and more sovereign and independent countries of assorted sizes and importance which nominally paid allegiance to the Holy Roman Emperor; specifically, it began in the Kingdom of Bohemia, the core of modern Czechoslovakia, which for long ages had formed one of the principal jewels in the crown of the Holy Roman Empire.

In 1609 (the year Hendryk Hudson discovered Manhattan Island), the aging Emperor Rudolf II had persuaded the

Bohemians to elect his brother Mathias as their king, and in exchange had granted them—for all that he disapproved of such things—a charter that guaranteed religious toleration. As the years of Mathias's reign went on, however, Bohemian Protestants had more than one violation of the charter to complain of, and they complained in vain. When, in 1617, the childless Mathias persuaded his subjects to accept his nephew, Ferdinand II, as their king and then offered a renewal of the charter to sweeten the bargain, certain restive leaders, especially Count Thurn, determined to press for more effective guarantees for Protestants' rights. A Diet was summoned to deal with the issue. Ferdinand II forbade the Diet to meet. The Diet defied him, and in his absence from Prague, assembled on the fateful May 21, 1618. An angry deputation made its way to the Hradshin Palace, confronted the absent King's Regents, Martinitz and Slawata, and demanded to know precisely who had declared the Diet illegal. When no satisfactory answer was forthcoming, the furious delegates seized the two Regents, together with their secretary, and threw them out of one of the upper-story windows of the building. The three men personally survived their fall in this "Defenestration of Prague" but the grotesque incident was the provocation to a vast war.

Not satisfied with this step, the Diet next demanded that Ferdinand himself relinquish the kingship so that a Protestant might be put in his place. Ferdinand understandably refused. The Diet defied him further, chose a rival king, and invited the latter to appear in Prague forthwith. Their choice had fallen on Frederick V, who from his capital in Heidelberg ruled the area known as the Rhine Palatinate—at the opposite extremity of the Empire. Frederick saw the peril in accepting such an invitation but was inclined to take the risk. He consulted with his royal father-in-law, King James I of England, who urged him to decline the dangerous offer. Still Frederick leaned toward acceptance. The autumn of 1618 found him in Prague. Opinion held that he would be lucky if he lasted the winter. He did last the winter—and no more. Ignominiously fleeing from Prague the following spring, he bore with him the name of "the Winter King'" into exile, for this grandfather of England's first King George was never again to enter either Prague or Heidelberg, and his existence was to be one long and sour peregrination with his consort and his large brood of children from one Protestant court of Europe to another, a superflous guest to the end of his days.

The Catholic armies of the Emperor which now moved into Bohemia found Protestant defiance strong but Protestant generalship divided. A series of minor victories marked their cause, and then, on November 8, 1620 (the month and year when the Pilgrims landed at Plymouth Rock), in the battle of White Hill outside of Prague, they inflicted a major defeat upon the insurgents. For five years thereafter sullen guerilla warfare brought the Protestants total loss of Bohemia in the east and total loss of Frederick's Palatinate in the west. The war seemed all but over.

Meanwhile the conflict had been watched with mounting concern by the Protestant monarchs of northern Europe, yet none had ventured to intervene. By 1625, however, Christian IV of Denmark decided to come to the aid of his fellow religionists. With money supplied in part by England and the Netherlands he began raising an army with which to oppose the Emperor's undefeated General Tilly. Alarm seized the Imperial council in Vienna. The victories had cost the Empire dearly. Finances were strained. How was a huge new counterforce to be paid for?

Unexpectedly the dilemma was solved when a private individual made the Emperor a flabbergastingly generous offer. Albrecht Waldstein, or Wallenstein, titled master of the district of Friedland in Bohemia, himself a Catholic convert from Lutheranism, proposed to recruit 20,000 men, pay them out of his personal fortune, and put them at the Emperor's disposal. There was no alternative but to accept, chafe as the Emperor might at the embarrassment of being bailed out of his troubles by one of his subjects and chafe as the generals might at the prospect of a rival to their prestige. General Tilly in particular did not relish sharing his power with the upstart. Religious bigots questioned the good faith of the convert.

The legend of Wallenstein's wealth attracted more nearly 30,000 than 20,000 men, and by early spring of 1626 the man himself seemed to be showing ample justification of the command with which the Emperor had felt obliged to invest him. While Tilly faced the Danes in the north, Wallenstein attacked the Protestant General Mansfeld, drove him through Silesia, through Moravia, into Hungary, and there defeated him utterly in 1627. With each victory the Emperor had felt bound to reward him with new titles, new authority, and new grants of lands. Tilly's noteworthy but inconclusive victory over the Danes meanwhile seemed slight by comparison with the spectacular pursuit and annihilation of Mansfeld's forces. Presently even that victory was eclipsed, for Wallenstein, heading north, joined Tilly, invaded Denmark itself, and conquered the whole country. In 1628 Wallenstein's opponents might gloat over his failure to reduce the independent seaport of Stralsund on the Baltic, which he had vowed to take, but the failure hardly dimmed the upstart's prestige. In 1629 the victors permitted Christian IV to resume his rule over Denmark on the condition of his solemn promise to interfere no further in the conflict. Again the war seemed all but over.

It was now the turn of Protestant Sweden to attempt what the Danes had failed to accomplish. In 1630 King Gustavus Adolphus, personally commanding a force of 12,000 Swedes, landed on the Baltic coast of the Germanies.

The entry of Sweden, however, was motivated by more than the defeat of their Danish friends. In the flush of victory over Denmark the Emperor, spurred on by the Catholic League, promulgated the Edict of Restitution, whereby all church lands lost since 1552—half a century before the war began!—had to be returned by the Protestants who had captured them. The Edict recognized the Lutheran faith, but, by ignoring the Calvinist minority, made the latter illegal and opened the way to its extermination. The Protestants thus had a fair idea of what would happen to them all in the event of total Catholic victory. As if this measure were not unwisdom enough, the Emperor proceeded to a second unwise act at the very moment of the arrival of the Swedish armies: he yielded to the jealous pressures of his advisors and dismissed Wallenstein from command. In fairness to the Emperor it must be said that the hapless monarch was forced to this step by desperate lack of money and by political forces completely beyond his control. Wallenstein, for his part, withdrew quietly to private life to await his inevitable recall, for the Swedes were fast advancing into the heart of Germany.

At first, Gustavus Adolphus, the Swedish king, sparred with General Tilly. Each took turns destroying a city held by his opponent and each sought to outdo the other in example-setting slaughter of civilians. In the sack of Magdeburg Tilly was estimated to have killed all but 5,000 of the town's 35,000 inhabitants. At last the two commanders met at Breitenfeld, near Leipzig, and in a battle which in retrospect could be identified as the turning point of the war, Tilly met disastrous defeat. It was the first real Protestant victory, and it brought into the war as active participants the Protestant states of Brandenburg, Saxony, and Weimar, as well as eliciting financial support for the Protestant cause from Catholic France! For Cardinal Richelieu, the head of the French state in all but name, understood that total victory for Catholic

Austria and the Empire would mean encirclement of France, as in the disastrous days of 1525, and possible annihilation, and he was determined to forestall that eventuality.

By October 1631 the Emperor's representatives were begging Wallenstein to resume command. Wallenstein declined. In November they urged anew, with the same result. In December a more urgent appeal was made to him at Znaim. Wallenstein agreed to raise a new army but refused to lead it. By April 1632 the magic of his name had attracted between 40,000 and 50,000 recruits. Still he refused to command them. The Swedes were now masters of something like a half of German territory and advancing toward the Catholic heartlands of Bavaria and Austria themselves. General Tilly, since his defeat near Leipzig, seemed unable to produce a victory. On April 15 he was killed in battle while resisting the Swedish thrust into Bavaria. Then a still more frantic appeal was addressed to Wallenstein. This time he accepted command, driving a hard bargain as he did so, and receiving powers as made him the equal of an independent sovereign. Little more than his personal word was left to make him responsible to the Emperor.

Immediately upon taking command of the new army Wallenstein recaptured Bohemia from the Protestant Saxons who had taken it the previous year. Next he marched against Gustavus Adolphus himself. To the amazement of everyone, he suddenly stopped short, avoided battle, and took up a strong defensive position near Nürnberg in northern Bavaria. Gustavus also halted. For nine weeks the two armies faced each other without making a move. On September 3 Gustavus attacked and lost heavily. Wallenstein, as if scorning to bother further with him, marched away toward Saxony, presumably to punish the Saxons for entering the war. In Saxony he directly captured Leipzig, the chief city. The Saxons urgently called for the Swedes, who had remained in Bavaria. The

INTRODUCTION xi

Swedes moved toward Saxony. On November 16 there was
fought the appalling battle of Lützen with its immense losses
in all the armies. Gustavus Adolphus himself was killed.

Wallenstein now proposed a general peace. The Emperor
refused the principal concession of granting religious toleration, without which the Protestants would not budge. The
Swedes also demanded territorial compensation in Germany
which the Emperor refused to consider.

From this point onward Wallenstein's conduct becomes
ambiguous. In May of 1633 he moved into Silesia, where
Protestant forces of Brandenburg and Saxony were massed,
but did not attack them. In a relatively small engagement at
Steinau on October 11 he did defeat a Protestant army, but
then took it upon himself to barter for the evacuation of the
rest of Silesia by setting free the captured Protestant leaders,
most particularly Count Thurn. When the Emperor urgently
warned him that Protestant Prince Bernhard of Weimar was
about to attack Bavaria, he claimed to be sure that Bernhard's
real plan was to attack Bohemia; when Bernhard attacked
Bavaria after all and captured the major town of Regensburg
(Ratisbon), Wallenstein belatedly set out to attack him. The
march, however, was halted midway and Wallenstein took up
winter quarters at Pilsen in Bohemia without coming anywhere near Bernhard. It began to look as though Wallenstein
were undertaking to conclude the war and make a European
peace over the heads of all parties belligerent. The Emperor,
having resigned to him all real power, could protest and plead
with him, but he could do little more than to protest and
plead. Catholic leaders were furious at what they considered
outright betrayal of their cause.

Such was the situation in the winter of 1633-1634, with
Protestant armies holding the northeast, the north, and the
southwest of German territory, with Catholic leaders having at
their disposal no really effective instrument other than

Wallenstein's army, and with Wallenstein deliberately refusing to move. With court approval he had been negotiating with the chiefs of certain Protestant states, but it was suspected and more than suspected that either he, or persons acting for him, was making secret bargains which the court would never approve. One rumor had it that he was planning a coup d'état to the end of becoming Emperor himself. In Vienna it became a fixed resolution to stop him at all costs, by assassination if necessary.

Schiller's drama opens at this point; it ends with the assassination of Wallenstein on February 25, 1634.

As for the war, fourteen years of its thirty-year course were yet to be run. Immediately after Wallenstein's murder events seemed to justify the deed. Catholic armies led by the Emperor's son, the future Ferdinand III, retook Regensburg from Bernhard and elsewhere fought the Swedes and Saxons to a standstill. Peace was again discussed in May of 1635, but it was frustrated by the Emperor's refusal to grant religious toleration to the Calvinists.

It was now that Cardinal Richelieu determined to widen his policy from indirect support of states opposing the Empire to active intervention. Invasion eastward from France into the Rhine districts would sever the lines of communication between the Empire's staunch ally, Spain, and the Spanish Netherlands and simultaneously break the iron ring that the Empire held girt around France. Ultimately there might be realized the age-old dream of making the Rhine the eastern boundary of France. Thus the major battles of the second half of the war were fought most often in the west and south of the Germanies, the very areas hitherto relatively unaffected. Campaigns followed campaigns, years followed years. Many of the principal personages associated with the war died: Emperor Ferdinand II in 1637, Prince Bernhard in 1639, Richelieu in 1642. Armistice was discussed in 1643 and 1644.

One by one, the Catholic leaders were conceding the necessity
of making peace. Not so Maximilian of Bavaria, one of the few
survivors from the heart of the events of 1618. French armies
under Marshal Turenne invaded Bavaria in 1646 and for two
years wrought such havoc in Maximilian's lands that even he
agreed to come to terms. The signing of the Treaty of Westphalia in 1648 at last brought the weary conclusion. Luther-
ism and Calvinism were officially recognized, and a less strin-
gent version of the Edict of Restitution established ownership
of church lands as of 1624. The independence of the Netherlands was recognized. Sweden was accorded relatively small
territoral compensation in northern Germany. Brandenburg
—the future Prussia—received significant extension of boundaries. France gained Alsace. Imperial Austria gained almost
nothing. Europe was now massively divided into Protestant
north and Catholic south, each too powerful for the other to
attack, each intensely hostile to the other. The Germanies
were an economic, physical, and moral wreck.

Into four days' time Schiller has condensed the events of the
entire winter of 1633-1634 which culminated in the assassination of Wallenstein on the midnight of February 25, 1634.
These events, and indeed the events of the entire war, were
perfectly well known to him, for, as Professor of History at the
University of Jena since 1789 and as author of a scholarly
History of the Thirty Years' War (written 1791-1799), he had
long been immersed in close study of them. It is therefore
extremely interesting to observe what changes and modifications of fact he made in the creation of his trilogy of dramas
as he gradually planned them through the middle 1790's and
finally wrote them in the years 1796-1799. By and large he was
faithful to history.

Two deputations to Wallenstein from court, one by Count
Trautmannsdorf in December of 1633 and one by Father

Quiroga on January 5, 1634, have been blended into one, with Questenberg as the bearer of their joint messages. Count Trautmannsdorf's deputation did occasion an officers' council very much like that represented in *Picc*. II. The banquet of *Picc*. IV took place on January 12, though the signing of the pledge of loyalty to Wallenstein by the forty-nine officers did not lead to the striking dramatic finale of that scene. Schiller, as dramatist, makes much of a contemporary legend which claimed that the pledge had originally contained a clause delimiting the terms to such acts as would not conflict with prior oaths of loyalty to the Emperor, but that Wallenstein himself struck out the clause when the document was submitted to his inspection before the banquet. On the following day, January 13, the historical Wallenstein assembled his officers to assure them that no attack was contemplated against either the Emperor or the Catholic religion. His sole purpose, he avowed, was to carry on negotiations for peace. News of the pledge-signing reached the court directly and Imperial orders dated January 24 relieved all officers of their allegiance to their "late commander-in-chief" and pardoned all signers except Illo and Terzky. Further *secret* orders to loyal officers issued directions to assist in the capture of Wallenstein, dead or alive. Count Gallas, not Octavio Piccolomini, was designated temporary Generalissimo. At the same time, however, the court maintained the pretense of normal relations with the Commander at Pilsen until February 17. When the open break came it took the form of a public accusation of treason, with plan to seize the kingship of Bavaria, and of confiscation of Wallenstein's considerable lands, their price of sale to be distributed among his army. This last detail is significant, for Wallenstein's men were bound to him less by the enthusiasms which Schiller attributes to them than by the money they had risked in his name. Thus Count Isolani's motives and conduct are more nearly typical of the historical state of affairs than

are those of either Buttler or Max Piccolomini, and indeed it
was the tenuously selfish nature of allegiances which enabled
the court to proceed so boldly against him.

Illo and Terzky were the ringleaders in Wallenstein's conspiracy, and together with Terzky's brother-in-law Kinsky,
who was in Dresden, the capital of Saxony, they did carry on
dubious negotiations with Protestant rulers. They did so, however, with Wallenstein's full knowledge. In some, but not all
instances Wallenstein displayed the reluctance, which Schiller
makes total, to commit documents to his handwriting. The
go-between was Sesina, but he was never captured by anyone;
he did purchase his own safety after Wallenstein's death by
making a long "confession." Chancellor Oxenstjerna of
Sweden was even more skeptical of Wallenstein's intentions
than his messenger in *Death* II indicates. Prince Bernhard of
Weimar, on the other hand, did take seriously Wallenstein's
appeal for help and did march to his defense. Had his own
doubts been less and his hesitation briefer, he might have
arrived at Eger in time to alter the outcome. Schiller assigns
this march to Wallenstein's assistance to the Rhinegrave
rather than to Bernhard, and makes relatively little of the
motif.

After the defection of his troops Wallenstein set out on
February 23 for the fortress town of Eger. He was ill enough
to require being carried, but his spirit was undaunted. On the
way his small force was augmented by Colonel Buttler with
some two hundred cavalry men. Gordon and Lessley, two
Scotch Presbyterians loyal to the Catholic faction in whose
services they were, admitted the fugitive to Eger, fully aware
of the plans for his capture, but not for his murder. At Buttler's implacable demands they balked considerably, but Lessley was finally persuaded to the murder of Illo and Terzky,
and he in turn persuaded the reluctant Gordon to take part.
The grim plan was carried out, as in the play, at a banquet

on the evening of the 25th. Illo, Terzky, Kinsky, and Wallenstein's secretary Neumann were there slain. Illo's ferocious
self-defense to the last is historical fact. Directly afterward
Buttler and Captain Deveroux, together with a few soldiers,
invaded the Commander's sleeping quarters. Wallenstein, just
awakened by the cry "Traitors!", stretched out his arms as
though welcoming the death blow, and said not a word.
Gallas, Piccolomini, and the other counter-conspirators were
well rewarded out of the dead man's estates.

The characters of the drama, however, by contrast with the
events, have been altered with greater latitude. The actual
Questenberg, for example, was one of Wallenstein's most
doggedly faithful supporters, and it is somewhat puzzling that
the author should have selected his name for the character
who blends three or four of the hero's adversaries. For quick
reference to the fact and fiction relative to the personages of
the drama the reader may consult the alphabetical *List of
Persons* (pages xxv-xxxix), but in considering the manipula-
tions of the major characters one may come close to the heart of
Schiller's poetic purpose.

The historical Wallenstein was a cold man, aloof from his
soldiers and even from his officers, objectively concerned with
generalship and diplomacy and with vast projects of government. In the management of his estates as in the administra-
tion of the territories awarded to him for his services to the
Emperor, he displayed severity combined with utter fairness
and shrewd common sense, but of personal affections there
was little trace. Rather, he cultivated an ostentatious cere-
mony around his person. He was fond of public pronounce-
ments of his own achievements as well as of his scathing judg-
ments on his rivals and opponents. In religious matters he was
a loyal Catholic but also a firm believer in religious toleration. In war he was consistently shrewd and cautious rather
than picturesquely gallant and bold. His concern with

astrology is factual, but he was simultaneously an able econo-
mist, an administrator of mines, factories, trades, and schools.
To his Duchess he was a devoted husband, but he did not
confide his plans to her nor did he have her with him at the
period represented in the play, any more than he had with
him his only child—a ten-year-old daughter named Marie.

Such was the man from the Age of Reason into whom
Schiller infused the qualities appropriate to the Age of
Romantic Sensitivity and juxtaposed with wife, maiden
daughter, affiliates by marriage, foster-son, and devoted friend,
in short, with all the objects of tender affection. In the drama
this personality from the age of Kepler and Newton must
move to its destiny while bearing in his bosom a Rousseauistic
heart.

In 1634 the historical Octavio Piccolomini was thirty-three
years old and unmarried. His connection with Wallenstein
dated only from 1629, and though he was highly regarded by
his chief, especially for his bravery at the battle of Lützen,
there was no question of an intimate trust such as the dramatist presents. It would seem that Schiller selected this officer
almost at random from among Wallenstein's cadre to develop
into the complex and fascinating figure of the play—older,
more subtle, deeper and more intense, faintly satanic for all
his devotion to law and duty, the rationalist and the realist.
He possesses precisely those qualities which would, in Wallenstein, have averted calamity, and there is a profound ironic
truth in Wallenstein's attraction toward him. And yet not
all the right is on Octavio's side by any means. He too betrays
and in the end finds his own hell in the loss of the son that,
in real life, he never had. For Max, like Thekla, is solely the
product of the dramatist's imagination.

Max and Thekla, fictitious though they are, were all but
indispensable if the drama was not to become an unrelievedly
sombre chronicle of a certain political disaster of long ago.

Their youthful love and youthful purity offer welcome contrast to the loveless persons of middle life by whom they are surrounded, and it was an admirable skill that integrated them so well with the historical characters. When, in the autumn of 1796, the image of them began to form in the author's mind, Schiller spoke of them as the "two figures for which alone I have an affection." The sinister villains of the drama stand in more awesome shadow for the light that emanates from this pair.

As for these villains, Illo and Terzky may be said to play their real life roles in the drama, though with magnified significance. In history they did no more than Wallenstein bade them do,—and just how much that was remains a subject of dispute among historians,—whereas in the play they engineer the conspiracy and try to bend Wallenstein to their purposes. The Countess Terzky of the play combines the name of the historical Countess with the actions of the Countess Kinsky, Terzky's *sister*, but her motivation and character owe even more to Lady Macbeth. In real life she survived the disaster and married again soon after, whereas in the play she emulates (somewhat too patently) the sleepwalking scene and the suicide by poison of her literary prototype. In Buttler's case, the deeds of the historical personage are rather faithfully reproduced, but the motivation for those deeds seems to have been, in fact, only base greed for reward and a certain religious fanaticism. Schiller has substituted a betrayal out of revenge for a prior betrayal, and the fine scene (*Death* II, 2) where Buttler learns of the offense to his honor and is wrought to fury, is the invention of creative genius.

A single principle underlies these modifications of historical fact, a principle which establishes artistic unity and infuses artistic intensity into a work which could in less gifted hands have turned into a cold and pompous tableau. Each transposition removes a character,—and this is true even for that

collective character, the army,—from relative independence
to a position of closer kinship or closer friendship, where
reciprocal duty and reciprocal trust are paramount. In this
new position each character is confronted with a conflict of
loyalties requiring a desperate choice. Throughout the drama,
the pledged word, the tie of kinship, the vows of love, the
soldier's oath, the obligation of gratitude, the steadfastness of
friendship, the responsibility of superior to subordinate and
of subordinate to superior, are all honored or betrayed, and
by such a wide variety of human types as to seem to encom-
pass the range of mankind. Immediately outside the scope of
these characters' lives there has been the Emperor's betrayal
of his word to Wallenstein, and the causes of this betrayal
recede into the circumstances of history, indeed into the
mystery of the human condition itself. Within the drama's
scope Wallenstein counters betrayal with betrayal, and from
him the moral dilemma devolves from level to level, affecting
all. Wallenstein himself, in the play, is made to perish because
Buttler counters betrayal with betrayal, for Wallenstein has
treated him as the Emperor treated Wallenstein. Every choice
is bitter, and holding fast seems to occasion as dire results as
outright treason. Octavio follows principle unswervingly, but
sacrifices friendship and gratitude to do so. His son, caught between the loyalties to his two fathers, sees that nothing remains
but to rush to battle and die fighting before the choice has to
be made in favor of the one or the other. The Countess
Terzky, who has actively participated in events, perishes; the
Duchess, who has remained in passive innocence, equally
perishes. The villains win our respect by their dogged loyalty
to their own principles,—even Buttler, whose only principle
seems to be his pride,—but we are distressed by the Corporal
of Cuirassiers who unhesitatingly deserts Wallenstein in order
to uphold his soldier's oath, and we feel a contempt mixed
with pity for Gordon who wrings his hands in anguish and

still betrays in order to uphold his soldier's oath. We admire Thekla's loyalty unto death to Max, but we must remind ourselves that in doing so she betrays her father. Even the touching obedience without question of Rosenberg, her equerry, is simultaneous disobedience to Wallenstein, where his prior loyalty lay. All things considered, we scarcely begrudge Buttler the reward which he hurries off to claim in Vienna, but we would hate "Prince" Piccolomini at the end of the play if we did not realize that he now has no son to inherit the title.

The trilogy as a whole is a sombre work pervaded by the Baroque grandeur of the seventeenth century in spite of Rousseauistic anachronisms. It has, undeniably, its blemishes. It is over-long. Rhetoric sometimes sweeps the speakers away, and some passages, e.g., the speeches of Max in *Picc.* I, have a tendency to become set pieces of a descriptive kind of poetry now in disfavor. The blank verse is technically faulty.[1] The Shakespeareanizing may strike the English reader as secondhand, not only the Countess Terzky-Lady Macbeth derivation and certain parallels between Octavio Piccolomini and the Octavius Caesar of *Antony and Cleopatra*, but numerous verbal echoes as well. Take, for example, *Death* II, 1, lines 896 ff., where in short compass one is reminded successively of *Henry IV, Julius Caesar, Hamlet,* and again *Julius Caesar.* The two scenes between the Piccolominis, father and son, have the single fault that there are *two* of them. The critic's

---

[1] Of the 6,518 lines of the blank verse sections, *Picc.* and *Death*, 268, or a little over four percent, are non-pentameter lines.

Picc. has three 7-foot lines, seventy-eight 6-foot lines, twenty-nine 4-foot lines, thirteen 3-foot lines, six 2-foot lines, and one 1-foot line.

Death has two 7-foot lines, sixty 6-foot lines, forty-one 4-foot lines, fifteen 3-foot lines, twelve 2-foot lines, and eight 1-foot lines.

These irregularities have been rendered with equivalent irregularities in the present translation, except in three instances (*Picc.* 2149, *Death* 1845, and *Death* 2368), where the procedure did not seem warranted.

Even *Camp* departs occasionally from its four-stress "Knittelvers" with 5-stress lines 117 and 549; the 2-stress lines 1046-1049 are, of course, deliberate. The present translation reproduces these irregularities also, along with the occasional blank lines amid the rhymed text.

talent, which could not have conceived and written either, complains that one such scene would have sufficed and two such impair the effectiveness of both; the poet, however, wrote *both*. The operatic finale of *Death* III, 2 is now unfashionable, but that does not mean that it may not be, in its own way, excellent. The passive death of Wallenstein entails a slackening of tension at a point in the drama when the heightening of tension would have been preferable, but the dynamics of the subject made that all but inevitable. Thekla is the *idea* of a heroine but not a convincing mortal.

To offset these flaws there are excellences beyond number: — the sustained elevation of mood, the vividness and variety of characters, the justice done each character by the poet in letting him live out his role naturally—what Schiller termed "objectivity" and what Keats termed Shakespeare's "negative capacity"—the uninterrupted flow of dramatic life from scene to scene, and, above all, the great scenes themselves. To take a single example from among many, the first interview between Octavio and Max Piccolomini in *Picc.* V may be ranked alongside Euripides and Shakespeare. There is no higher tribute. The *Wallenstein* trilogy is probably the loftiest achievement in the dramatic literature of the German language.

CHRONOLOGY OF SCHILLER'S LIFE

1759   Born November 10 at Marbach on the Neckar in Württemberg.

1763-66   Lived at Lorch.

1767-72   Lived at Ludwigsburg.

1773-80   Attended the Academy established by the Duke of Württemberg, first at Solitude, later at Stuttgart.

1780-82   Regimental surgeon at Stuttgart.

1781   *Die Räuber* (The Robbers).

1782   Flight from Stuttgart to Mannheim.

1783   *Fiesco.*

1783-85   At Mannheim as theatre poet.

1784   *Kabale und Liebe* (Intrigue and Love), first entitled *Luise Müllerin.* (Basis for Verdi's opera *Luisa Miller.*)

1785-87   At Leipzig and at Dresden; friendship with Körner.

1787   *Don Carlos.* (Basis for Verdi's opera, *Don Carlo.*)

1787-99   At Jena.

1789   Professor of History at Jena.

1790   Married Charlotte von Lengefeld.

1791-93   *Geschichte des dreissigjährigen Krieges* (History of the Thirty Years' War).

1792-96   Philosophic and aesthetic essays.

1794   Beginning of his intimate friendship with Goethe.

1798   *Wallensteins Lager* (Wallenstein's Camp).

1799   *Die Piccolomini* (The Piccolominis); *Wallensteins Tod* (The Death of Wallenstein).

1800   *Maria Stuart.*

1801   *Die Jungfrau von Orleans* (The Maid of Orleans).

1803   *Die Braut von Messina* (The Bride of Messina).

1804   *Wilhelm Tell* (William Tell). (Basis for Rossini's opera,
       William Tell.)
1805   Fragment of a drama on the Boris Godunov theme, en-
       titled *Demetrius*. Died May 9.

CHRONOLOGY OF THE *WALLENSTEIN* TRILOGY

1791   December 1, letter to Körner: first mention of the sub-
       ject for possible dramatic treatment.
1793   Prose sketches reported as having been made for a five-
       act play.
1796   Letters to Körner and to Humboldt, both dated March
       21, announce the beginning of serious work on the
       drama; delays; work begun anew in October.
1797   Letter of February 1 first mentions *Wallenstein's Camp*,
       designated simply as "Prologue."
       June 18, Schiller mailed Körner a manuscript of
       Wallenstein's Camp approximately half the length of
       the final version and lacking the Capuchin friar scene.
       November 4, announcement of the intention to com-
       pose the play proper in iambic pentameter.
1798   September 21, Schiller wrote his publisher, Cotta, to
       advertise a trilogy of dramas to be printed for Easter
       1799.
       September 30, completion of *Wallenstein's Camp* in
       final form.
       October 2, composition of the poem now entitled
       Prologue.
       Première of *Wallenstein's Camp* at Goethe's theatre in
       Weimar, October 12, under the title of *The Wallen-
       stein Men* (Die Wallensteiner). Since the work was too
       short to occupy a whole evening, it was preceded by
       Kotzebue's *The Corsicans* (Die Korsen), and thus the
       prologue poem was spoken somewhat awkwardly in
       the middle of the program. The occasion was the

reopening of the renovated theatre, which had originally been built in 1779.

First draft of *The Piccolomini* mailed to Iffland on November 11; a second draft was sent on December 24, and still further changes were made in the manuscript up to December 31.

1799 Première of *The Piccolomini,* January 30, as a five-act play which extended through what is now the second act of *The Death of Wallenstein.*

March 17, completion of *The Death of Wallenstein.*

Première of *The Death of Wallenstein,* April 20, as a five-act play beginning at Act III of the present text and entitled simply *Wallenstein.*

October 16, Schiller sent Cotta "both plays" for publication.

1800 June, publication by Cotta of the total work in two volumes. An edition of four thousand copies was rapidly exhausted.

LIST OF PERSONS

Names are given first as they occur in the play; the alternate spellings freely used by Schiller are given in capital letters; common or more accepted spellings are given immediately after in parenthesis.

ALTRINGER, ALTRING (Aldringen, Altringen), Count Johann, a Catholic general. Distinguished himself at Dessau, 1626, and at the siege of Mantua. After Tilly's death he became general of the Catholic League, operating in southwestern Germany in 1633 in conjunction with the Duke of Feria. Killed in battle a few months after Wallenstein.

Referred to: *Picc.* 21, 338, 806, 809, 2578, 2580; *Death* 664, 1171, 2656.

ARNHEIM (Arnim), Johann Georg von, a Saxon noble and distinguished general. Served successively under Sweden, Poland, and Austria. Became intimate with Wallenstein and was made field marshal in 1628. Unable to secure his pay from the Emperor, he entered the service of the Elector of Saxony and was the negotiator with Gustavus and Wallenstein until the latter's death. He took part in the battle of Breitenfeld and captured Prague in 1631. Mistreated by the Swedes, he again entered imperial service. Died 1641.

Ref.: *Picc.* 850, 1096, 1107, 1337; *Death* 51.

ATTILA, the famous "Scourge of God," King of the Huns, who was defeated at the battle of Chalons in 451.

Ref.: *Death* 287.

BANNIER, BANNER, one of the chief Swedish generals after the

death of Gustavus, with a record of many victories and scarcely
any defeats. Died 1641.

Ref.: *Picc.* 1034; *Death* 940.

THE BAVARIAN—see MAXIMILIAN.

BERNHARD, Prince of Saxony-Weimar, one of the greatest
generals of the war. Born 1604, he served under various Protestant
leaders but submitted in 1628 to the Emperor. On the arrival of
Gustavus, however, he joined the Swedish king, rose to high rank,
and at age 29 helped to win the battle of Lützen after the death
of Gustavus. At the time of Wallenstein's death Bernhard was in
command of the Swedish forces that were to join Wallenstein.
This portion of his career is assigned in the play to the Rhinegrave in order not to give offense to the court of Saxony-Weimar,
where the drama was presented, by representing one of their
ancestors in the quality of a traitor.

Ref.: *Picc.* 1034, 1068, 2022, 2119.

BOURBON, Charles of, Constable of France, deserted his King,
Francis I of France, and entered into a league with the king's
enemies, Charles V of the Holy Roman Empire and Henry VIII
of England, whereby he was to receive a throne. He was killed
in the siege of Rome in 1527.

Ref.: *Death* 419, 442.

BURGOMASTER PACHHÄLBEL, one of the burgomasters of Eger,
but not in 1634.

Appears: *Death* IV, 1; V, 2.   Ref.: *Death* 2602.

BUTTLER (Butler), Colonel Walter, one of Wallenstein's commanders. He directed the assassination of Wallenstein, but not
for the motives alleged in the play. As far as is known, he was
motivated by greed for reward and by devotion to the Catholic
faith. His reward came in the form of a Count's title.

Appears: *Picc.* I, II, IV; *Death* II, 2; III, 1, 2; IV, 1; V, 1, 2.
Ref.: *Camp* 440 ff.; *Picc.* 94, 273, 282, 285, 1005, 1147, 2374;
Death 1440, 1580, 1821.

CARAFFA—see KARAFFA.

CARDINAL INFANTE, Don Fernando of Spain. His brother, Philip
IV of Spain, desired to send him in 1663 to the Netherlands via

Germany, and to furnish him an escort Wallenstein was directed to detach six regiments.

Ref.: *Camp* 697; *Picc.* 1226, 1250; *Death* 1370.

CHARLES V, the great Emperor in the first half of the sixteenth century, during whose reign the Empire included the largest territory ever brought under the control of a single individual in the course of European history.

Ref.: *Death* 440.

CHRISTIAN, Duke of Brunswick-Wolfenbüttel and administrator of the Lutheran bishopric of Halberstadt, a commander in the first period of the war. His warfare was particularly irregular, leading to the nickname "The Mad Halberstädter." He fought in conjunction with Mansfeld, and died June 1626.

Ref.: *Picc.* 2024.

CONTE AMBASSADOR OF SPAIN, Count Oñate, special envoy to Vienna to secure the escort for the Cardinal Infante, and finally one of the most vigorous workers against Wallenstein.

Ref.: *Picc.* 682.

DEODAT (Deodati), an Italian, joined the counter-conspiracy against Wallenstein, entered Pilsen after Wallenstein's withdrawal and directed Gordon to admit him to Eger. This part is assigned to Buttler in the play.

Ref,: *Picc.* 879, 1005, 1147, 2122; *Death* 989, 1565.

DEVEROUX, an Irish captain, the actual assassin of Wallenstein. Appears: *Death* V, 1.

DÜBALD (Duwall), a Swedish colonel who was captured at Steinau with Thurn.

Ref.: *Death* 1846.

EGGENBERG, Duke of, a member of the imperial council in Vienna and of the faction friendly to Wallenstein. Wallenstein's second wife was a sister of Eggenberg's son-in-law. In December 1631 it was Eggenberg who finally persuaded Wallenstein to resume command of the imperial forces. His part is taken by Questenberg in the drama.

Ref.: *Picc.* 680, 1919.

ESTERHAZY, name of an ancient Hungarian family of many branches; one member of it was Palatine of Hungary in the third decade of the 17th century. No member of the family took a conspicuous part in the war.

Ref.: *Death* 989, 1567.

FERDINAND II, Emperor of Germany 1619-1637, called from his birthplace (Gratz), "der Grätzer." A mild-mannered man, fond of hunting, having no executive ability. Only in matters of religion did he have a fixed purpose, which may best be seen in his own words: "Better a desert than a land full of heretics."

Ref. (among many others): *Picc.* 1022 ff, 1970, 2094; *Death* 549 ff., 645 ff.; 2119, 3378, 3532, 3647.

FERDINAND III, the King of Hungary 1625 and Emperor of Germany 1637-1657, son of Ferdinand II. He became commander-in-chief of Wallenstein's army after the latter's assassination and, through 1634-1635, until the active intervention by France, won important victories.

Ref.: *Picc.* 208 (as "the child"), 800; *Death* 501, 504, 1934, 2792.

FERIA, Duke of, commander of the Spanish regiments which came in 1633 from Italy, intended as escort for the Cardinal Infante. Died Jan. 1634.

Ref.: *Camp* 144.

FORGATSCH (Forgach), Palatine of Hungary in 1618; not known to have been in the conspiracy. In one draft of the drama Esterhazy stood in stead of Forgatsch.

Ref.: *Picc.* 1005.

FREDERICK V—see PALATINE.

FRIEDLAND, "the FRIEDLANDER," Wallenstein's title from his estate of Friedland in Bohemia. See WALLENSTEIN.

GALLAS, Count Matthias, important general under and succeeding Wallenstein. He served throughout the war and with fair ability. His most brilliant performances were at the taking of Mantua, 1630, for which he was ennobled, and the battle of Nördlingen, 1634, won over Bernhard of Weimar. Among Wallenstein's generals Gallas was the one on whom the court depended. He received Friedland as his reward for Wallenstein's death. Died 1647. Much of his real role is in the play assigned to Octavio Piccolomini.

Ref.: *Picc.* 21, 40, 338, 807, 2387, 2560; *Death* 41, 48, 666, 889, 1036, 1064, 1171, 2410, 2668, 2793.

GERALDIN, Buttler's sergeant-major who conducted the assassinations of Illo, Terzky, Kinsky, and Neumann.

Appears: *Death* V, 1. Ref.: *Death* 3305.

GÖTZ, served first in the Protestant cause but joined Wallenstein's army in 1626. Infamous for his atrocities in the sack of Pasewalk, 1630. The most important part of his career followed Wallenstein's death.

Appears: *Picc.* II, IV. Ref.: *Picc.* 18; *Death* 1568.

GORDON, a Scotch soldier of fortune, lieutenant-commander of Eger.

Appears: *Death* IV, 1; V, 2. Ref.: *Death* 3461.

THE GRÄTZER—see FERDINAND II.

GUSTAVUS ADOLPHUS, born 1594, King of Sweden 1611-1632. From 1630 his deeds were an essential part of the war. Killed in the battle of Lützen, Nov. 16, 1632. (Before writing *Wallenstein*, Schiller had contemplated a work with Gustavus as hero.)

Ref.: *Camp* 256; *Picc.* 1035, 1063, 1095, 1220; *Death* 239, 241, 367, 374, 1800.

THE HALBERSTÄDTER—see CHRISTIAN.

HARRACH'S DAUGHTER, Wallenstein's wife, the Duchess of Friedland. Count Harrach was a leading intriguer at the Austrian court, being connected with Eggenberg and Wallenstein. He often served as deputy to Eggenberg. He died 1628.

Ref.: *Picc.* 660.

HENRY, King of Navarre, subsequently King of France, assassinated 1610 by the Catholic fanatic Ravaillac.

Ref.: *Death* 3491.

HINNERSAM (Henderson), one of Wallenstein's commanders, of Scotch birth. He is mentioned as one of the committee of officers that visited Wallenstein Jan. 12, 1634 to urge him not to lay down his command.

Ref.: *Picc.* 18.

HOLK, General von, an imperial commander famous for the brutality of his warfare. Devastated the Voigtland in 1632.
Ref.: *Camp* 121, 216, 230.

HUSS, Jan, founder of Bohemian Protestanism, burned at the stake at Constance by order of the Council of Constance, 1415.
Ref.: *Picc.* 2082.

ILLO (Ilow), one of Wallenstein's generals, a native of Brandenburg. He was apparently the ringleader of the conspiracy, especially at the officers' meeting of January 12, 1634.
Appears: *Picc.* I, II, III, IV; *Death* I, II, 1; III, 1, 2; IV, 1.
Ref.: *Picc.* 281, 2129, 2374, 2396, 2403; *Death* 1739, 2680, 2740, 3300, 3520, 3699.

ISOLANI, ISOLAN, one of Wallenstein's commanders.
Appears: *Picc.* I, II, IV; *Death* II, 2. Ref.: *Camp* 826; *Picc.* 93, 875, 1006, 2374; *Death* 1458, 1563, 1617, 1640.

KAUNITZ, an Austrian family. A Count Kaunitz married Wallenstein's daughter, but took no prominent part in the war. Like Esterhazy, the name Kaunitz may have been introduced by Schiller less for historical reasons than from familiarity with them from his own time.
Ref.: *Death* 989, 1568.

KARAFFA, CARAFFA, Prince Geronimo, member of a distinguished Italian family. Fought in the battle of White Hill, 1620, was made Prince and Vice-King of Aragon. Died at Genoa, 1633. His enumeration among Wallenstein's generals is an error.
Ref.: *Picc.* 1006, 1146; *Death* 1655.

THE KING OF HUNGARY—see FERDINAND III.

KINSKY, Count William, a Bohemian noble, a leader in the insurrection of 1618, and an active intriguer for Wallenstein with the French, whether authorized or not is uncertain. He was with Wallenstein at Pilsen and at Eger and was murdered together with Illo and Terzky. His wife was Terzky's sister and the original of the Countess Terzky of the play.
Ref.: *Picc.* 2374; *Death* 50, 1716, 1739.

KOLALTO (Collalto), a native of Mantua, became one of Wallenstein's generals in 1625, President of the War Council in 1627. Led 20,000 troops to Italy and took Mantua in July, 1630; died a month later.

Appears: *Picc.* II, IV. Ref.: *Picc.* 18, 878; *Death* 1568.

LAMORMAIN (French corruption of Lämmermann), a Jesuit priest, confessor of Ferdinand II and actual director of the latter's policies; an active intriguer against Wallenstein.

Ref.: *Picc.* 689, 1233.

LAUENBURG, Duke Franz Albert von, a Saxon field marshal, was engaged in negotiations between the Elector of Saxony and Wallenstein.

Ref.: *Death* 1549.

LESSLEY (Lessly), a Scotch soldier, Lieutenant-commander of Eger; a friend of Buttler; represented as having taken part in the murder of the officers.

Ref.: *Picc.* 2032; *Death* 3309.

LIECHTENSTEIN, Prince Karl von, made prince in 1618 by Ferdinand II, a member of the imperial council, and friendly to Wallenstein. He is one of the precious jewels (Steine) in the Emperor's crown, along with Dietrichstein and Wallenstein, and is thus indirectly referred to in *Picc.* 1164.

Ref.: *Picc.* 680, 1919.

LORRAINE, Duke Charles of, who, persecuted by Richelieu, joined the imperial army. After Tilly's death he even aspired to the chief command.

Ref.: *Death* 1267.

MACDONALD, confederate of Deveroux.

Appears: *Death* V, 1, 2.

MANSFELD, Ernst von, a natural son of Count Peter Ernst von Mansfield. Reared a Catholic, he was driven into the Protestant opposition by the ingratitude of Archduke Leopold, but fought as a free-lance during the first period of the war till, in 1625, he raised an army as general of the Palatine. He attacked Wallenstein at the Dessau Bridge, but was defeated and pursued through

Silesia till he joined Bethlen Gabor in Hungary. The latter making peace, Mansfeld set out for Venice, but died on the way, 1626.

Ref.: *Camp* 140; *Picc.* 2024; *Death* 1926.

MARÁDAS (Marradas, Marrados), a Spaniard and loyal imperial general, commander in Bohemia and later in Silesia.

Appears: *Picc.* II, IV. Ref.: *Picc.* 18, 1005, 2135; *Death* 1567.

MARTINEZ, Jaroslas von, a prominent Bohemian noble, member of the Committee of Regency; one of the three men "defenestrated" at Prague in 1618. (See SLAWATA.)

Ref.: *Picc.* 151, 2109.

MAXIMILIAN, Duke and Elector of Bavaria, leader of the Catholic League, the rival and determined enemy of Wallenstein. As the Emperor's son-in-law he had great influence at court, and with that influence combined the qualities of statesmanship and generalship which Ferdinand II wholly lacked. Along with General Tilly, Maximilian bore the primary responsibility for the dismissal of Wallenstein at the meeting of the Diet at Regensburg in July 1630. Again in 1633 he urged the replacement of Wallenstein by Aldringen, and when Wallenstein failed to save Bavaria from the invasion of Bernhard of Weimar in the autumn of that year, he exerted such pressure upon the Emperor as to precipitate the actions leading directly to Wallenstein's assassination. Maximilian was the last of the Catholic leaders to agree to a peace, and only the major campaigns against Bavaria by the French marshal Turenne in 1646-1648 forced him to consent to the Treaty of Westphalia which brought the war to its conclusion in 1648.

Ref.: *Camp* 858; *Picc.* 694, 1073; *Death* 565.

MOHRBRAND, must be a careless or deliberate alteration of Mohra, who was Lieutenant-commander of Prague when Schlief was captured.

Ref.: *Picc.* 2566.

MONTECUCULI (Montecuccoli), Count Ernst, an Italian and friend of Wallenstein, chief of ordnance. He was killed in Feria's campaign in 1633. Uncle of the more famous Count Raimund Montecuccoli.

Ref.: *Picc.* 1953; *Death* 1655.

NEUMANN, historically Wallenstein's secretary; in the play, Terzky's adjutant.

Appears: *Picc.* IV; *Death* III, 2. Ref.: *Death* 2381.

OXENSTIRN (Oxenstjerna), Swedish Chancellor and Regent after the death of Gustavus Adolphus. A shrewd and successful diplomat, but lacking in the military ability of Gustavus.

Ref.: *Camp* 502; *Picc.* 815, 850, 1034; *Death* 51, 238, 258, 282, 291 ff., 336, 384, 406.

THE PALATINE, THE COUNT PALATINE, Frederick V, "the winter king." See Introduction. Died 1632.

Ref.: *Picc.* 2058, 2096; *Death* 448, 1759.

PAPPENHEIM, General, arrived at the battle of Lützen, Nov. 16, 1632, just in time to save the day for the imperial armies. He was killed in that same battle.

Ref.: *Camp* 677; *Death* 1266.

PALFFY, Stephen von, distinguished himself in wars with the Turks. Made Count in 1634; was also Palatine of Hungary.

Ref.: *Picc.* 2054, 2133.

PESTALUTZ, a captain under Terzky, but reported to have joined the conspirators.

Ref.: *Death* 3282 ff., 3309.

PICCOLOMINI, Max, a fictitious character invented by Schiller. Perhaps suggested by Max von Waldstein (Wallenstein), a favorite nephew and heir of Wallenstein.

PICCOLOMINI, Octavio, one of Wallenstein's generals, member of an old Italian family. At the close of the war he was made Duke of Amalfi.

PROKOP, name of two leaders of the Taborites in the Hussite wars, Prokop the Great and Prokop the Small. The former, for years a victorious general, was defeated and slain at Lipau in 1434.

Ref.: *Picc.* 2104.

PYRRHUS, a king of Epirus, who ruled and warred against the Romans in the first half of the third century B.C.

Ref.: *Death* 287.

THE QUEEN OF HUNGARY, wife of Ferdinand III, the Spanish Infanta Mary, sister of Queen Anne of France.

Ref.: *Picc.* 634, 671.

QUESTENBERG, QUESTENBERGER, member of the Imperial Privy Council and a staunch friend of Wallenstein. Schiller has rather curiously selected his name to stand in place of several of Wallenstein's enemies.

Appears: *Picc.* I, II. Ref.: *Camp* 71; *Picc.* 72, 116, 1007, 2481; *Death* 885, 1371, 1660.

QUIROGA, a Capuchin monk, confessor to the Queen of Hungary. It was he who, on January 5, 1634, brought to Wallenstein at Pilsen the request for the detail of 6,000 men to escort the Cardinal Infante to the Netherlands. His role at this point is assigned in the play to Questenberg.

Ref.: *Camp* 173 ff.; *Picc.* 2127.

THE RHINEGRAVE, Otto Ludwig von Salms, Count of the Rheingau, took a prominent part in the war after the arrival of Gustavus. Commanded in Alsace in 1633 and made conquests in Breisgau. At the time of Wallenstein's death he was on the upper Rhine. In the play he is assigned a considerable share of the role historically played by Bernhard of Weimar. (See BERNHARD.)

Ref.: *Picc.* 1034; *Death* 332, 2633, 2665, 3040, 3066, 3070, 3638.

RUDOLPH II, the Emperor who preceded Ferdinand II. It was he who originally granted the Bohemians their charter of religious toleration in 1609.

Ref.: *Picc.* 2090.

SCHAFGOTSCH, Count Ulrich, member of an ancient Silesian family. Though a Lutheran, one of Wallenstein's most trusted generals. Was commissioned in February 1634 with the command in Silesia. The only one of Wallenstein's officers who tried to resist after the ban had been pronounced against his chief. He was captured and executed in 1635.

Ref.: *Picc.* 2371.

SCHERFENBERG, Wallenstein's High Steward, a loyal adherent. After Wallenstein's death he was sentenced to death, then to life imprisonment.

Ref.: *Death* 2022.

SECKENDORF, name of a distinguished Austrian general and diplomat of the first part of the 18th century; also a young poet who was a friend of Schiller; neither has any connection with the Swedish command of 1634.

Ref.: *Death* 3082.

SENI (Senno), Wallenstein's astrologer.

Appears: *Picc.* II; *Death* II, V, 2. Ref.: *Camp* 372; *Picc.* 1348, 1581 ff.

SESINA, SESIN (Sesyma Raschin), a Bohemian employed by Terzky as messenger in negotiations with the Swedes. He was not captured at all, but after Wallenstein's death purchased his own safety by a detailed confession of all his transactions.

Ref.: *Picc.* 812, 1337, 2564, 2576, 2596; *Death* 40 ff., 98 ff., 392.

SLAWATA, Wilhelm von, a prominent Bohemian noble who took the part of Austria against the Protestant Estates of Bohemia. He was one of the three men "defenestrated" in Prague in 1618. In spite of the fall of eighty feet the men were not seriously injured, and escaped with the aid of friends. Wallenstein's second wife was connected with the Slawata family. (See MARTINEZ.)

Ref.: *Picc.* 151, 1919, 2109.

STERNBERG, Adam von, chief burggrave of Bohemia, one of the imperial regents, and father-in-law of Martinitz. He was present at the defenestration, but, being less aggressively imperialistic, was not assailed.

Ref.: *Picc.* 1920.

SUYS, a colonel under Wallenstein, was in charge of four regiments in Upper Austria. Historically he did precisely the opposite of what he is represented as having done in the play: he did not obey the Emperor and disobey Wallenstein by advancing, but refused to advance as the Emperor ordered. For this he was severely reprimanded by the Emperor. Later, however, Suys was put in charge of Prague when the Emperor assumed command.

Ref.: *Picc.* 1196 ff.; *Death* 2660.

TERZKY, TERSCHKA, TERZKA, Count Adam, one of Wallenstein's officers, brother-in-law of the Duchess Wallenstein. For dramatic purposes Schiller has greatly magnified the relatively slight conspiratorial role that Terzky had in history.

Appears: *Picc.* II, III, IV; *Death* I; II, 1; III, 1, 2; IV, 1. Ref.: *Camp* 84, 1017; *Picc.* 17, 904, 1690, 1717, 1914, 2051, 2372, 2574; *Death* 63, 1739, 1820, 2740, 3300, 3520, 3767.

COUNTESS TERZKY, daughter of Count Harrach and sister of the Duchess Wallenstein. In history she knew little of Wallenstein's plans. In the drama she takes over the historical role of Terzky's *sister*, the Countss Kinsky, who *was* an intriguer. Her character has about it something of the character of Terzky's mother, "the old Countess" (referred to in *Picc.* 1915, 2037, 2146-2148), but in larger part she derives from Lady Macbeth.

Appears: *Picc.* II, III; *Death* I; III, 1, 2; IV, 2; V, 2. Ref.: *Picc.* 1379, 2146.

THURN, Count Matthias, a Bohemian noble and leader of the Protestant opposition to the Austrian encroachments. After the Protestant loss of Bohemia in the early stages of the war he fought under Bethlen Gabor, and under Gustavus Adolphus at Leipzig and at Lützen. In October 1633 he was captured by Wallenstein together with his force of allied Protestants. Wallenstein set him free in return for certain guarantees to evacuate Silesia, a move which would favor the imperial armies but which aroused bitter criticism of Wallenstein at court. Thurn died soon afterward.

Ref.: *Picc.* 814, 1095, 1119, 1336, 2111; *Death* 50.

TIEFENBACH, a Moravian colonel who served in the imperial army as early as 1618 but not mentioned in connection with Wallenstein's closing career.

Appears: *Picc.* II, IV. Ref.: *Picc.* 17, 879, 2047; *Death* 964, 1268, 1577, 1862, 2250.

TILLY, Johann von, after Wallenstein, the most famous Catholic general in the Thirty Years War. A Walloon by birth, he served under many flags; was made field marshal of the Catholic League;

won the battle of White Hill, 1620; was made Count, 1623; defeated the King of Denmark in the battle of Lutter, 1626; succeeded Wallenstein as imperial generalissimo, 1630. He met his first great defeat at the hands of Gustavus Adolphus in the battle of Breitenfeld, 1631, and was mortally wounded April, 1632 in the battle on the Lech.

Ref.: *Camp* 273, 343; *Picc.* 112; *Death* 1798.

TOSKANA (Tuscany), a representative of the decaying house of the Dukes of Tuscany.

Ref.: *Death* 1267, 1861.

WALLENSTEIN (Waldstein), Albrecht von, Duke of Friedland, generalissimo of the Catholic armies, central character in Schillers' drama.

born 1583 at Hermanitz, in Bohemia, of Lutheran parents.

educated first by the Bohemian (Moravian) Brothers, then by the Jesuits at Olmütz, where he was converted to Catholicism, then at the University of Altdorf (near Nürnberg).

travelled in Europe with a friend of Kepler, from which time dates his interest in astrology.

military service against the Turks; application for a position at the court of Austria; service, for Austria, against Venice; marriage to a wealthy and elderly widow; ennoblement (1617); second marriage to Count Harrach's daughter, a lady with important connections at court.

1618, outbreak of war; he raised a regiment of Walloons for the Emperor and led them with distinction. In the early stages of Catholic victories he bought up, at low prices, the confiscated lands of the Protestant Bohemian nobles.

1623 made Prince of Friedland.

1625 he voluntarily recruited and paid for an army to serve the Emperor; rewarded by being made Duke of Friedland and "Capo d'Armada" of the new army.

1626 defeated the Protestant General Mansfeld; made Duke of Sagan.

1627 totally defeated Denmark; given the Duchy of Mecklenburg temporarily.

1629 made Duke of Mecklenburg outright and hereditary prince of the empire.

1630 removed from command upon complaints from the Emperor's advisors.

1631-1632 was repeatedly urged to resume command and finally did so in April of 1632 after having received almost the powers of an independent ruler; defeat of the Swedes under Gustavus Adolphus at the battle of Lützen, Nov. 16, 1632.

1633 carried on peace negotiations, with the approval of the court; new victory in Silesia; Bernhard of Weimar invaded Bavaria, but Wallenstein failed to attack him.

1634, February 21, received news that he had been declared a traitor.

February 23, fled to Eger with a small force.

February, 25 assassinated.

Assessment of his motives and actions has been a subject of unending controversy, depending on the religious and political attitudes of historians, who have portrayed him as everything from a common traitor to a visionary, ahead of his time, who sought to end the Thirty Years War and establish the principle of religious toleration in Europe.

WALLENSTEIN, ELIZABETH (her real name was Isabella Katherina), second wife of the generalissimo, daughter of Count Harrach, Duchess of Friedland. She was a devoted wife but she was not present at either Pilsen or Eger, nor was she aware of her husband's plans.

Appears: *Picc.* II; *Death* III, 1, 2; IV, 2. Ref.: *Camp* 57; *Picc.* 32, 269; *Death* 1301, 1338 ff., 3769, 3819.

WERDENBERG, a member of the imperial council, several times employed on commissions to Wallenstein.

Ref.: *Picc.* 116.

WRANGEL, Gustav, a famous Swedish general and admiral who was only thirty-one years old at the time of Wallenstein's death. His father, Hermann Wrangel, led the Swedish forces in Poland, but was not at Stralsund.

Appears: *Death* I. Ref.: *Death* 95, 132, 481, 643, 657, 845 ff.

ZISKA, a famous Hussite general, leader of the extreme Taborite party. He lost one eye in youth and the other in battle, yet continued to command.

Ref.: *Picc.* 2140.

WALLENSTEIN'S CAMP

CHARACTERS

A Sergeant ⎫
A Trumpeter ⎬ from one of Terzky's carbineer regiments
A Bombardier
Sharpshooters
Two Mounted Jägers (chasseurs) from General Holk's forces
Dragoons from Buttler's regiment
Arquebusiers from Tiefenbach's regiment
A Cuirassier from a regiment of Walloons
A Cuirassier from a regiment of Lombards
Croats (light cavalrymen)
Uhlans (lance cavalrymen)
A Recruit
A Civilian
A Peasant
The Peasant's son
A Capuchin friar
A Field-school Master
A Sutlerwoman
A Barmaid
Soldiers' children
Musicians

Time: February 1634
Place: Wallenstein's camp outside the town of Pilsen in Bohemia.

PROLOGUE

*Spoken at the reopening of the stage in Weimar in
October, 1798*

The sport of jesting and of earnest masks,
To which you have lent willing ears and eyes
So often, and committed tender hearts,
Unites us once again within this hall.
Behold how it has been rejuvenated.
Art has adorned it as a cheerful temple,
And a harmonious lofty spirit speaks
To us out of these noble ranks of columns
And stirs our minds to high and solemn feelings.

Yet this is still the well known stage of old,   10
The cradle of how many youthful spirits,
The highroad of how much evolving talent.
We are ourselves the same who formerly
Acquired our skills with eager warmth before you.
A noble master has stood on this stage
Who charmed you to the heights of his great art
By virtue of his own creative genius.
O, may this room's new-founded dignity
Attract the worthiest into our midst,
And may *one* hope that we have cherished long   20
Be realized in brilliance of fulfillment.
A splendid model rouses emulation,
Establishes more lofty laws of judgment.
Hence let this building stand, and this new stage,
In testimony of perfected talent.
Where better might it test its powers out,

3

Refreshing and regaining former fame,
Than here before this chosen audience,
Which, sensitive to every stroke of Art's
Enchantment, seizes with responsive feeling   30
Upon the mind's most fleeting apparitions?

    For swiftly over our awareness passes
The wondrous art of mimes without a trace,
Whereas the sculptor's statue and the song
Of poets live beyond the centuries.
Here, when the artist ends, his magic ends,
And as the sound recedes upon our ears
The moment's quick creation dies in echoes,
Its fame preserved by no enduring work.
Hard is this art, its praise is transitory;   40
For mimes, posterity entwines no garlands.
Therefore they must be greedy of the present
And fill the moment which is theirs, completely,
Assure themselves of their contemporaries
And in the feelings of the best and noblest
Build living monuments. In this way they
Anticipate their names' eternity.
For he who does sufficient for the best
Of his own time, has lived for all the ages.

    And this new era which today begins   50
For Thalia's art upon this stage has made
The poet bold as well, to quit old paths
And from the narrow sphere of middle class
Existence lift you to a higher scene
Not unbefitting the exalted moment
Of time in which we strive and have our life.
For only subjects of high consequence
Can stir the deepest depths of human kind;
The mind grows narrow in a narrow sphere
And man grows great with greater purposes.   60

    Now at this century's impressive close,
As actuality itself is turned

To art, as we see mighty natures locked
In struggle for a goal of lofty import,
As conflict rages for the mighty ends
Of man, for masterdom, for freedom, now
Art is allowed assay of higher flight
Upon its shadow-stage; indeed it must be,
Lest it be put to shame by life's own stage.

    Amid these days we see the old fixed form   70
Disintegrate, which in its time a hundred
And fifty years ago a welcome peace
Imposed on Europe's realms, the precious fruit
Acquired by thirty dismal years of war.
Now once. again permit the poet's fancy
To bring before your eyes that sombre age,
While more content you gaze about the present
And toward the hopeful distance of the future.

    Into the middle of that war the poet
Now takes you. Sixteen years of devastation,   80
Of pillage, and of misery have passed.
Dark masses of the world are still in ferment
And from afar there shines no hope of peace.
The Empire is a rumpus-field for weapons,
Deserted are the cities, Magdeburg
In ashes, art and industry are prostrate,
The citizen is naught, the soldier all,
Unpunished insolence makes mock of custom,
And rude hordes, lawless grown in lengthy war,
Make couches on the devastated ground.   90

    Against this lowering background there is painted
An undertaking of audacious pride
And an impetuous, headstrong character.
You know him—the creator of bold armies,
The idol of the camp and scourge of countries,
The prop and yet the terror of his Emperor,
Dame Fortune's fabulous adopted son,
Who, lifted by the favor of the times,

Climbed rapidly the highest rungs or honor
And, never sated, striving ever further,   100
Fell victim to intemperate ambition.
Blurred by the favor and the hate of parties,
His image wavers in our history.
But Art shall now bring him more humanly
And closer to your eyes and to your hearts.
For Art, which binds and limits everything,
Brings all extremes back to the sphere of Nature.
It sees this man amid the press of life
And shows the greater half of his wrong-doing
To be the guilt of inauspicious stars.   110

    It is not he who will appear upon
This stage today. But in the daring hosts
Which his command with power sways, his spirit
Inspires, you will behold his shadow-self
Until the cautious Muse shall venture to
Produce him in his living form before you.
It is his power which misleads his heart:
His camp alone will make his crime quite clear.

    Forgive the poet therefore if he does not
Sweep you with rapid step and all at once   120
Straight to his story's goal, but only ventures
To set his mighty subject forth before you
In series, one by one, of pictures merely.
May this day's play persuade your ears and win
Your hearts as well to unfamiliar tones;
May it transport you to that former epoch
And to that far-off theatre of war
Which soon will be preempted by our hero
And his exploits

            And if today the Muse,
Unfettered goddess of the dance and song,   130
Should modestly claim her old German right
Once more to sport with rhyme,—do not reprove her.
But thank her for transposing that grim picture

Of truth into the cheerful realm of Art,
Herself destroying her illusion in
Good faith, not substituting with deceit
The semblances of Truth for Truth itself:
For life is stern, but art serenely joyous. [138]

Sutlerwomen's tents. In front of them a peddlar's booth and a second-hand dealer's booth. Soldiers in all varieties of uniforms and insignia are milling about. All tables are occupied. Croats and Uhlans are cooking at a coal fire. A sutlerwoman is dealing out wine. Soldiers' children are rolling dice on a drumhead. Singing is going on inside the tent.

(Enter a peasant and his son.)

THE PEASANT BOY: Father, I tell you it just won't do.
  We'd better steer clear of this soldier crew.
  They're a tough lot of rascals, I tell you again,
  If only they leave us with our whole skin.
THE PEASANT: They may carry on a bit high and mighty,
  But they won't eat us. Don't be so flighty.
  Do you see over there? New troops in the line,
  All fresh in from the Saal' and the Main,
  With booty besides, the choicest stuff,
  And that will be ours if we're smart enough.   10
  A Captain that somebody thought to kill
  Left me some loaded dice in his will
  And I want to try them out today
  And see if they've kept their old winning way.
  Now look your bedraggledest, act thoroughly cowed,
  This is a dead-game-sport of a crowd.
  They love to be praised, they love to be flattered,
  But what is won is just as soon scattered.
  If they take our goods by the bushel load,
  Then we'll spoon it back from where it is stowed.   20
  If they play it rough, show swords in the fray,
  Then we'll play it smooth in the slyest way.

*(Singing and hilarity are heard
from the tent.)*

8

God save us!—What a hullaballoo!
They take all that from the peasant's hide.
It's eight months now that this whole crew
In our homes and barns has been bedded and styed.
It's ages since the barnyard saw
The white of a feather, the print of a claw,
Till we in our want, with starvation near,
Are forced to gnaw at the joints of our hands;   30
Things were no topsy-turvier here
When the Saxons swaggered the length of our lands.
Think they're Imperials! What do they mean!

THE PEASANT BOY: There come a few now from the canteen,
By the looks, they've got little blood to be bled.

THE PEASANT: They're locals, Bohemians born and bred,
Part of Count Terschka's Carbineers,
They've been in quarters here for years.
They're the worst of a lot that's bad at best,
They strut and straddle and swell the chest,   40
Pretend that they would lose their class
If they sat with a peasant over a glass.
But there to our left by the fire I see
Three sharpshooters sitting. They look to me
As if they were of Tyrolian breed.
Emmerich, come on! They're just our speed,
Gay dogs fond of talk as bears of honey,
Sharp in their dress and loaded with money.

(Enter a Cavalry Sergeant, a Trumpeter,
and an Uhlan.)

THE TRUMPETER: And what do *you* want, you peasant scum?

THE PEASANT: Gentlemen, just a sip and a crumb,   50
All day long we've had nothing warm.

THE TRUMPETER: Ah, gorge and swill, then you're in form.

THE UHLAN *(with a glass)*:
No breakfast? Here! Drink this, you brute!

(He leads the peasant toward the tent.)

The Cavalry Sergeant and the Trumpeter
come down stage.)

THE SERGEANT *(to the Trumpeter)* :
  Do you think they paid us double to boot
  Without any reason at all today
  Just so we could be jolly and gay?
THE TRUMPETER: The Duchess arrives today, you know,
  With her daughter the Princess—
THE SERGEANT: That's just for show.
  The troops that are in from foreign regions
  And gathered here with the Pilsen legions,   60
  We are supposed to butter them up
  With morsel in trencher and dram in cup
  To make them feel at home right away
  And knit them to us and get them to stay.
THE TRUMPETER: Yes, something's brewing on the sly.
THE SERGEANT: The Generals and the Commandants—
THE TRUMPETER: It's something more than meets the eye.
THE SERGEANT: Are not crowded in here just by chance—
THE TRUMPETER: Or for lack of something better to do.
THE SERGEANT: And this sending and calling, this ho-ing and
    humming—   70
THE TRUMPETER: Yes, yes.
THE SERGEANT: And this old geezer coming
  Here from Vienna with his golden chain
  And stalking the camp since yesterday,
  There's something behind it, mark what I say.
THE TRUMPETER: Another bloodhound that they have set
  To snoop on the trail of the Duke, I'll bet.
THE SERGEANT: You see? They don't trust us here in this place.
  They're afraid of Friedland's inscrutable face.
  He has climbed too high for them, I say,
  They'd love to force him down a way.   80
THE TRUMPETER: But we will keep him right up on high,
  If all of us feel as you and I.
THE SERGEANT: Our regiment and four others led by
  Count Terschka, the Duke's brother-in-law,

The ruggedest corps the camp ever saw,
We are all loyal to him and true,
And he was the man that trained us too,
And all the commanders were named by him,
And they are all his with life and limb.

> (Enter a Croat with a neckchain.
> A sharpshooter is following him.)

THE SHARPSHOOTER: Croat, where did you steal that chain? 90
I'll trade you for it, it's no good to you,
I'll give you these pistols, and yours is the gain.
THE CROAT: Nix, Nix! You'll cheat me if I do.
THE SHARPSHOOTER: Here's this blue cap, I'll give you that too.
I staked on the Wheel of Fortune and won.
You see? With this you'll dazzle the girls.
THE CROAT (letting the neckchain flash in the sunlight):
Why's it's made of rubies and pearls.
Look how it glitters in the sun.
THE SHARPSHOOTER (takes the neckchain):
I'll throw in this field flask for extra measure.
> (examining the chain)
It's the pretty shining that gives me pleasure. 100
THE TRUMPETER: Just see that fellow swindling the Croat.
Halves, Rifleman, and I'll keep mum!
THE CROAT (has put the cap on):
I like your cap. So let's have a go at
A swap!
THE SHARPSHOOTER: It's a deal! With witnesses. Come!

> (Enter a Bombardier.)

BOMBARDIER (steps up to the Cavalry Sergeant):
What's going on, Brother Carbineer?
Are we going to sit here and keep our hands warm
While the enemy takes the field in a swarm?
SERGEANT: What's the hurry, Constable?
The roads are still impassable.
BOMBARDIER: I'm in no hurry, I'm cozy here. 110
But a courier has just arrived with the word

That Regenspurg has fallen, I heard.
TRUMPETER: Oh, then we'll take to horse in a wink.
SERGEANT: To protect the Bavarian's land, you think,
Who's so offish with our Duke? Oho!
There's once we won't go over the brink.
BOMBARDIER: You fancy?—There's a lot that you don't know!

(Enter two Jägers.)

FIRST JÄGER: See, see!
Here are some jolly company.
TRUMPETER: Who are those green-coats coming there?
They step it off smartly with quite an air.   120
SERGEANT: Holk's Jägers. That silver lace they wear
They didn't buy at the Leipzig Fair.

(Enter a Sutlerwoman with wine.)

SUTLERWOMAN: Welcome, Gentlemen.
FIRST JÄGER: Hey! Why, it's
Gustel the barmaid from Blasewitz.
SUTLERWOMAN: It's nobody else! Then you, M'sio,
Must be Big Pete from Itzehoe?
The one that brought his father's till
To our regiment one jolly night
In Glückstadt and left it pretty light.
FIRST JÄGER: And got me a rifle in place of a quill.   130
SUTLERWOMAN: O we've known each other quite a while!
FIRST JÄGER: And here we meet on Bohemian soil.
SUTLERWOMAN: This place today, tomorrow another,
Just as the harsh broom of war
Sweeps us from place to place, Brother.
I've seen quite a lot of the road so far
Myself.
FIRST JÄGER: I believe you there. You look it.
SUTLERWOMAN: Way over to Temesvar I took it
Travelling with the baggage train
When we chased Mansfeld on *that* campaign.   140
At the siege of Stralsund with Wallenstein
My business suffered a mortal decline.

South with relief troops to Mantua,
Back north again with Feria,
And with a Spanish regiment
I made a side trip over to Ghent.
In Bohemia here I'm going to try
To collect some money that I am shy
And see if the Duke's good influence
Will help me get it. Those are my tents.   150

FIRST JÄGER: Well, all your debtors are here in camp.
 But what happened to that Scottish scamp
 That you were seeing so much of then?

SUTLERWOMAN: That tramp! He up and left me. And when
 He went he took every penny I'd saved
 By scrimping and starving. The way he behaved!
 He left me just this brat of a lad.

SOLDIER'S SON (running up):
 Mommy, you're talking about my dad?

FIRST JÄGER: Well, the Emperor feeds them. While operating,
 An Army must be self-perpetuating.   160

(Enter a Field-school Master.)

FIELD-SCHOOL MASTER: Off to Field-school! March, you boys!
FIRST JÄGER: For them, cramped schoolrooms hold few joys.

(Enter a Barmaid.)

BARMAID: They're leaving, dearie.
SUTLERWOMAN: I'll be there right away.
FIRST JÄGER: Hey, who's *that* little rogue of a piece?
SUTLERWOMAN: My sister's girl—she's here on a stay
 From the Empire.
FIRST JÄGER: Oh, a dear little niece.

(Exit the Sutlerwoman.)

SECOND JÄGER (holding the girl back):
 Stay here with us, you sweet little thing.
BARMAID: There are guests in there and wine to bring.

(She disengages herself and leaves.)

FIRST JÄGER: That girl is a pretty tempting bit—

And her friend is not bad either, By Thunder!   170
The regiment lads, I shouldn't wonder,
Have had their tussles for that pert chit.
What a lot of people you get to know,
And how time flies and the seasons go!
What all won't I live to experience yet!
      (*To the Cavalry Sergeant and the Trumpeter.*)
A health to you gentlemen standing there!
Let's have a seat as long as we're here.
SERGEANT: Thanks a lot. If you move over, we'll share
   The space. I give you Bohemia's cheer!
FIRST JÄGER: You have it snug here. Our life of late   180
   In enemy lands was mighty grim fare.
TRUMPETER: You don't show it, you look like a fashion-plate.
SERGEANT: Yes, the Saal district doesn't have too much praise,
   Nor Meissen either, for you fellows' ways.
SECOND JÄGER: Oh, quiet! What do you mean: "don't praise"?
   The Croats' methods on that same score
   Left us with only the leavings to glean.
TRUMPETER: That's a fine piece of lace you have at your throat,
   And the fit of those breeches, the cut of that coat!
   That dainty linen, that plume on your hat!   190
   What an effect you get with all that!
   It's queer how Luck will beam on some,
   While to us nothing ever will come.
SERGEANT: But, then, we are Friedland's regiment,
   And that makes respect and honor our due.
FIRST JÄGER: That's not much of a compliment
   For the rest of us who bear his name too.
SERGEANT: You have your place in the general mass,
   As it were.
FIRST JÄGER: While you're of a special class?
   The only difference is tunic design,   200
   And I'm perfectly happy to stick to mine.
SERGEANT: Jäger, you have my sympathy,
   Living out there with the peasantry.
   The genteel touch, the proper tone,

Can be learned from the General's self alone.
FIRST JÄGER: The lesson missed you like a stone,
    I observe. You're quite correct in hitting
    The manner he uses in hawking and spitting,
    But his genius is lacking—his spirit, I mean—
    When you drill on parade, as far as I've seen.   210
SECOND JÄGER: Just you ask, by the Lord! You'll learn that we
    Are Friedland's Flying Cavalry
    And do not discredit the name. We go
    Right through the lands of friend or foe,
    Over planted seed, through yellow corn,
    And everyone knows Holk's hunting horn!
    In a wink of time, from near or far,
    Swift as the deluge, there we are,—
    Or as flames in the dark of night that sweep
    Over houses when all are fast asleep.   220
    Resistance is useless, flight no avail,
    Order and discipline equally fail;
    A girl may resist our sinewy arms,
    But war has no mercy for such alarms.
    Just ask, I'm not talking to boast,
    In Baireuth, in the Voigtland, wherever the host
    Of Holk and his huntsmen has once passed through,
    Children and children's children too
    Will still be telling the tale of how
    They passed a hundred years from now.   230
SERGEANT: Well, there you are! Riot and bluster,
    You think, will make a soldier pass muster?
    Alertness makes him, and skill and sense,
    Sure grasp, sharp eye, and intelligence.
FIRST JÄGER: Freedom makes him, that's what! Why snivel
    This way and waste my time with such drivel?
    Do you think I quit school, dodged 'prentice shop,
    Forced labor, the galleys, in order to drop
    Back into a secretarial clamp
    Of an office out here in the midst of a camp?   240
    I want to live lightly and leisurely,

Find something new every day to see,
Yield to the present and never mind
What lies ahead, what lies behind.
That's why I sold the Emperor my hide,
So I'd have have no more worries and cares to abide.
Take me out on the firing line,
Or across the deep and rushing Rhine,
Tell me every third comrade of mine
Will be killed, and I won't whimper or dally.   250
But apart from these things, I'm telling you flat,
Just see that it's kept clear out of my alley.

SERGEANT: Come, come, your aim is higher than that?
You found this much in the tunic you're wearing.

FIRST JÄGER: What trials we suffered with that overbearing
Gustavus of Sweden, tormentor of men!
He made a church of his camp and then
Had prayer meetings held in the morning right
After Reveille and also with Taps at night.
Let us once get lively, and down he would crack   260
With a sermon preached from Dobbin-back.

SERGEANT: He was a god-fearing man, that's sure.

FIRST JÄGER: No wenches allowed, except as we
Rushed them to church immediately.
I lit out. I couldn't stand any more.

SERGEANT: I hear things have changed now on that score.

FIRST JÄGER: So I rode to Magdeburg and down
To the Catholic League besieging the town.
Now that was quite a different affair!
Everything looser and lustier there,   270
With liquor and dice and wenches galore!
No fooling, there was fun to be had for fair,
For Tilly knew something about command.
He would drive himself till he was sore
But he let his soldiers have a free hand,
Just so long as he was not out of purse.
Live and let live: that was his verse.
But Luck would not keep him for a master,

And ever since the Leipzig disaster
It seemed as if nothing he did would succeed. 280
Things slowed to a walk—to a halt, indeed.
Wherever we showed up and knocked,
We got no greeting, no door unlocked.
We practically sneaked from place to place,
We got no respect, we had simply lost face.
So I went for pin money to a Saxon source,
Thinking my luck would thus shift course.

SERGEANT: Just in time to share the Bohemian plunder,
I would guess.

FIRST JÄGER: Not at all. It proved a blunder.
Discipline galled us, and niceties 290
Forbade us to act as enemies;
We had to guard the Emperor's places,
And bow and scrape with solemn faces;
We played at war as if in jest,
With half a heart for the business at best;
No one was to be offended really,
Nor honor gained—to speak quite freely.
I was so irked I would have gone home
To my high clerk's stool and accounting tome
If Friedland hadn't begun just then 300
To scour the highways recruiting men.

SERGEANT: How long do you think you'll last out here?

FIRST JÄGER: Scoff away! While *he's* in charge, never fear,
I won't be thinking of running away.
Can a soldier do better in living or pay?
Here, customs of war alone prevail,
With everything done on magnificent scale,
And the spirit that lives in the entire force
Sweeps a man on like the wind in its course,
Down to the lowliest trooper. Now I, 310
With a spring in my step and a light in my eye,
Can walk right over civilians as bold
As the Chief when he walks over Princes' heads.
We have things here as in days of old

When the rule of the rapier was the rule that told.
Here there's just one crime or offense:
To brook an order with insolence.
Where there isn't a rule, you may do as you please;
Nobody asks what a man believes.
Just two things to watch, and they are these: 320
What belongs to the Army and what does not.
The flag is the only duty I've got.
SERGEANT: Jäger, I like you! I like the way
You say what a soldier of Friedland should say.
FIRST JÄGER: He doesn't command as if in confinement
By rules and a post of the Emperor's assignment.
For the Emperor's service he cares not a whit.
When did he help the Emperor one bit?
For all that his power is immense,
What has he done in the country's defense?   330
He would like to found a soldier state,
Set the world on fire and initiate
Unheard-of ventures and innovate—
TRUMPETER: Quiet! Who dares to speak of this kind
Of thing!
FIRST JÄGER: I speak what's on my mind.
Speech is free, the General says.
SERGEANT: So he does. In several instances
I heard him say it. "Speech is free,
Actions are mute, obedience is blind."
Those are the actual terms he defined.   340
FIRST JÄGER: Whether he used those words, I don't know,
But the facts of the case are exactly so.
SECOND JÄGER: For him war's luck will never swerve
As happens with others, even the best.
Tilly outlived his fame. I serve
Under Friedland's banners, with warranty
That we shall therefore have victory.
He holds luck in thrall, it does his behest.
Beneath the signs that are his and ours
A man is protected by special powers.   350

For as the whole world knows full well
Friedland has in his paid employ
A devil out of the depths of hell.
SERGEANT: He is proof by magic to things that destroy,
No doubt of that. See how he bestrode
His horse in the Lützen battle and rode
Calmly amid the smoke and flame.
His hat was riddled with bullets, the same
Was true of his boots and doublet: traces
Of bullets were plain as the nose on your faces. 360
Not one of them had grazed his skin,
For hellish ointment had been rubbed in.
FIRST JÄGER: What miracles are being touted?
A bullet-proof doublet he wears, made of moose's
Hide, they say, and I don't doubt it.
SERGEANT: No, it's an ointment of herbs and their juices
Spell-brewed by witches who know their uses.
TRUMPETER: Yes, there's something uncanny about it!
SERGEANT: They also say he tells by a star
Of things of the future, both near and far. 370
But I know better, I'm not so dumb:
A little grey man is known to come
To him through doors that are locked for the night.
The sentries have challenged him when he neared.
And something great always follows the sight
Whenever that grey coat has come and appeared.
SECOND JÄGER: Oh yes, he has given himself to the Devil.
That's how we can have a life of revel.

(Enter a recruit, a civilian, and a Dragoon.)

RECRUIT *(emerging from the tent with a tin helmet on his head
    and a bottle of wine in his hand):*
Farewell to my father and all his men!
I'm a soldier and won't be back again. 380
FIRST JÄGER: Look, they're bringing a new one our way.
CIVILIAN: Franz, take care! You'll rue this day.
RECRUIT *(sings):* O the drum and the fife

And a soldier's song,
And a wandering life
The world along,
On horse to the field,
Reined up and wheeled,
A sword at my side,
And off far and wide,   390
Quick as a word,
Free as a bird
In the tree so high
Or up in the sky,
Hurrah! I follow the Friedlander's banners!
SECOND JÄGER: Well, there's a lad with jolly manners!

(They welcome him.)

CIVILIAN: He comes of good people, O, I entreat
  You to leave him.
FIRST JÄGER: Well, *we* weren't found on the street.
CIVILIAN: I tell you he has fortune and birth.
  Just feel his coat cloth, the best on earth.   400
TRUMPETER: The Emperor's coat is the highest worth.
CIVILIAN: He's heir to a little cap manufacture.
SECOND JÄGER: To do as he wills is man's true rapture.
CIVILIAN: His grandmother leaves him a shop and wares.
FIRST JÄGER: Bah, dealing in sulphur matches! Who cares!
CIVILIAN: His godmother leaves him a retail store
  With a cellar of twenty butts of wine.
TRUMPETER: On that his comrades will go shares.
SECOND JÄGER: Say, we must be tentmates, brother mine!
CIVILIAN: His betrothèd is left to her grief and tears.   410
FIRST JÄGER: Fine, there his iron heart appears.
CIVILIAN: His grandmother'll die of grief and despair.
SECOND JÄGER: So much the sooner he'll be her heir.
SERGEANT *(steps up gravely and lays his hand on the recruit's helmet):*
  It's right and proper, what you have done.
  You have put on a new man, my son.

With your helmet here and that sword on its thong,
You have joined up with a worthy throng.
Now a lofty spirit must enter your soul—
FIRST JÄGER: And don't stint your money, that's the main goal.
SERGEANT: On Fortuna's ship that rides the gales   420
You're about to embark and hoist your sails.
Open before you is the world's great globe.
With nothing ventured, there's nothing to hope.
Civilians are dullards and only drag
Themselves in a circle like a treadmill nag.
A soldier can reach anything of worth,
For War is now the watchword on earth.
Take *me*, now! This coat that I have on
Has the force of the Emperor's own baton.
From that baton all government   430
On earth, you know, takes its descent;
And the scepter in the royal hand
Is just a baton, you understand.
Once a man gets Corporal in front of his name
He has started the ladder to supreme fame
And power. You too can reach that height.
FIRST JÄGER: If you just know how to read and write.
SERGEANT: I'll give you an instance so you can see,
This came to my notice just recently.
There's a chief of dragoons up this way   440
Named Buttler; some thirty years ago
We were privates together in Köln; and you know:
They call him Major General today.
He worked his way up, that is to say,
And filled the world with his martial name.
But I have been left in the shadow of fame.
Yes, and this Friedland himself, you observe,
This exalted master whom we serve,
Who rules now all his eyes can scan,
Was a simple squire when he began.   450
By reliance upon the goddess of war
He achieved the peak he was striving for,

And after the Emperor he's the top man.
Who knows how high he still may get,—
          (slyly)
For the end of this business is not yet.
FIRST JÄGER: Yes, he started so small and is now so great.
At school in Altdorf he caused quite a scandal,
If I may speak so, acting the Vandal
And carrying on at a high old rate.
His famulus, whom he dared mishandle,   460
Came near dying. The Nürnberg men
Decided to jail him there and then.
The jail was brand new and the first to reside there
Was supposed to lend the place his name.
But what happened before he got inside there?
He sent on his dog before he came,
And the jail to this day is named for the pup.
A clever cuss may be seen warming up
In that story. Of all the things he has done,
That little trick is my favorite one.

    (The waitress has meanwhile been serving
    and the Second Jäger has been making up to her.)

DRAGOON *(stepping between them)*:
Comrade, you've gone far enough, do you hear?
SECOND JÄGER: Why the Devil should you interfere!
DRAGOON: I just want to tell you the wench is for me.
FIRST JÄGER: He wants a sweetheart exclusively
For himself. Dragoon, are you out of your mind?
SECOND JÄGER: Here in camp something private of this kind!
A wench's pretty face must be
Like sunlight, shared with the company.

            (He kisses her.)

DRAGOON *(wrenches her away)*:
I won't stand for this. I say, let her be!
FIRST JÄGER: Hey, hey! Here come the Praguers!
SECOND JÄGER: You'll find   480
That I'm your man if it's trouble you're making.

SERGEANT: Peace, peace! A kiss is free for the taking.

([*Prague musicians dressed as*] *miners appear and play a* *waltz, slowly at first, then faster and faster. The first Jäger* *dances with the waitress, the sutlerwoman with the recruit.* *The girl slips away. The Jäger pursues her and mistakenly* *seizes the Capuchin friar who is just coming on the scene.*)

CAPUCHIN FRIAR: Halloo! Hurray! Fiddle-dee-dee!
Fine doings! I'll join you in your spree!
Is this an army of Christians or Turks?
Or Antibaptists maybe, that shirks
Its Sabbath respect to mock and flout
As if Almighty God had gout
In His hands and couldn't interfere?
Is this the time for orgies here,   490
For banquets and bouts and holyday cheer?
Quid hic statis otiosi?
Why do you stand with your hands in your laps?
By the Danube war's Fury is loose; in collapse
Is Bavaria's bulwark, fallen and low
Regenspurg lies in the claws of the foe.
And the Army lies here in Bohemia, sees
That its belly is stuffed, and takes its ease,
More concerned about its wear than its war,
Wetting its whistle, not whetting its sword,   500
Gallivanting around with doxies,
Eating not Oxenstirn but oxes.
In sackcloth and ashes Christendom grieves,
But the soldier just fills his pockets and leaves.
The time is for tears and lamentation,
Marvels and portents occur in the sky,
Blood-red out of clouds the Lord of Creation
Unfurls His mantle of war from on high.
He has placed the comet like a whip before
The window of heaven, and here we languish   510
While the whole world is a house of anguish
And the ark of the Church is swimming in gore.

The Roman State in its present position—
Which God amend!—is the Rummy Condition.
The Rhine runs tears till it's known as the Brine,
The cloisters are sacked and renamed the roisters,
The dioceses are changed into dire seas,
The convent walls and monasteries
Are brigand-stalls and robber-eyries,
And our blessed German territories   520
Are all transformed into terrortories.
Whence comes this? Where was its beginning?
I tell you it comes from your vices and sinning,
From the heathenish life and abomination
Which are soldiers' and officers' ruination.
For sin is the magnet in your hands
That draws cold steel into our lands.
Out of wrongdoing will evils arise.
As sure as onions draw tears from your eyes.
V is for vice, with double-v next,   530
Which will W woes throughout the text.
        Ubi erit victoriae spes
Si offenditur Deus? What hope can there be
Of triumph when cutting your sermon and Mass
And lying in taverns perpetually?
The woman in the Gospel story
Sought her lost groat and found it again,
Saul found his father's lost asses again,
And Joseph his lovely bretheren,
But among soldiers a man may plod   540
Seeking discipline, the fear of God,
A sense of shame, and find them never,
Though a hundred lanterns light his endeavor.
To the preacher in the wilderness
Soldiers once came with eagerness,
As we read in the Gospel, who realized
Their sins, repented, and were baptized.
They asked him: *Quid faciemus nos?*
What is needful that we may in Abraham's bosom repose?

Fate Started by you—not imposed.

Et ait illis, and to them he spoke: 550
Neminem concutiatis,
Harass no man, neither provoke,
Neque calumniam faciatis,
See no man maligned nor no man belied,
Contenti estote, be satisfied,
Stipendiis vestris, with your pay,
And accursed be every bad habit and way.
The Commandment says: Thou shalt refrain
From taking the Lord God's name in vain.
And can more blasphemies be found   560
Than here in Friedland's Headquarters abound?
If for every Damn! that skips
In a flurry of sparks from the spouts of your lips
The bells were to ring in the land around,
Soon not a sexton more would be found.
And if for every evil word
That from your unwashed mouths is heard
A single hair were lost and shed,
Overnight you'd be shorn and bald, it is true,
Though your hair were as thick as on Absolom's head.   570
Now Joshua was a soldier too,
And Goliath it was that David slew,
But where will you find it stated plain
That they were foul-mouthed and profane?
Yet the mouth requires no wider stretching
To say "Please God!", I know full well,
Than to pronounce "God damn it to hell!"
But with whatsoever a vessel is filled,
That is what overflows and is spilled.
    Another Commandant is: Thou shalt not steal.   580
Well, that one you follow quite literally,
You carry things off when all can see.
From your vulture claws and talon vises,
From your rascals' tricks and your rascals' devices,
Cash is not safe in the till where it hides,
The calf is not safe in the cow's insides,

You take the egg and the hen besides.
Contenti estote the Preacher has said,
Be content with your regimental bread.
But how can the menials be spoken of   590
With praise? The mischief comes from above!
As the head does, so the members must,
And nobody knows in whom *he* puts trust!

FIRST JÄGER: Priest! Us soldiers you can slander,
But don't you dare rail at our Commander!

CAPUCHIN FRIAR: *Ne custodias gregem meam!*
He is like unto Ahab and Jerobeam,
Corrupting men's faith and making them bow
Unto false idols in spite of their vow.

twist
faith
for own
use

TRUMPETER AND RECRUIT: Don't you dare repeat what you're
saying now!   600

CAPUCHIN FRIAR: Of all the loud-mouths and fire-eating clowns!
He wants to take over all fortified towns.
His godless mouth once made the boast
He would take Stralsund on the coast
Though it were bound to heaven by chains.
But he wasted his powder for all his pains.

TRUMPETER: Will nobody stop his blasphemous screed?

CAPUCHIN FRIAR: He's a summoner of fiends, a King Saul indeed,
A Jehu, a Holofernes; he'll deny
His Master and Lord, like Peter; that's why
He cannot endure to hear the cock crow—   610

BOTH JÄGERS: Priest! You've gone far enough, you know!

CAPUCHIN FRIAR: A cunning fox of a Herod as well—

TRUMPETER AND BOTH JÄGERS (*advancing upon him*):
Shut up! Or it's your death knell!

CROATS (*intervening*):
Stay put, monk old boy, stand your ground,
Speak your piece and we'll gather round.

CAPUCHIN FRIAR (*shouting louder*):
He's a downright Nebuchadnezzar for pride,
An arch-sinner, a heretic deep-dyed,
And he goes by the name of Wallenstein,

And he is indeed a Wailing Sign,
A stone of stumbling and a rock of offense,   620
And as long as the Emperor lets this Friedland
Hold power, this won't be a war-freed land.

(*Little by little during these final words, which he speaks in a loud voice, he effects his retreat, while the Croats protect him from the other soldiers.*)

FIRST JÄGER (*to the Sergeant*):
Say, what's this about roosters, I'd like to know,
That the Chief can't stand to hear them crow?
He meant some slur, I saw in a minute.
SERGEANT: That I can tell you. There *is* something in it.
Our Chief was oddly born, it appears;
For one thing, he has most finicky ears.
He cannot abide the meow of a cat
And the crowing of roosters he shudders at.   630
FIRST JÄGER: The same way with lions.
SERGEANT: All around
He wants it mouse-still, without a sound.
That's the order that all his guards are assigned.
Things much too deep are on his mind.

(*Uproar inside the tent.*)

VOICES: Grab him, the rascal! Belt him a few!
VOICE OF THE PEASANT: Help! Have mercy!
OTHER VOICES: Quiet, you!
FIRST JÄGER: Devil take me, here's a squabble!
SECOND JÄGER: I must get into it! (*They run to the tent.*)
SUTLERWOMAN (*emerging*): Thieving rabble!
TRUMPETER: Hostess, what's got you all of a sputter?
SUTLERWOMAN: The tramp! The scoundrel! The scum of the
  gutter!   640
To think this should happen in my own tent!
I'll be hooted in every regiment.
SERGEANT: What's the fuss, my dear?
SUTLERWOMAN: The fuss?

They've caught a peasant in there, and the cuss
Was playing with loaded dice.

TRUMPETER: And here
They come with him now, and his son to the rear.

(Soldiers drag the peasant forward.)

FIRST JÄGER: He'll swing for this.

SHARPSHOOTER AND DRAGOON: Provost! Provost!

SERGEANT: The order was issued just recently.

SUTLERWOMAN: I'll see him this hour high in a tree.

SERGEANT: Bad dealings bring bad compensation.   650

FIRST ARQUEBUSIER *(to the second)*:
All this comes of their desperation.
We ruin them first, which amounts to appealing
To them ourselves to take up stealing.

TRUMPETER: Do you go so far as to speak in his favor?
The swine! Is the Devil in you today?

FIRST ARQUEBUSIER: A peasant is human too—in a way.

FIRST JÄGER *(to the Trumpeter)*:
They're Tiefenbachers, let them pass.
All tailors and glovers and men of that class.
They're up from Brieg, a garrison spot;
When it comes to warfare they know a lot.   660

(Enter Cuirassiers.)

FIRST CUIRASSIER: What's going on with that peasant there?

FIRST SHARPSHOOTER: It's a rascal they caught not playing fair.

FIRST CUIRASSIER: Do you mean to say he cheated *you?*

FIRST SHARPSHOOTER: Yes, and took everything on me too.

FIRST CUIRASSIER: What? And you a Friedland man,
Can you lower yourself and play the fool
To risk your luck with a peasant tool?
Off with him now as fast as he can.

*(The peasant slips away.
The others gather together.)*

FIRST ARQUEBUSIER: He makes short work, he knows his mind.
That's the way to deal with that kind.   670

He's not a Bohemian, I expect?

SUTLERWOMAN: A Walloon, and he deserves your respect!
One of the Pappenheim Cuirassiers.

FIRST DRAGOON (steps up):
It's Piccolomini the younger who rears
Their standard. They chose him themselves to wield
Their command on the Lützen battlefield
After Pappenheim was killed in action.

FIRST ARQUEBUSIER: They had the nerve for such a transaction?

FIRST DRAGOON: That regiment has special rights.
It was always first in all the fights,   680
In cases of law has autonomy,
And Friedland loves it especially.

FIRST CUIRASSIER (to the second one):
Are you sure? Who started these rumor flights?

SECOND CUIRASSIER: I have the Colonel's word that it's so.

FIRST CUIRASSIER: Damn it! We're not their dogs, you know.

FIRST JÄGER: What's eating them? They look poisonous.

SECOND JÄGER: Is it something, Sirs, that touches us?

FIRST CURASSIER: Nobody will like it overmuch.
            (Soldiers gather around.)
They're going to lend us to fight the Dutch.
Cuirassiers and Jägers and riflemen   690
Eight thousand strong are to ride again.

SUTLERWOMAN: What? What? We're to be again on our way?
I got here from Flanders just yesterday.

SECOND CUIRASSIER (to the Dragoons):
You Buttler men, too, will be riding on.

FIRST CUIRASSIER: It means us Walloons, first on the spot.

SUTLERWOMAN: Why, those squadrons of yours are the best of the
    lot!

FIRST CUIRASSIER: It's for us to escort the man from Milan.

FIRST JÄGER: The Infante? That's curious now, I'd say.

SECOND JÄGER: The priest! Then there'll be the Devil to pay.

FIRST CUIRASSIER: We are supposed to leave Friedland, the
    best   700
Of generals, who keeps us in royal style,

To take the field with this Spaniard, this vile
Skinflint, whom we in our hearts detest?
Not on your life! We'll run away.

TRUMPETER: Once we got there, what part would we play?
We've sold our blood for the Emperor's endeavor,
But to that Hispanic red hat—never!

SECOND JÄGER: We accepted service under the sign
Of Friedland on Friedland's word. And thus,
Were it not for our love to Wallenstein,   710
Ferdinand never would have had us.

FIRST DRAGOON: It was Friedland who organized our forces;
His Fortuna shall guide our courses.

SERGEANT: Listen to me, I will explain:
This kind of talk is pointless and vain.
I see further than all of you there:
Behind all this is a treacherous snare.

FIRST JÄGER: The Manual speaks! Quiet! Be still!

SERGEANT: Gustel, my girl, be so good as to fill
A glass of Melneck for my digestion,   720
And then I'll tell you my suggestion.

SUTLERWOMAN (pouring out the wine for him):
Here, Sergeant.—You scare me. I hope there is
Nothing too bad behind all this!

SERGEANT: Now, you see, each man is doing quite right
When he keeps his immediate concerns in sight.
But as our Commander likes to say,
The whole must also be kept in survey.
We call ourselves, all of us, Friedland's troops.
The civilian quarters us, shares his stocks,
Takes care of us, and cooks us hot soups;   730
The peasant must hitch his nag or his ox
To our baggage carts. He may complain,
But all his complaining will be in vain.
Just let a Corporal with seven men
Come near a town to which he's been sent:
He's the authority there, and then
He can rule and give orders to his heart's content.

None of them like us, whoever they are.
They'd rather behold the Devil by far
Than our yellow jerkins. Then why don't they   740
Throw us off their land and drive us away?
They have us outnumbered, by the Lord!
They're as handy with cudgels as we with the sword.
Why can we laugh at them? Because,
In a group, we inspire a terror that awes!

FIRST JÄGER: Yes! Power lies in the group. That's so!
Friedland himself discovered that fact
When he raised the great Army the Emperor lacked
Eight—or was it nine?—years ago.
Twelve thousand, they said, was the most they would need. 750
That many, said he, I couldn't feed;
But I *will* raise sixty thousand. I know
That *they*'ll never starve wherever they go.
And Wallensteiners we thus became.

SERGEANT: For example, if one of you should maim
This right hand of mine by lopping away
My smallest finger of five, could you say
You'd taken my finger only?—No!
By gad, I'd have lost my hand *in toto*!
It's only a stump and of no avail.   760
And these eight thousand horse they want to detail
For service in Flanders now entail
The Army's little finger clearly.
And if they let them go, do you think
We lose a fifth of our forces merely?
Not much! The whole thing's over the brink.
Respect is gone and awe wears thin,
The peasant's comb will swell once again,
The Vienna War Office will begin
To issue us orders for billets and board,   770
And there's the Starvation Line restored.
And just how long will it be before
Our Commander won't be with us any more?
They're down on him now at Court as it is,

But everything's shot if it gets to this.
Who'll help us then to get our pay?
Who'll see that contracts are kept anyway?
Who has the energy, who can command
The nimble wit and the steady hand
To keep this catchall force in control   780
And weld it together in a workable whole?
For instance—Dragoon—What was the place
You hail from? What fatherland and race?

FIRST DRAGOON: Ireland, in my particular case.

SERGEANT (to the two Cuirassiers):
You're a Walloon, I happen to know,
And you're a Latin, as your talk will show.

FIRST CUIRASSIER: Who *I* am I never could find out:
I was kidnapped in childhood and carried about.

SERGEANT: You also are not from up this way?

FIRST ARQUEBUSIER: I'm from Buchau on the Federsee.   790

SERGEANT: And you there, neighbor?

SECOND ARQUEBUSIER: From Canton Schwyz.

SERGEANT (to the second Jäger):
And what's the district you're from, Jäger?

SECOND JÄGER: Beyond Wismar lay my ancestors' seats.

SERGEANT (pointing to the Trumpeter):
And this lad and I, we're from Eger.
Now who could tell from the look of this flock
That we were snowed and blown together
From South and North by all kinds of weather?
Don't we look hewn from a single block?
Don't we stand united against the foe
As if we were moulded and glued in a row?   800
Don't we mesh like cogwheels as neat as you please
At a word or a sign from authorities?
Who forged us together with such fine art
That no one can ever tell us apart?
Why, Wallenstein! Who else could it be?

FIRST JÄGER: Why, that had never occurred to me
In all my days, that we blend so well;

I just went along however things fell.

FIRST CUIRASSIER: I must agree with the Sergeant. They would
    Destroy the Army if they could.   810
    They like to keep the soldier down
    So they can rule and have renown
    For themselves. It's a plot, a conspiracy.

SUTLERWOMAN: O Lord above! A conspiracy!
    Then the gentlemen couldn't pay their debts.

SERGEANT: That's right! They're headed for bankruptcy.
    Many a Captain's and General's assets
    Were staked to furnish regiments,
    And, aiming at show and magnificence,
    They went in deeper than they could afford,   820
    Thinking they'd get a great reward.
    And they will be ruined, one and all
    If the head, if the Duke himself should fall.

SUTLERWOMAN: Lord save us! I am on tenterhooks.
    Half of the Army are on my books.
    Count Isolani, a risky credit,
    Has two hundred Thalers alone in debit.

FIRST CUIRASSIER: Comrades, what's to be done in this plight?
    One thing can save us if anything can:
    They can't do us harm if we unite,   830
    So we'll stand together to a man.
    Then let them send and issue orders,
    We'll root ourselves fast in Bohemia's borders,
    We won't give way, not a march will we make,
    The soldier's honor is now at stake.

SECOND JÄGER: We won't be led round about this way!
    Just let them come and try it, I say!

FIRST ARQUEBUSIER: Consider carefully, Sirs, your stand.
    This is the Emperor's will and command.

TRUMPETER: A lot *we* care what the Emperor wants!   840

FIRST ARQUEBUSIER: You'd better not say that more than once.

TRUMPETER: It's so, all the same, just as I stated.

FIRST JÄGER: Yes, *I*'ve always heard things put that way:
    Here Friedland alone has it to say.

SERGEANT: And it's true. His contract stipulated
  Absolute power, if you please,
  For waging war and concluding peace.
  Money and goods he can confiscate,
  He can hang or pardon, and nominate
  Commanders and officers of every sort.   850
  He has all the prerogatives, in short,—
  And all in the Emperor's handwriting too.

FIRST ARQUEBUSIER: The Duke is powerful and clever, it's true,
  But like us all, say what you will,
  He remains the Emperor's vassal still.

SERGEANT: Not like us all! There you are ill
  Informed. He's a sovereign, equalitarian
  Prince of the Realm, just like the Bavarian.
  Didn't I see with my own eyes
  When I was one of the guards at Brandeis   860
  The way the Emperor gave him leave
  To cover his princely head?

FIRST ARQUEBUSIER: I believe
  That was because the Emperor had just
  Given him Mecklenburg Duchy in trust.

FIRST JÄGER (to the Sergeant):
  What? In the presence of Majesty?
  That's pretty special—a rarity.

SERGEANT (reaching into his pocket):
  Well, if my word doesn't meet your demands,
  You shall touch and feel with your own hands.
          (Producing a coin)
  Whose stamp and image is this?

SUTLERWOMAN: Let's see!
  Why, that's simple. This is a Wallenstein penny.   870

SERGEANT: There you are! What better proof can there be?
  Isn't he a Prince as much as any?
  Doesn't he mint coins like Ferdinand?
  Doesn't he own subjects and rule a land?
  He's termed Serene Highness in everyone's sight.
  Then maintaining soldiers must be his right.

FIRST ARQUEBUSIER: Nobody is arguing that point with you.
　But the Emperor's allegiance is our due.
　And the man who pays us is the Emperor.
TRUMPETER: I deny that right to your face! It's not true!　880
　The man who does *not* pay us, that is the Emperor!
　For forty weeks have they not been deceiving
　Us with promise of pay we should be receiving?
FIRST ARQUEBUSIER: It's in good hands, as everyone knows.
FIRST CUIRASSIER: Peace, gentlemen! Must you end with blows?
　Must there be wrangling and disaccord
　Over whether the Emperor is our Lord?
　Precisely because we would like to be
　His loyal and honorable cavalry
　We refuse to act like his silly sheep.　890
　We won't be led and transported around
　By priests and toadies on foreign ground.
　If troops take pride in themselves, it's plain,
　Is it not, that their master stands to gain?
　Who but his soldiers maintains his state
　And makes him the mighty potentate?
　His controlling voice, from whom does it come,
　That he wields throughout all Christendom?
　Let those who feed on his favor assume
　His yoke, and who dine in a golden room　900
　With him. Of all his splendor and glitter
　We, we have nothing but the bitter
　Trials and pains,—and the thing which we
　Know ourselves, in our hearts, to be.
SECOND JÄGER: What all the great Emperors used to do
　Was this, and wiser they were for it too:
　They neglected and browbeat the rest of the sheep
　But they put the soldier on top of the heap.
FIRST CUIRASSIER: The soldier must feel a sense of his worth,
　And one who does not act nobly would　910
　Do well to steer clear of the trade for good.
　If I am to risk my life on this earth,
　There must be something more precious to vie for,

Or I herd to the slaughter as Croats go—
And despise myself for doing so.

BOTH JÄGERS: Yes, honor is something a man must die for.

FIRST CUIRASSIER: The sword is no spade, no plow, and to
    use it
To dig in the fields would be to abuse it.
For us neither grass nor seed grows tall,
Upon the earth soldiers must all   920
Wander homeless in a vagrant swarm;
They may not at native hearthsides warm;
They must forego the splendor of towns;
And village greens with their frolicking,
The garnered grapes and the harvest crowns
They must glimpse from afar in their wandering.
Unless he takes pride in himself, what on earth
Does a soldier have of value or worth?
A man must call something his own; if not,
Murder and arson will be his lot.   930

FIRST ARQUEBUSIER: God knows, it's a dismal existence, brother.

FIRST CUIRASSIER: But I wouldn't exchange it for any other.
I've gotten around in the world, you know,
And had experience of how things go.
I've served the Hispanic monarchy;
The Venetian Republic recalls what I gave her,
As does the Kingdom of Napoli;
But Fortune has never shown me favor.
I have seen the merchant and the knight,
The artisan and the anchorite,   940
And of all their garbs not one made me feel
The pleasure I take in my jerkin of steel.

FIRST ARQUEBUSIER: On that, now, I take another position.

FIRST CUIRASSIER: If a man aspires to some condition,
Let him stir and let him show some ambition.
If honors and rank are his goal, let him poke
His head underneath the golden yoke;
If he yearns for family blessedness
Where sons and grandsons around him will press,

Let him ply some honest trade in peace.   950
I—I lack the temperament for these.
Free will I live and as freely die,
Rob no one, be no one's heir, and high
Above the furor around me cast
My carefree gaze as I ride past.

FIRST JÄGER: That's just the lot that I would cast!

FIRST ARQUEBUSIER: It's more fun riding any day
Over others' heads and off and away.

FIRST CUIRASSIER: Comrade, times are hard, and the scales
With the sword beside it no longer prevails.   960
And no one can criticize me therefore
For preferring the life of the sword. In war
I can still be human and not like a drum
To be beaten upon by any who come.

FIRST ARQUEBUSIER: Who but we soldiers deserves the blame
If productive civilians have got a bad name?
This hateful war with its woes and tears
Has now dragged on some sixteen years.

FIRST CUIRASSIER: Brother, the dear Lord above cannot be
Praised by all simultaneously.   970
One man wants sunshine, his brother's bane,
One wants the drought, one wants the rain.
Where *you* see trouble and misery,
There bright daylight may shine for *me*.
If civilians and peasants suffer thereby,
I'm truly sorry, so say I.
But I cannot change it.—You see, it's just
Like when we make an attack or a thrust:
The horses are snorting and race to the charge,
Whoever then lies in my path at large,   980
My brother, my very son though he be,
Though his piteous cry rend the soul of me,
Over his body I must ride,
I cannot carry him gently aside.

FIRST JÄGER: Aye, who could think then of another man's side?

FIRST CUIRASSIER: And since things are such, for once in a way,

all it takes is "peace" by leaders irreg. of people

war declared & stopped without vote — that you know.

That Fortune smiles on the soldier, I say
Let's grab it and hold it with hands that are strong,
They won't let us keep it for very long.
Peace will be made overnight by the Powers   990
And put an end to this life of ours.
The soldier dismounts, and Dobbin does
The farm work, and there's the world as it was.
We're still all together in this land,
We still have the helm firmly in hand,
But once we're dispersed, you can look up higher
Where they dangle our breadbasket on a shorter wire.

socialism?

FIRST JÄGER: No, that we must never allow to be done!
Let's all stand together united as one!

SECOND JÄGER: Yes, let's agree. Quiet! Be still!   1000

FIRST ARQUEBUSIER (*taking out a leather moneysack, to the
     sutlerwoman*):
Tell me, hostess, how much is my bill?

SUTLERWOMAN: Oh, hardly worth mention, this little bill!

(They reckon up.)

TRUMPETER: It's good that you're leaving. All you've done
Is put a damper on our fun.

Comedy

(The Arquebusiers leave.)

FIRST CUIRASSIER: What a shame! They're really nice fellows,
     you know.

FIRST JÄGER: They think like a pack of soap boilers, though.

SECOND JÄGER: Now we're by ourselves, let's see what we can
Concoct to upset this latest plan.

TRUMPETER: Why, we just won't march from the place we're in.

FIRST CUIRASSIER: Nothing, Sirs, counter to discipline!   1010
Each man will go now to his own corps
And there he will lay the matter before
His comrades till they understand the way
Things stand: We can't go so far away.
My Walloons I can safely guarantee,
There every man agrees with me.

SERGEANT: Terzka's regiments, foot and horse,
  Are all agreed upon this course.
SECOND CUIRASSIER (*turning to the first one*):
  Lombard from Walloon shall not be rent.
FIRST JÄGER: Freedom's the Jäger's element.   1020
SECOND JÄGER: With power alone can freedom combine.
  I'll live and die with Wallenstein.
FIRST SHARPSHOOTER: The man of Lorraine follows the tide
  Where mirth and spirit are ever allied.
DRAGOON: The Irishman follows his fortune's star.
SECOND SHARPSHOOTER: The Tyrolian serves his lord in war.
FIRST CUIRASSIER: Let every regiment then inscribe
  A *Pro Memoria* bold and plain:
  All together we mean to remain,
  And any force or trick they think of   1030
  To drive us from Friedland will be in vain,
  For he bears his soldiers a father's love.
  This we shall tender in humble devotion
  To Piccolomini—I mean the son—
  He knows how to handle these things with skill
  And with Friedland he can do as he will;
  He also has an ace in the hole
  With the King and the Emperor at the other pole.
SECOND JÄGER: That's it, then! Shake hands to show we agree!
  Our spokesman shall be Piccolomini.   1040
TRUMPETER
DRAGOON
FIRST JÄGER   (*simultaneously*):
SECOND CUIRASSIER   Our spokesman shall be Piccolomini.
SHARPSHOOTER   (*They start to go.*)
SERGEANT: First, comrades, one more glass: To the health
  Of Piccolomini's noble self!
                    (*He drinks.*)
SUTLERWOMAN (*bringing a bottle*):
  No charge for that. I can do no less.
  I wish you gentlemen all success.

FIRST CUIRASSIER: May soldiers flourish!

BOTH JÄGERS: May civilians furnish!

DRAGOON AND SHARPSHOOTERS: May the Army thrive in the land!

TRUMPETER AND SERGEANT: With Friedland in command!

SECOND CUIRASSIER: Then up with you, comrades, to horse, to
horse,   1050
  To battle, to freedom ride forth.
  Out there a man's worth is still in force
    And the heart is weighed for its worth.
  None other out there can take his place,
  He must stand for himself alone in space.

  (During the singing the soldiers in the rear have come
  forward and now form the chorus.)

CHORUS: None other out there can take his place,
  He must stand for himself alone in space.

DRAGOON: Freedom has vanished out of the land,
    Only masters and slaves will you find;
  Deceit and treachery now command   1060
    Among craven human kind.
  Looking death in the face, as only he can,
  There's none but the soldier who is a free man.

CHORUS: Looking death in the face, as only he can,
  There's none but the soldier who is a free man.

FIRST JÄGER: The cares of life, he casts them aside,
    He's finished with fear and sorrow;
  Out against Fate he makes bold to ride,
    Today's miss is the meet of tomorrow.
  And if it's tomorrow, then let us today   1070
  Drink Time's delights to the dregs while we may.

CHORUS: And if it's tomorrow, then let us today
  Drink Time's delights to the dregs while we may.

    (The glasses have been filled again. They
        clink glasses and drink.)

SERGEANT: His lot falls to him from Heaven on high,

It takes him no effort to win it;
The serf, he searches the soil to try
    For the treasure he fancies is in it.
He digs and grubs and lives like a slave,
And grubs till finally he grubs his grave.
CHORUS: He digs and grubs and lives like a slave,
And grubs till finally he grubs his grave.

put down farmer as slave & romantic soldier when really more of a slave — to killing/iction to Emp. while serf is ruled by nature & Emp. is killing nature? after yes but before - NO

1080

"Grub"

FIRST JÄGER: Rider and steed rushing in flight
    Are guests to be feared at the least.
Lamps gleam in the wedding castle by night,
    Unbidden he comes to the feast.
His wooing is brief and gold he denies,
He captures by storm his lovely prize.
CHORUS: His wooing is brief and gold he denies,
He captures by storm his lovely prize.

Nonsense

SECOND CUIRASSIER: Why weeps the wench, wasting away? 1090
    Let him go, let him go, it is vain.
There's no home on earth where he will stay,
    True love he cannot sustain.
Swift Fate impels his onward fleeing,
To his peace he will leave no place of being.
CHORUS: Swift Fate impels his onward fleeing,
To his peace he will leave no place of being.

babbling-cheerleading

it's fate "I have a disease"

FIRST JÄGER (*takes the hands of the two nearest to him. The others follow suit. All the speakers form a large semicircle.*)
Up then, comrades, saddle your steeds,
    With hearts in battle delighted!
Youth seethes, life foams! So onward to deeds 1100
    Before the spirit is blighted.
Till life has been staked for the rise or the fall
Your life will never be won at all.
CHORUS: Till life has been staked for the rise or the fall
Your life will never be won at all. [1105]

die to live? except kill is slid in there

(*The curtain falls before the Chorus
has finished singing.*)

poop

THE PICCOLOMINIS

in Five Acts

CHARACTERS

ALBRECHT WALLENSTEIN, Duke of Friedland, Imperial
      Generalissimo in the Thirty Years War
OCTAVIO PICCOLOMINI, Lieutenant General
MAX PICCOLOMINI, his son, Colonel of a regiment of Cuirassiers
COUNT TERZKY, Wallenstein's brother-in-law, commander of
      several regiments
ILLO, Field Marshal, Wallenstein's confidant
ISOLANI, General of Croats
BUTTLER, Commander of a regiment of Dragoons
TIEFENBACH ⎫
DON MARÁDAS ⎬ Generals under Wallenstein
GÖTZ   ⎪
KOLALTO   ⎭
CAVALRY CAPTAIN NEUMANN, Terzky's adjutant
WAR MINISTER VON QUESTENBERG, envoy from the Emperor
BAPTISTA SENI, an astrologer
THE DUCHESS OF FRIEDLAND, Wallenstein's spouse
THEKLA, Princess of Friedland, her daughter
COUNTESS TERZKY, sister of the Duchess
A CORNET
CELLAR MASTER of Count Terzky
Pages and servants of Friedland
Servants and musicians of Terzky's retinue
Various Colonels and Generals

Time: February 1634.
Place: The town of Pilsen in Bohemia.

ACT I

An old Gothic hall in the City Hall at Pilsen, decorated with flags and other military objects.
Enter Illo with Buttler and Isolani.

ILLO: You're late—but still you're here. The lengthy journey,
  Count Isolan, excuses your delay.
ISOLANI: And we do not arrive with empty hands!
  Near Donauwerth it was reported to us
  A Swedish transport train was on its way
  With rations, some hundred wagons of it.—
  My Croats found the time to grab it up;
  We have it with us.
ILLO: It will come in handy
  To feed the noble crowd that's gathered here.
BUTTLER: It's pretty lively here, I see.
ISOLANI: Yes, yes,   10
  The very churches are jam-packed with soldiers;
                    (looking around)
  And in the City Hall, I see, you've fixed
  Up quarters of a sort.—Well, soldiers must make shift
  And help themselves as best they can.
ILLO: Commanders from no less than thirty of
  The regiments are gathered here already;
  Terzky, you'll find here, and Tiefenbach,
  Kolalto, Götz, Marádas, Hinnersam,
  The Piccolominis, both son and father,—
  You'll meet a lot of old familiar friends.   20
  Just Gallas yet to come, and Altringer.
BUTTLER: Gallas you needn't wait for.
ILLO *(startled)*:   Why? You know—?

45

ISOLANI *(interrupting him):*
  Max Piccolomini here? O lead me to him.
  I see him yet—it was ten years ago—
  When we were fighting Mansfeld down by Dessau—
  Jumping his horse down from the bridge and battling
  Against the rushing waters of the Elbe
  To reach his father who was in a pinch.
  The first fuzz on his chin had barely sprouted;
  I hear he's quite the seasoned warrior now.   30
ILLO: You'll see him yet today. He's bringing up
  The Duchess Friedland and the Princess from
  Carinthia. They should arrive this morning.
BUTTLER: The Duke has sent for both his wife and daughter?
  It's quite a crowd he's gathered.
ISOLANI: All the better.
  Just when I thought we'd get to hear of nothing
  But marches, rough-and-tumbles, and attacks,
  Why, here the Duke has gone and taken pains
  To furnish something sweet to catch the eye.
ILLO *(who has stood in thought, to Buttler, taking him aside
    a bit):*
  How do you know Count Gallas will not come?   40
BUTTLER *(meaningfully):*
  Because he tried to talk *me* out of coming.
ILLO *(warmly):*
  And you stood firm?
                    (pressing his hand)
                Ah, that's our good old Buttler!
BUTTLER: Well, after the indebtedness in which
  I stand now to the Duke—
ILLO: Yes, Major General. Congratulations!
ISOLANI: Yes, wasn't it a regiment to which
  The Duke appointed you? What's more, I hear,
  The one where you had worked up from the ranks?
  How true it is! It spurs an entire corps,
  You know, when every now and then an old   50
  Deserving soldier makes his way.

BUTTLER: I am embarrassed
  About accepting the congratulations.
  —The Emperor has not sent his confirmation.
ISOLANI: Take it! Take it! The hand that put you there
  Is strong enough to keep you there in spite
  Of Emperors and Ministers.
ILLO: If we
  Were all as scrupulous as that!
  The Emperor gives us nothing—from
  The Duke comes all we have or hope to have.
ISOLANI (to Illo):
  I've told you, haven't I, old boy? The Duke   60
  Is going to satisfy my creditors,
  Says he himself will henceforth be my purser
  And make an honest man of me at last.
  And this is now the third time, just remember,
  That regal-minded man has plucked me from
  Destruction and returned me to my honor.
ILLO: If he could always do the way he liked!
  He'd give his soldiers everything in sight.
  But then the way they tie his hands there in Vienna—
  And clip his wings for him at every turn!—   70
  Now, just take these nice new demands sent up
  Here by this fellow Questenberg!
BUTTLER: I've heard a bit
  About these new Imperial demands myself,—
  But I can do no more than hope
  The Duke will not give way on any point.
ILLO: Not from his rights, that's sure, if only not
  —From his position!
BUTTLER (struck):   You know, you frighten me.
ISOLANI (simultaneously):
  We'd all be ruined!
ILLO: Let us drop the subject.
  I see the man in question coming now with
  Lieutenant-General Piccolomini.
BUTTLER (shaking his head dubiously):   I fear   80

We won't leave here the way we came.

(Enter Octavio Piccolomini
and Questenberg.)

OCTAVIO *(still some distance away):*
  What? Still more guests? Acknowledge it, my friend,
  It took this war with all its tears to gather
  The fame-crowned heads of such a host of heroes
  Within the confines of a single camp.
QUESTENBERG: Let no man who prefers to think war evil
  Come into any one of Friedland's camps.
  Its scourges all but vanished from my mind
  When I beheld the lofty rule of order
  By which it lives while it destroys the world   90
  And all the grandeur it establishes.
OCTAVIO: And look at that brave pair that worthily
  Concludes the hero line. Count Isolan
  And Colonel Buttler.—There we have before
  Our eyes the total handiwork of war.

(presenting Buttler and Isolani)

  This one is Strength, my friend, and this one Swiftness.
QUESTENBERG *(to Octavio):*
  And Shrewdness of Experience stands between them.
OCTAVIO *(introducing Questenberg to the others):*
  This guest we honor here is Chamberlain
  Questenberg and Minister of War,
  The bringer of Imperial commands,   100
  Patron and intercessor of the soldier.

(general silence)

ILLO *(approaching Questenberg):*
  This is not the first time, Excellency,
  That you have honored us this way in camp.
QUESTENBERG: No, once before I stood beneath these flags.
ILLO: Do you remember where that was? It was
  At Znaim, down in Moravia, when you
  Came on the Emperor's behalf to beg
  The Duke to take charge of the regiment.

QUESTENBERG: To *beg* him, General? That far my commission
   Did not extend, I fancy,—nor did my zeal.   110

ILLO: Well, to compel him, then, if that's the way
   You'd have it. I recall quite well—Count Tilly
   Had been defeated at the Lech—exposed
   Lay all Bavaria to the enemy—
   Nothing could stop his thrusting to the heart
   Of Austria. Then *you* and Werdenberg
   Appeared before our master, urging him
   And threatening Imperial displeasure
   If he would not take pity on your plight.

ISOLANI *(stepping up):*
   Oh yes, we understand, your Excellency,   120
   Why you with your commission of today
   Should not like to recall that former one.

QUESTENBERG: Why not? Between them lies no contradiction.
   We needed *then* to wrest Bohemia from
   The clutches of the foe; *today* I must
   Deliver it from friends and from protectors.

ILLO: A fine task! After we have fought and shed
   Our blood to get Bohemia from the Saxons,
   They want to kick us out for all our pains.

QUESTENBERG: If *one* misfortune is not merely to   130
   Replace another, this poor country must
   Be saved from scourge of friends and foes alike.

ILLO: Rubbish! The season has been good, the peasants can
   Contribute once again

QUESTENBERG: Yes, if you mean
   Contribute herds and pastures, my Lord Marshal—

ISOLANI: War lives on war. If peasants are the price,
   Well, then the Emperor will acquire more soldiers.

QUESTENBERG: And just to that degree have fewer subjects!

ISOLANI: Bah! When it comes to that, we're all his subjects.

QUESTENBERG: With differentiation, Count. Some by   140
   Their useful occupations fill the purse,
   Others know only how to empty it.
   The sword has made the Emperor poor; it is

The plow that must restore him to his strength.
BUTTLER: The Emperor would not be so poor if fewer
—Leeches were sucking at the country's marrow.
ISOLANI: Things cannot be that bad. I see not all
          (*standing in front of him and scanning*
                his uniform)
The gold has yet been minted by a long shot.
QUESTENBERG: Thank God for that! A few things have been kept
  As yet—beyond the fingers of the Croats.   150
ILLO: Take that Slawata now, and that Martinitz,
  On whom the Emperor, to the fury of
  All good Bohemians, lavishes his favors,
  Who fatten on the spoils of people dispossessed,
  Who thrive upon the general decay,
  Feather their nests alone amid the public
  Calamity, and in their regal splendor
  Taunt the country's misery,—let *them*
  And all their ilk pay for this monstrous war,—
  Which, after all, they kindled, they alone.   160
BUTTLER: And take those parasites who have their feet
  Forever stretched beneath the Emperor's table
  And greedily snap up all benefices,
  They want to ration bread and whittle down
  The soldier's pay who fronts the enemy.
ISOLANI: I never will forget when I came to
  Vienna seven years ago to get
  Supply of horses for our regiments
  How they dragged me from *antecamera*
  To *antecamera* and left me standing   170
  Among the flunkeys hour after hour
  As if I were a beggar begging bread.
  And finally—they sent me down a friar,
  A Capuchin. I thought it was to hear
  My sins, but no, he was the man with whom
  I was supposed to bargain for the horses.
  And *then* I had to leave with empty hands.
  The Duke later procured me in three days

What I had failed to get in thirty there.

QUESTENBERG: Ah yes! The item got into the bill.   180
I know, because we're paying on it yet.

ILLO: War is a rough and rugged trade. Its ends
Are not achieved with dainty measures, nor
Can everyone get out of it scot-free.
If one sat by till down there in Vienna
They picked the least of four and twenty evils,
He'd have a lengthy wait!—Pitch headlong in!
That's best. And devil take the hindmost. People
Have as a rule the knack of piece and patch
And in a nasty pinch come better off   190
By far than when they have a bitter choice.

QUESTENBERG: Yes, that is true! The Duke spares us the choice.

ILLO: The Duke bears all his troops a father's love;
We know what thought the Emperor takes of us.

QUESTENBERG: He has an equal heart for each estate
And cannot sacrifice one for the other.

ISOLANI: And so he drives us to the wilderness
With beasts of prey to guard his well-loved sheep.

QUESTENBERG (mockingly):
The metaphor is yours, Lord Count,—not mine.

ILLO: But if we were what the court takes us for,   200
It was a risk to give us liberty.

QUESTENBERG (seriously):
Such liberty is taken and not given;
And hence the need for putting on a check-rein.

ILLO: You'll find you have a wild horse on your hands.

QUESTENBERG: A better horseman then will tame it down.

ILLO: It bears one rider only, who *has* tamed it.

QUESTENBERG: *If* it has been tamed, a child can lead it.

ILLO: The child, I gather, has been found already.

QUESTENBERG: Duty is *your* concern and not the name.

BUTTLER (who up to now has been standing off at one side with
    Piccolomini yet with obvious interest in the conversation,
    approaching):
Lord President! The Emperor has a fine   210

Array of fighting men in Germany,
Some thirty thousand more here in Bohemia,
And in Silesia sixteen thousand more;
Ten regiments are ready on the Weser
And by the Rhine and Main; in Swabia six,
And in Bavaria twelve defy the Swedes,
Without including garrisons that hold
The fortified positions at the border.
Now, every man of these obeys commanders
Of Friedland's. Every one of these commanders   220
Went to *one* school, was nourished by *one* milk,
One heart and one heart only animates them,
They stand as foreigners upon this soil;
The service is their only house and home.
No zeal for fatherland impels them; thousands
Were born, as I was, in a foreign land.
Not for the Emperor did a good half of them
Come to us fugitive from alien armies
To fight quite equally for Double Eagle
Or for the Lion or for the Fleur-de-Lys.   230
Yet by one rein of equal force one man
Leads all of them, by equal love and fear
Conjoining them into a single folk.
And as the lightning's fire runs guided swift
And sure along the lightning rod, just so
Does his command prevail from the last outpost
That hears the Baltic pounding on the dunes
Or looks into the fertile valleys of
The Adige, up to the watch that has
Its sentry box by the Imperial palace.   240
QUESTENBERG: The brief sense of this lengthy speech is what?
BUTTLER: Just this: the confidence, the favor and
Respect that make us serve the Duke of Friedland
Will not endure transplanting to a random
Second the court may send us from Vienna.
We have a vivid recollection still
How the command came into Friedland's hands.

Was it, you think, Imperial Majesty
Who gave an army to him ready formed
And merely chose a leader for the troops?   250
—The army did not yet exist. And Friedland
Created it. No question of *receiving*.
He *gave* it to the Emperor! We did not get
Our Wallenstein as leader from the Emperor.
Not so, not so at all. From Wallenstein
We first received the Emperor as a master.
He, he alone unites us to these flags.

OCTAVIO *(stepping between them)*:
Let me remind you merely, Minister,
That you are here with soldiers in a camp,
And liberty and boldness make the soldier.   260
Could he act boldly if he were forbidden
To speak out boldly?—One thing entails the other.—
The boldness of this worthy officer,
          (pointing to Buttler)
Which just now was but merely misapplied,
Once when his boldness could alone prevail
Amid a frightful garrison revolt,
Saved Prague, his capital, for the Emperor.
          (Martial music is heard in the distance.)

ILLO: They're coming! That's the guards' salute.—This signal
Informs us that the Duchess has arrived.

OCTAVIO *(to Questenberg)*:
Then my son Max is back as well. He acted   270
As escort to her here up from Carinthia.

ISOLANI *(to Illo)*:
Shall we go down together now and greet her?

ILLO: Fine! let us go! Come, Colonel Buttler, come
Along!
          (to Octavio)
Remember that by noon we meet
This gentleman in the presence of the Duke.

          (Exeunt Illo, Buttler, and Isolani;

Octavio Piccolomini and Questenberg
remain behind.)

QUESTENBERG *(with marks of astonishment):*
  General! The things I've had to listen to!
  What uncontrolled defiance! What ideas!
  —If this is the predominating spirit—
OCTAVIO: Three quarters of the army spoke to you.
QUESTENBERG: Alas, then! Where to find a second army   280
  To keep a watch on this one!—And this Illo thinks,
  I fear, more evilly by far than he gives words to.
  Nor can this Buttler hide his bad intentions.
OCTAVIO: Hurt pride—resentment—nothing more than that!
  This Buttler I will not surrender yet; I know
  How *that* dark spirit can be exorcised.
QUESTENBERG *(pacing restlessly back and forth):*
  No, this is worse, oh this is far worse, friend,
  Than in Vienna we had ever dreamed!
  We saw it only with our courtiers' eyes
  Dazzled with the splendor of the throne,   290
  And we had not beheld the field-commander
  Omnipotent out here amid his camp.
  This is quite different!
  There is no Emperor here. The Duke is Emperor!
  The walk that I have taken at your side
  Here through the camp has shattered all my hopes.
OCTAVIO: You now see for yourself how dangerous
  A task you have brought down for me from court—
  How delicate a rôle I have to play here.
  The least suspicion on the General's part   300
  Would cost me freedom and my life to boot,
  And only serve to hasten his foolhardy
  Intention.
QUESTENBERG: Where was caution at the time
  When we conferred the sword upon this madman
  And placed such power in a hand like this?
  Oh, *that* temptation was too powerful

For this ill-guarded heart! It would have proved
A danger in a better man than he.
He will refuse, I tell you now,
To give obedience to Imperial orders.— 310
He can and will.—His unrepressed defiance
Will shamefully reveal our impotence.

OCTAVIO: And do you think that he has had his wife
And daughter brought up here to camp for nothing
Just when we were preparing for a war?
His calling in of final pledges of
His loyalty out of Imperial lands
Points to the sudden outbreak of rebellion.

QUESTENBERG: Alas, then! How shall we withstand the storm
That hems us in and threatens from all quarters? 320
The Empire's foes are at the borders, masters
Already of the Danube and reaching further—
The tocsin of rebellion in our heartlands—
The peasants up in arms—all classes restive—
And now the army where we look for help
Seduced, run wild, and void of discipline,
Wrenched from the State, wrenched from its Emperor,
Gone crazy and led by a crazy man,
A fearful instrument entrusted blindly
In service to the rashest of all men. 330

OCTAVIO: But let us not despair too soon, my friend.
Speech always tends to be more bold than deeds.
And many who in blind excitement now
Seem bent upon the uttermost extremes
Will find, when least was thought, a heart within their bosoms,
If one but name the crime by its right name.
Besides—we are not wholly unprotected.
Count Altringer and Gallas, as you know,
Are holding their small army to its duty—
And every day they make it stronger.—Take 340
Us by surprise he cannot, for, you know
I have him ringed about with my informants;
His slightest step is brought to my awareness

At once,—in fact, his very lips report it.

QUESTENBERG: It is incredible that he does not divine
The foe that walks beside him.

OCTAVIO: Do you think
That I have crept into his favor by
Deceit and artful bending with his will
Or that I feed his trust with flattery?
Though cunning and the duty which I owe   350
To Empire and to Emperor require
That I conceal my inmost heart from him,
I never yet have shown him any false one.

QUESTENBERG: It is the manifest device of Heaven.

OCTAVIO: I don't know what it is—that draws and binds him
So mightily to me and to my son.
We always have been friends, brothers in arms;
Long habit and adventures shared brought us
Together early,—yet I can single out
The day when all at once his heart to me   360
Was opened and his trust in me grew strong.
It was the morning of the Lützen battle—
Some evil dream drove me to seek him out
And offer him a different horse to ride
That day. Far from the tents, beneath a tree,
I found him fast asleep. And when I woke him
Recounting all my dubious fears, he gazed
At me in long astonishment, then fell
Upon my neck displaying such emotion
As that small service could not have deserved.   370
And since that day his confidence pursues me
In equal measure as mine flees from him.

QUESTENBERG: You'll draw your son, of course, into the secret?

OCTAVIO: No!

QUESTENBERG: What? You will not even serve him warning
Of in what evil hands he finds himself?

OCTAVIO: I must commit·him to his innocence.
Frank hearts must always feel deception alien.
By unawareness only can he keep

His open mind which reassures the Duke.
QUESTENBERG (worried):
My worthy friend, I have the best opinion   380
Of Colonel Piccolomini—yet—if—
Consider how—
OCTAVIO: I still must risk it.—Quiet! There he comes.
(Enter Max Piccolomini.)

MAX: Why, there he is himself now. Welcome, father!
(He embraces him; as he turns around he catches
sight of Questenberg and coldly steps back.)
You're occupied, I see? Then I shall not
Intrude.
OCTAVIO: Why, Max! Observe this guest more closely.
An old friend merits some attentiveness;
Respect is due the envoy of your Emperor.
MAX (drily):
Von Questenberg! Welcome, if something good
Brings you to our Headquarters.
QUESTENBERG (taking his hand):   Do not draw   390
Your hand away, Count Piccolomini!
I clasp it not on my behalf alone
And signify no small thing when I speak thus.
(taking both their hands)
Octavio—Max Piccolomini!
These are propitious and portentous names!
Fortune will never turn on Austria
As long as two such stars of blessing shine
Protectively above its armies' heads.
MAX: You're out of character, your Excellency.
You have not come to praise us here. I know   400
That you were sent to blame and to find fault—
I claim no excellence above the others.
OCTAVIO (to Max):
He comes from court, where satisfaction with
The Duke is not quite so complete as here.
MAX: What new thing is there then to tax him with?

The fact that he alone decides what he
Alone can understand? Well, he is right,
And furthermore things will remain this way.
Once and for all, he was not made to twist
And bend with pliancy at others' bidding;   410
It goes against his nature and he cannot.
In him a ruler's soul has its existence
And it is posted in a ruler's place.
And we rejoice that it is so! Few men
Know how to rule themselves and how to use
Their reason reasonably.—The many profit
If but one man is found who forms a center
For many thousands, a support who stands
A firm-fixed pillar round which men may gather
With confidence and joy. And such a man   420
Is Wallenstein, and even if some other
Should suit the court much better, only he
Will suit the army.
QUESTENBERG: Oh, of course! The army!
MAX: The way he has of rousing everyone
Around him, giving them new life, new strength!
How every force finds its expression, every
Talent is made clearer to itself
Within his presence! He evokes the strength
Unique in every man, develops it,
Lets every man remain the man he is,   430
Concerned alone that he should always be so
In proper place; the way he can transform
The powers of all men to his own power.
QUESTENBERG: Who will deny that he knows men, and knows
Moreover how to use them? But, in being
The ruler, he forgets his stewardship
Completely as though he were born to office.
MAX: Well, wasn't he? By every talent for it
He was, and with the further talent of
The literal executive of Nature   440
Who conquers ruler's rank for ruler's talent.

QUESTENBERG: Thus on his generosity depends
  To what degree and whether we prevail!
MAX: Unusual men require unusual trust.
  Grant him the scope and *he* will set the goal.
QUESTENBERG: That has been shown!
MAX: Yes, so it has! *They* shrink
  From anything with any depth at all,
  Grumble if everything is not quite flat.
OCTAVIO *(to Questenberg):*
  You may as well give in with grace, my friend,
  You'll never get the best of *him*.   450
MAX: Thus in distress they summon spirits up
  And quail in terror when the spirits come,
  Expect extraordinary things produced,
  Supremest things, like commonplaces. In
  The field the present moment presses,—here
  One will must give command, one eye must see.
  The General uses Nature's every greatness:
  Allow him then to live amid her great
  Conditions. He must ask the oracle,
  The vital oracle within his heart,   460
  He must not ask dead books and moldy papers
  And ancient ordinances for his guidance.
OCTAVIO: My son, those ancient and confining ordinances
  Must not be scorned. They are inestimable
  Counterbalances which oppressed men
  Attached to the wild will of hot-head leaders;
  For arbitrary will was ever dreadful.—
  The path of order, though its course meanders,
  Is still no false path. Lightning's path is straight,
  Straight is the cannon ball's appalling path,—   470
  Swift, by the shortest way, it reaches goal,
  And, maiming in its flight, it lands to maim
  Still more. My son, the road that mankind travels,
  The road upon which blessings fare, must follow
  The course of streams and freely winding valleys,
  Must pass around the fields of grapes and wheat

And honor measured bounds of ownership—
And late but safely reach its destination.

QUESTENBERG: O listen to your father—pay him heed,   480
Who is at once a hero and a man.

OCTAVIO: The child of camps speaks with your voice, my son.
You have been formed by fifteen years of war,
—You never knew a time of peace! There are
Things more of worth, my son, than things of war.
In war itself the final goal is still not war.
The swift and mighty deeds of violence
And the astounding marvels of an instant,
It is not these that make our happiness,
That found serene and massive permanencies.
In haste and flurry will a soldier build   490
His flimsy canvas city; in a twinkling
There is a noise and movement to and fro,
The market bustles, roads and rivers are
Bedecked with cargoes, business is astir.
And then one morning suddenly the tents
Are struck, and onward moves the horde to leave
The field deserted like a death-still graveyard,
With seeded grain all trampled and no hope
Remaining for the harvest of the year.

MAX: O father, let the Emperor make peace!   500
I will forego with joy the bloodstained laurel
To gain the violets that March will bring,
The fragrant pledge of earth made young again.

OCTAVIO: What's this? What moves you thus all of a sudden?

MAX: You say I never knew a time of peace?
O father, but I have, I have! Just now—
I have just come from it.—My way took me
Through countries where the war has never been.—
O life has lovely aspects, father,
That we have never known.—We have but edged   510
Around the dreary coasts of lovely life
Like vagrant predatory pirate folk
Cramped in their close and evil-smelling ships

And dwelling with rude manners on rude seas,
And of the mainland knowing but the bays
Where they dare risk a landing for a raid.
What glorious things the land contains within
Its hidden valley—Oh, of those, of those
Our barbarous voyage has disclosed no view.

OCTAVIO *(becoming attentive)*:
   And can this journey have disclosed these things?   520
MAX: This was the first real leisure of my life.
   Tell me, what is the goal and prize of this
   Ungrateful work that has robbed me of youth
   And left my heart all bleak and left my mind
   Unstirred and unadorned with any training?
   The thronging hurly-burly of this camp,
   The neighing horses and the trumpets' clangor,
   The clocks monotonously set for service,
   The weapons drills, the shouting of commands,—
   The parched heart profits nothing from all these,   530
   This wretched business has no soul.—But there
   Are other joys and other happiness.

OCTAVIO: You have learned many things on this brief journey,
   Max.
MAX: O happy day when finally the soldier
   Comes home to life and to humanity,
   When in the glad procession flags unfurl
   And homewards plays the gentle march of peace;
   When every hat and helmet is adorned
   With sprigs of May, the final plunder of
   The fields; the cities' gates yield of themselves   540
   With no petards required to burst them open;
   The walls around are crowded full of people,
   With peaceful people who shout up to the sky,—
   Clear ring the bells from all the towers sounding
   Happy Vesper to the bloody day.
   Then from the towns and from the cities throng
   Exulting folk who by their kindly, eager
   Officiousness prevent the army's march,—

Then, glad that he has lived to see the day,
The old man shakes his son's hand coming home;   550
He comes a stranger to his native place
That he left long ago; and his return
Is shaded by the tree with boughs grown broad
That once bent down for sticks when he departed;
And modestly the maiden comes to meet him
Whom last he saw upon her nurse's arm.
O happy he for whom a door is opened,
For whom arms open in a sweet embrace.

QUESTENBERG (touched):

O why must it be of a far, far time
You speak, not of today, not of tomorrow!   560

MAX (turning to him with vehemence):

Whose fault is it but yours down in Vienna?—
I will confess quite frankly, Questenberg,
That when I saw you standing here just now,
A rush of anger choked my heart.—It's you,
You in Vienna, who prevent this peace.
And it's the soldier who by force must win it.
You stir up trouble for the Duke, you hinder
His every step, heap him with slander,—why?
Because he values Europe's welfare more
Than certain paltry hides of land which may   570
Be gained or lost for Austria;—you term him
Seditious and God knows what more besides
Because he spares the Saxons and attempts
To foster confidence among our foes,
Which is the only way to peace when all
Is said and done, for if war does not bring
Its own conclusion, then whence *shall* peace come?
—Go on! For as I love the Good, I hate you,—
And I will take a vow to shed my blood
For him, this Wallenstein, yes, shed my blood   580
By drops, down to the last drop of my heart,
Before you shall exult above his fall! —

                    (Exit Max.)

QUESTENBERG: Alas, Do things stand thus?

> *(urgently and impatiently)*

Friend, must we let him leave with this delusion?
Shall we not call him back again
Immediately and open up his eyes?

OCTAVIO *(rousing out of profound thought)*:
Ah, he has opened *my* eyes up completely,
And I behold more than I like.

QUESTENBERG: What is it, friend?

OCTAVIO: A curse upon this journey!

QUESTENBERG: How so? What is it?

OCTAVIO: Come with me! I must   590
At once track down this unpropitious clue,
I must see for myself,—Come on with me

> *(He starts to lead him away.)*

QUESTENBERG: But why? Where to?

OCTAVIO *(urgently)*:   To her!

QUESTENBERG: To—

OCTAVIO *(correcting himself)*:
No, to the Duke! Let's go. I fear the worst.
I see the net cast over him, for he
Has not returned to me the way he left.

QUESTENBERG: Will you explain for me—

OCTAVIO: Why did I not
Foresee? Why did I not forstall this journey?
Why did I hide it from him?—You were right,
I should have warned him.—Now it is too late.   600

QUESTENBERG: What is too late? You realize, my friend,
That you are talking utter riddles to me.

OCTAVIO *(more calmly)*:
We'll go now to the Duke. Come on. It is
Almost the hour that he has set aside
For audience. Come along!—
A curse, a threefold curse upon this journey!   [606]

> *(He leads him away. The curtain falls.)*

ACT II

A Hall in the quarters of the Duke of Friedland.
Servants are placing chairs and laying down carpets. Enter
directly Seni the Astrologer clad in black, somewhat fantastically,
like an Italian doctor. He advances to the middle of the room, a
white wand in his hand, with which he designates the regions of
the sky.

FIRST SERVANT *(going about with a censer):*
    Get started! Finish up the task! The watch
    Has called "To Arms", and they will soon appear.
SECOND SERVANT: But why, now, was the tower room declined,
    The red one that is full of shining light?   610
FIRST SERVANT: Ask the astrologer. He claims it is
    An evil-omened room.
SECOND SERVANT: Of all the nonsense!
    That's taking people in. A room's a room.
    How can a place have that significance?
SENI *(with gravity):*
    My son, there is no thing in all this world
    Without significance. But first and foremost
    In earthly matters are the place and hour.
THIRD SERVANT: Don't get yourself mixed up with him,
    Nathanael.
    Our master must himself do as he bids.
SENI *(counting the chairs):*
    Eleven. Evil number. Set twelve chairs.   620
    Signs twelve are in the zodiac. Five and seven,
    The sacred numbers lie within the twelve.
SECOND SERVANT: What's wrong, now, with eleven? Tell me that.
SENI: Eleven is for sin. It overreaches

64

The Ten Commandments.

SECOND SERVANT: So? And why do you
Call five a sacred number?

SENI: Five is for
The soul of man. And just as man is mixed
Of good and evil, so is five the first
Of numbers to be mixed of odd and even.

FIRST SERVANT: The fool!

THIRD SERVANT: Oh, let him be. I like to hear him talk. 630
His words bring lots of things to mind, you know.

SECOND SERVANT: Away! They're coming! Here, let's take the
side way out.

> *(They hurry away. Seni follows slowly.*
> *Enter Wallenstein and the Duchess.)*

WALLENSTEIN: Well, Duchess? You have touched upon Vienna,
Appeared before the Queen of Hungary?

THE DUCHESS: Before the Empress too. Both Majesties
Received us in a private audience.

WALLENSTEIN: How did they take the fact that I have summoned
My spouse and daughter to my camp in winter?

THE DUCHESS: I did as you enjoined and stated that
You had made disposition of our child   640
And wished before the start of your campaign
To show the future bridegroom his betrothed.

WALLENSTEIN: Did they divine the choice which I have made?

THE DUCHESS: The hope was voiced that she had not been given
To any foreign lord or Lutheran.

WALLENSTEIN: And what, Elizabeth, is *your* wish?

THE DUCHESS: Your will, you know, was ever my will too.

WALLENSTEIN *(after a pause):*
And—your reception otherwise at court?

> *(The Duchess lowers her eyes in silence.)*

Hide nothing from me.—How were things on that score?

THE DUCHESS: O my dear Lord—nothing was any more   650
As formerly.—A change has come about.

WALLENSTEIN: What! Were they lacking in the old respect?

THE DUCHESS: Not in respect. Full dignity and honor
Marked their reception of me.—But instead
Of nobly trustful condescension, I
Encountered solemn ceremoniousness.
O that discreet consideration shown me,
It had about it more of pity than
Of favor. No! Duke Albrecht's princely consort,
Count Harrach's noble daughter never should   660
Have been received in that way—not in that way!

WALLENSTEIN: Of course they found fault with my recent
conduct?

THE DUCHESS: If only they had done so!—I have long
Since grown accustomed to excusing you,
To pacifying outraged feelings.—No,
No one found fault with you.—They wrapped themselves
In such a ponderously solemn silence.
This was no commonplace misunderstanding, no
Mere transitory sensitivity.—
Some mischief irretrievable has happened.—   670
Till now the Queen of Hungary was wont
To call me always her beloved cousin
And put her arms around me when we parted.

WALLENSTEIN: This time she failed to do so?

THE DUCHESS (drying her tears; after a pause):
                            She embraced me,
But not until I had already taken leave and
Was walking toward the door, did she come to me,
Quickly, as if she only then remembered,
And pressed me to her bosom, more with painful
Than tender feelings.

WALLENSTEIN (seizing her hand):   Come, compose yourself!
And what of Eggenberg, of Lichtenstein,   680
And of our other friends?

THE DUCHESS (shaking her head):   I saw not one
Of them.

WALLENSTEIN: And the Conte Ambassador of Spain

Who used to speak so warmly in my favor?

THE DUCHESS: He had no further word to speak for you.

WALLENSTEIN: So *those* suns shine no more for us. Henceforth
We must derive our light from our own fire.

THE DUCHESS: Then has it come, dear Duke, then has it come
To what the court is whispering, to what
Is elsewhere said aloud,—what Father Lamormain
In several hints has—

WALLENSTEIN (*quickly*):   Lamormain! And what   690
Does *he* say?

THE DUCHESS: That you are accused of willful
Abuse of powers given to your trust,
Of criminal disdain of orders from
His Most Imperial Majesty. The Spaniards,
Bavaria's haughty Duke, stand your accusers.—
A storm is gathering above your head,
A storm more menacing by far than that
Which once before at Regenspurg brought downfall
For you. They speak, he said,—Oh, I can't tell it—

WALLENSTEIN (*tensely*):   Well?

THE DUCHESS: About a second— (*She is unable to go on.*)

WALLENSTEIN: Second—

THE DUCHESS: Still more shameful   700
—Removal.

WALLENSTEIN: *Do* they?
(*pacing the room in violent excitement*)
          Oh, they drive me to it, thrust me
By force, against my will, right into it.

THE DUCHESS (*clinging to him pleadingly*):
Oh, if there still is time, my husband,—if this
Can be averted by submission or
By yielding to their will—I beg you: yield—
Compel your proud heart to it, for it is
Your Lord and Emperor to whom you yield.
Do not permit your good intentions to
Be blackened any longer by sardonic
Malice or by a poisoned misinterpretation.   710

Triumphant with the strength of truth, stand up
And shame these liars, shame these slanderers.
Of loyal friends we have so few already.
You know our rapid fortunes have exposed us
To people's spitefulness.—What *are* we if
Imperial favor turns away from us?

(*Enter Countess Terzky leading
Princess Thekla by the hand.*)

COUNTESS TERZKY: What, sister, what! Already talking business
And, as I see, not happy business either,
Before he has rejoiced to see his daughter?
First moments should belong to happiness.   720
Here, father Friedland, here: this is your daughter.

(*Thekla shyly approaches him and starts to
kiss his hand; he takes her in his arms
and stands for a time lost in gazing at her.*)

WALLENSTEIN: Yes, yes. My hope has sprung up beautifully.
I take her as a pledge of greater fortune.

THE DUCHESS: She was a tender child when you went off to
Assemble the great army for the Emperor.
Later, when you came home from Pomerania
And the campaign, your daughter was already
At convent school, where she remained till now.

WALLENSTEIN: And while we in the field have toiled to make
Her great and win her highest earthly things,   730
Old Mother Nature in the quiet cloister
Has done her part and given godly gifts
Out of her generous bounty to the child,
And now produces her adorned with beauty
For her resplendent fate and for my hopes.

THE DUCHESS (*to the Princess*):
You never would have recognized your father,
Would you, my child? You were but scarcely eight
When last you looked upon his countenance.

THEKLA: Of course I would, at first glance, Mother.—Father
Has not grown old.—Just as my mind remembered him   740

He stands in flower now before my eyes.

WALLENSTEIN *(to the Duchess)* :
The lovely child! How cleverly observed,
How understanding! I had complained of Fate's
Denying me a son to bear my name
And be my fortune's heir and in a proud
Descendancy of princes carry forward
My own existence all too soon extinguished.
I have done Fate injustice. Here upon
This maiden vernal brow I shall emplace
My crown of warrior's life. I shall not deem it   750
A thankless task if on some future day
It is transformed into a royal crown
Wherewith I may encircle this fair head.

*(He is holding her in his arms as
Max Piccolomini enters.)*

COUNTESS TERZKY: Here comes the paladin who shielded us.
WALLENSTEIN: You're welcome, Max. For me you always were
The bringer of some joyous thing or other,
And like the happy star of morning now
You have brought forth for me the sun of life.
MAX: General—
WALLENSTEIN: Up to now it was the Emperor
Who by my hand rewarded you. Today   760
You have a happy father in your debt,
And this debt Friedland must himself repay.
MAX: My Prince, you have already cancelled it
In haste. It is with shame I come, with sorrow,
For I had been but fresh arrived, had scarcely
Brought to your arms the mother and the daughter,
When from your royal stables, richly harnessed,
A splendid four-in-hand was given me
To pay me off for my poor service rendered.
Oh yes, to pay me off. It was a service,   770
A duty merely, not a favor for
Which I so rashly took it and with full

Heart came to thank you. It was not intended
That duty should become my highest pleasure.

*(Enter Count Terzky with letters for the Duke,
which the latter quickly opens.)*

COUNTESS TERZKY *(to Max)*:
Should he reward your service? He rewards
You for his joy. To think so tenderly
Becomes you; but my brother-in-law does well
To show himself at all times great and princely.

THEKLA: Then I as well should have to doubt his love
Because his generous hand had lavished gifts   780
On me before his father's heart had spoken.

MAX: He always must be giving, granting happiness!
(He seizes the Duchess's hand; with rising ardor)
What all do I not have to thank him for,—
What all do I not tell in that dear name of Friedland!
My life long I shall be a prisoner of
That name.—Within it there shall bloom and flourish
My every fortune and my every hope.
Fast, as if in a magic circle, Fate
Holds me enthralled and charmed within that name.

COUNTESS TERZKY *(who meanwhile has been anxiously watching
the Duke, observing that he has become pensive over the
letters)*:
My brother wants to be alone. Let us   790
Withdraw.

WALLENSTEIN *(turning quickly around, masters himself and
speaks cheerfully to the Duchess)*:
Again, Duchess, I bid you welcome here.
You are the mistress of this court.—You, Max,
Shall once again act in your former office
While we transact the master's business here.

*(Max Piccolomini offers the Duchess his arm;
The Countess Terzky leads the Princess away.
Wallenstein remains with Count Terzky.)*

COUNT TERZKY *(calling after Max)*:

Don't fail to be here for the Conference.

WALLENSTEIN *(in profound thought, to himself)*:
She saw correctly.—So it is. It fits
Precisely with the rest of the reports.—
They have their minds made up there in Vienna,
They have already chosen my successor.
The King of Hungary, that Ferdinand,   800
The Emperor's fair-haired boy, is now their savior,
The newly risen star! And they intend
To rid themselves of us, and we are here
As if we were already dead and buried.
Then no time must be lost!
          *(As he turns he notices Terzky and hands
                    him a letter)*
Altringer begs to be excused, and Gallas
Likewise.—I don't like it.

COUNT TERZKY: Wait still longer
And they will all desert you one by one.

WALLENSTEIN: Altringer has the passes of the Tyrol.
I must send someone to him so he will not   810
Let in the Spaniards coming from Milan.
—Well, there's Sesin, our go-between of old,
Who just put in a new appearance lately.
What does he bring us from Count Thurn?

COUNT TERZKY: The Count sends word
                                              to you
That he has sought the Swedish Chancellor out
At Halberstadt, where now the War League meets.
But he said he was sick and tired of it
And wants to have no further dealings with you.

WALLENSTEIN: How so?

COUNT TERZKY: He said you never mean the things you say,
You only want to make fools of the Swedes,   820
Ally yourself with Saxony against them
And in the long run leave them nothing but a sum
Of paltry money.

WALLENSTEIN: So! And does he fancy

I'll give him some fine German state for booty
Till we wind up not being our own masters
Upon our native soil? They must get out,
Out, out! We do not need that kind of neighbors.

COUNT TERZKY: Oh let them have a plot of land. It won't
    Come out of yours. What do you care who pays,
    So long as you are winner of the game?   830

WALLENSTEIN: Out, out with them!—You do not understand.
    No one shall say of me that I dismembered
    Germany, betrayed it to outsiders,
    To snitch my portion of it on the sly.
    In me the Realm shall honor its protector,
    And by my conduct as Prince of the Realm
    I shall deserve to sit with the Realm's Princes.
    No foreign power shall strike root within
    The Realm if I can stop it, least of all
    These Goths, these plunder-greedy starvelings, who   840
    With looks of envy cast their eyes upon
    The blessed bounty of our German land.
    Support me in my plans they shall, and still
    Get nothing for their pains by doing so.

COUNT TERZKY: But with the Saxons are you going to deal
    More honorably? They're running out of patience
    Because you tread such crooked paths.—
    Why all these masks? Tell me, what do they mean?
    Our friends are puzzled and in doubt of you;—
    Oxenstjerna, Arnheim, no one can   850
    Make out your vacillation. In the end
    I am the liar, for all is done through me.
    I do not even have your signature.

WALLENSTEIN: I will give out nothing in writing; you know that.

COUNT TERZKY: But how can anyone believe you mean it,
    If deeds do not succeed your words? Admit
    That your transactions with the enemy
    Till now could quite well have been carried on
    With no thought on your part but making fools
    Of all of them.   860

WALLENSTEIN (*after a pause during which he eyes him sharply*):
   How do you know that I have not made fools
   Of them deliberately? that I have not
   Made fools of all of you? Do you know me
   That well? I don't recall revealing to you
   My inmost heart.—The Emperor, it is true,
   Has shamefully misused me.—If I wished,
   I could return him no small bit of mischief.
   It pleases me to realize my power.
   But whether I shall actually make use of it,
   Of *that* you know no more than any other.   870
COUNT TERZKY: Then you've been trifling with us all along!

(Enter Illo.)

WALLENSTEIN: How do things stand out there? Are they
   prepared?
ILLO: You'll find them in a mood to suit your wishes.
   They know about the Emperor's demands
   And they are wild.
WALLENSTEIN: What stand has Isolan
   Adopted?
ILLO: Yours in soul and body since you
   Set up his faro bank for him again.
WALLENSTEIN: Kolalto, how does he stand? Did you make
   Quite sure of Deodat and Tiefenbach?
ILLO: They'll do as Piccolomini will do.   880
WALLENSTEIN: You think, then, I may dare to count on them?
ILLO: —If you can trust the Piccolominis.
WALLENSTEIN: I trust them as myself. *They* won't desert me.
COUNT TERZKY: And yet I wish you wouldn't trust that fox
   Octavio quite so much.
WALLENSTEIN: Instruct me how
   To know my men. No less than sixteen times
   I've entered battle with the elder one.
   —Besides—I've cast his horoscope and found
   That we were both born under equal stars.—
   In short—

(mysteriously)
    there's something quite mysterious about it. 890
So if you can vouch to me for the others—
ILLO: One voice prevails among them all; you shall not
 Give up the regiment. I hear they plan
 To send a deputation up to see you.
WALLENSTEIN: If I must obligate myself to them,
 Then they must do the same for me.
ILLO: Of course.
WALLENSTEIN: They must give me their word in writing, under
 oath,
 To do my service *unconditionally*.
ILLO: Why not?
COUNT TERZKY: But *unconditionally*? They will
 Always reserve their duties to the Emperor 900
 And Austria.
WALLENSTEIN *(shaking his head)*:
      No! Unconditionally
 It has to be. No kind of reservations!
ILLO: I have a thought.—Count Terzky gives a banquet
 For us this evening, does he not?
COUNT TERZKY: Why, yes.
 And all the Generals have been invited.
ILLO *(to Wallenstein)*:
 If you will let me have my hands completely
 Free, I will get the Generals' word for you
 The way you want it.
WALLENSTEIN: Get their signatures.
 Whichever way you manage that, is your affair.
ILLO: If I succeed in getting it for you 910
 In black and white that all Commanders present
 Support you without question, will you then
 Play seriously at last and try your luck
 With hearty action?
WALLENSTEIN: Get me that in writing!
ILLO: Consider what this means! You cannot meet
 The Emperor's demands—nor let the army

Be weakened,—nor allow the regiments
To join the Spaniard, if you do not mean
To drop the power forever from your hands.
Consider the alternative as well!   920
You cannot flout the Emperor's solemn orders
Or seek evasions any longer, and temporize,
Unless you mean to break clean from the Court.
Make up your mind! Will you by some bold action
Anticipate him? Or, delaying further,
Will you wait for the worst?

WALLENSTEIN: That is befitting,
   Before one goes to last extremes.

ILLO: O, use this hour before it slips away.
   The moments truly meaningful and great
   Occur so rarely in our lives. If one   930
   Decision must be made, then many things
   Must with felicity conjoin and meet.—
   Sporadically and scattered only do
   The threads of fortune, opportunities,
   Converge into a single point of life
   To form the clustered flower's pregnant pistil.
   See how decisively and fatefully
   Conditions gather round you now!—The army's
   Best and astutest chiefs are gathered here,
   Assembled here with you, their royal leader.   940
   They wait but for your beckoning sign.—O do
   Not let them go away again dispersed!
   So single-minded you will not recall them
   A second time, not in the war's whole course.
   It is full tide that lifts the heavy ship
   Away from shore.—And each man feels his spirits
   And courage grow amid the throng's great stream.
   You have them with you now. Soon war will scatter
   Them far asunder, one place and another.—
   In private petty cares and self-concern   950
   The common will is dissipated. A man
   Today caught up amid the current will

Forget himself; alone, he will turn sober,
Feel nothing but his helplessness, and quickly
Rein back into the old, the broadly trodden
Highroad of common duty, seeking solely
To find his comfort and a place of shelter.

WALLENSTEIN: The time has not yet come.

COUNT TERZKY: You always say that.
When *will* it be the time, then?

WALLENSTEIN: When I say so.

ILLO: Oh, you will tarry for the starry hour   960
Until the earthly one is lost! Believe me,
Your stars of destiny are in your bosom.
Reliance on yourself, decisiveness,
There is your Venus: Your "Maleficus",
The only one that works you harm, is *doubt*.

WALLENSTEIN: That's all *you* know. How many, many
    times
Have I explained to you:—When you were born
The clear god Jupiter was in decline;
You have no vision for these arcane things.
You can but burrow darkly in the earth,   970
Blind like the Subterranean One who with his pale
And leaden shine then lighted you to life.
Mundane and common things, these you can see,
And cunningly combine near things with near;
And there I trust you and believe in you.
But that which moves with mystic meaning, forming
And fashioning within the depths of Nature,—
The spirit ladder rising from this world of dust
With thousand rungs into the world of stars
Whereby celestial powers operative   980
Descend and then again ascend at will,
—The circles in the ring of circles which
Converge and close about the central sun,—
These are beheld alone by eyes unsealed,
The eyes of bright-born, cheerful sons of Jove.
    (*After taking a turn through the room he stops*

and continues speaking.)
The constellations of the sky do not
Make merely day and night, springtime and summer,—
And not to sowers merely do they signal
Seedtime and harvest. Actions of mankind are also
A sowing of the seeds of destinies   990
Cast forth upon the dark land of the future,
Entrusted hopefully to fateful powers.
Thus it is needful to inquire the seedtime,
To make the right choice from the hours of stars,
To search with care among the heavens' houses
Lest lurking in the corners to our harm
The foe of growth and thriving may be hidden.
     So give me time. Do what you can meanwhile.
I cannot say now what I plan to do.
Surrender, that I will not do. Not I!   1000
Depose me, that they shall not either.—That
You may depend upon.

                    (Enter a servant.)
THE SERVANT: The Generals.
WALLENSTEIN: Show them in.
COUNT TERZKY: Is it your will that all Commanders be here?
WALLENSTEIN: No need of that. Both Piccolominis,
     Maradas, Buttler, Forgatsch, Dcodat,
     Karaffa, Isolani may come in.
                 (Exit Terzky with the servant.)
     (to Illo)
Have you had watch kept on this Questenberg?
Has he seen anyone in secret?
ILLO: I've had him sharply watched. He was with no one
     Except Octavio.   1010

     *(Enter Questenberg, both Piccolominis, Buttler, Isolani,
     Maradas, and three other Generals. At a sign from the
     General, Questenberg steps up opposite him. The
     others follow according to rank. There is a momentary
     silence.)*

WALLENSTEIN: I am informed about and I have weighed
   The import of your mission, Questenberg,
   And my decision has been made, which nothing
   Will change. But it is fitting these Commanders
   Should hear from your own lips the Emperors' wishes.—
   Be kind enough, then, if you please, to state
   The nature of your errand to these noble leaders.
QUESTENBERG: I shall. But I must beg you bear in mind
   It is Imperial Authority
   That speaks through me, not my audacity.   1020
WALLENSTEIN: Spare us your preface.
QUESTENBERG: When His Majesty
   The Emperor upon your valiant armies
   Conferred a head, fame-crowned and battle-seasoned,
   In the person of the Duke of Friedland,
   He did so in the joyous confidence
   War's luck might quickly be turned favorable.
   Nor was the outset hostile to his hopes.
   Bohemia was swept clear of the Saxons,
   The Swedes' victorious course was checked;—those lands
   Fetched easy breath once more when Friedland's Duke   1030
   From all the streams of Germany assembled
   The scattered armies of the enemy together
   And conjured to a single meeting place
   The Rhinegrave, Bernhard, Banner, Oxenstjerna,
   And even that unconquered king himself,
   In order there within the sight of Nürnberg
   To make a final end of this vast struggle.
WALLENSTEIN: Come to the point, I beg you.
QUESTENBERG: Then new spirit
   Proclaimed immediately the new commander.
   Blind fury raged no more against blind fury.   1040
   In battle clearly drawn we then beheld
   Staunch-heartedness resisting insolence
   And wise skill wearing bravery down. In vain
   They lure you toward engagements, you entrench
   Yourself more deeply in your camp than ever,

As though to found an everlasting home.
At last the desperate king makes his attack,
And to the slaughterhouse he herds his troops
Whom hunger and the raging pestilence
Are slowly killing in the corpse-strewn camp.   1050
Through barrier hedges of the camp, where death
Lurks in a thousand muzzles, he attempts
The never-yet-curbed man, to carve a path,
Then came attack, then came resistance, such
As eye of mortal man had never seen.
In rout at last the king draws off his men,
And not a foot of territory did he
Gain with his ghastly human sacrifice.
WALLENSTEIN: Spare us recitals from the chronicle
That we with horror have ourselves lived through.   1060
QUESTENBERG: It is my task and mission to accuse,
My heart prefers to linger over praise.
In Nürnberg's camp the King of Sweden lost
His fame—on Lützen's plains he lost his life.
But who was not astounded when the Duke
Of Friedland, after that great day, fled like
One conquered to Bohemia, vanished from
The scene of war, while Weimar's youthful hero
Quite unresisted pushed into Franconia,
Made sweeping inroads right up to the Danube,   1070
And all at once confronted Regenspurg,
Thus striking terror in all Catholic Christians.
Whereat the just Prince of Bavaria cried
For sudden help amid his extreme peril.
With this request the Emperor sends Duke Friedland
No less than seven mounted messengers,
Imploring, when as Lord he may command.
In vain! For at that time the Duke has ear
For nothing but his ancient grudge and hatred,
Sells out the common welfare to achieve   1080
Revenge against an enemy of old.
And thus falls Regenspurg!

WALLENSTEIN: What time was that he refers to, Max?
  I just can't seem to place it now.
MAX: He means
  When we were in Silesia.
WALLENSTEIN: So! so! so!
  What was it that we had to do just then?
MAX: We had to drive the Swedes out and the Saxons.
WALLENSTEIN: Right! His description there made me forget
  The war entirely.
    (to Questenberg)
            Would you please continue.
QUESTENBERG: Beside the Oder was recouped perhaps   1090
  What by the Danube shamefully was lost.
  Things of astounding greatness were expected
  To happen in that theatre of war
  When Friedland took the field in person and
  Discovered facing him Gustavus' toadies,
  That Arnheim and that—Thurn. And actually
  They did approach each other closely,—
  Exchanging hospitalities as friends.
  All Germany might groan beneath war's burden,
  But there was peace where Wallenstein was camped.   1100
WALLENSTEIN: How many bloody fights are fought for nothing,
  Because some young commander needs a victory.
  The proved commander offers this advantage:
  He does not have to fight to show the world
  That he knows how to win. I would have gained
  But little, using luck on Arnheim; but
  My moderation would have done great good
  To Germany, had I succeeded in
  Dissolving that unfortunate alliance
  That held the Swedes and Saxons in conjunction.   1110
QUESTENBERG: But it did not succeed, and so began
  Anew the bloody game of war. And then
  The former reputation of the Duke
  Was justified at last. On Steinau's fields
  The Swedish army laid its weapons down

Without a blow.—There Heaven's justice
Delivered to avengers' hands, with others,
The first originator of the mischief,
The curse-steeped brand of war, Matthias Thurn.
—But he had fallen into generous hands.   1120
Instead of punishment he found reward,
The Duke dismissed with gifts his Emperor's
Arch-foe.
WALLENSTEIN *(laughing):* I know, I know. Down in Vienna
The windows and the balconies were rented
Ahead of time to view him in the tumbril.¹—
Loss of a battle would have made no difference,
But never will the Viennese forgive me
For cheating them out of their spectacle.
QUESTENBERG: Now with Silesia free, all voices called
The Duke to save hard-pressed Bavaria next.   1130
He actually begins his march. He crosses
Bohemia leisurely and by the *longest*
Routes; but, before the enemy is sighted,
He turns around, goes into winter quarters, burdens
Imperial lands with his Imperial troops.
WALLENSTEIN: The army's state was pitiable, with every need
And comfort lacking,—winter coming on.
What does his Majesty think troops are made of?
Are we not men, and like all mortals subject
To cold and wet and all necessities?   1140
The soldier's fate is damnable! Whenever
He comes, the people flee from him. Whenever
He goes, they curse him. He must take whatever
He gets, with nothing given; and compelled
To seize from everyone, he is a monster
To everyone. Here stand my Generals. Count
Karaffa! Deodati! Buttler! Tell him
How long the troops have gone without their pay.
BUTTLER: One whole year's pay is lacking.
WALLENSTEIN: And the soldier
Must have his "solde"; he takes his name from that.   1150

QUESTENBERG: This has a different ring from what the Duke
  Of Friedland said eight or nine years ago.
WALLENSTEIN: Quite so. The fault is mine, I realize.
  I've spoiled the Emperor so myself. Nine years ago
  When we were fighting Denmark, I provided him
  A force of forty thousand head or fifty
  Without its costing him a single farthing
  From his own purse.—Through fields of Saxony
  Up to the Baltic reefs war's Fury raged
  And all the way bore terror in his name.   1160
  That was a time worth living in! Throughout the Empire
  No name was honored and exalted more
  Than mine, and the third jewel in his crown
  Was christened Albrecht Wallenstein.
  But at the meeting of the Princes' Diet
  In Regenspurg it all came out as clear
  As day from whose purse I had paid expenses.
  And as a faithful servant of my master,
  What thanks did I receive for taking on
  Myself the burden of this curse of nations,   1170
  This war, which made *him* great, and having paid
  The Princes? What? I was the scapegoat for
  Their grievances. I was deposed.
QUESTENBERG: Your Grace
  Well knows his freedom was encumbered badly
  At that ill-fortuned meeting.
WALLENSTEIN: Death and devils!
  I *had* that which would have procured his freedom.
  —No, Sir! Since I have found it pays so poorly
  To serve the throne for what the Empire gives,
  I've learned to think quite differently about
  The Empire. From the Emperor, to be sure,   1180
  I have this staff; but now I wield it as
  Imperial General for the good of all,
  The common welfare, not for one man's greatness!—
  But to the point. What is it they desire of me?
QUESTENBERG: First, his Majesty desires the army

To quit Bohemia without delay.
WALLENSTEIN: This time of year? And where is it proposed
That we should travel?
QUESTENBERG: Where the enemy is.
It is his Majesty's desire to see
That Regenspurg is cleansed of foes by Easter   1190
So that in the cathedral no more Lutheran
Is preached,—and no more monstrous heresy
Defile the feast day's pure solemnity.
WALLENSTEIN: Can this be done, my Generals? What say you?
ILLO: It is not possible.
BUTTLER: It can't be done.
QUESTENBERG: The Emperor has already issued orders
To Colonel Suys to advance into
Bavaria.
WALLENSTEIN: And what did Suys do?
QUESTENBERG: His duty. He advanced.
WALLENSTEIN: Advanced! And I,
His chief, gave him specific orders not   1200
To leave his post. Is this the way things stand
With my command? Is this the obedience
That is my due, without which discipline
Of war is quite unthinkable? Judge now,
My Generals, here. What does the officer deserve
Who in defiance of his oath flouts orders?
ILLO: To die!
WALLENSTEIN (raising his voice, since the others keep dubious
    silence): Count Piccolomini, what does he
Deserve?
MAX (after a long pause):
            According to the law—to die.
ISOLANI: To die!
BUTTLER: By laws of war, to die!

(Questenberg gets up. Wallenstein follows suit.
            All rise.)

WALLENSTEIN: It is the law condemns him, and not I!   1210

And even if I pardon him, I do so
From the respect I owe my Emperor.

QUESTENBERG: If things stand thus, I have no more to say here.

WALLENSTEIN: I took command here on conditions only,
The first of which was that no human being,
Not even Majesty himself, should speak
In criticism of me with the army.
If I must answer with my head and with
My honor for the outcome, I must be
Full master here. What was it made that Gustav   1220
Unconquered, irresistible on earth?
Just this: that he was *king* above his *army!*
However, any king who is a king
Was never conquered yet, except by equals.—
But to the point. The best is yet to come.

QUESTENBERG: The Cardinal Infante will this spring
Be coming from Milan and leading up
Through Germany a Spanish army to
The Netherlands. That he may travel safely
It is the Monarch's wish that from this army   1230
Eight regiments of horsemen should escort him.

WALLENSTEIN: I see, I see.—Eight regiments.—How well,
How well worked out, O Father Lamormain!
Were not the thought so damnably astute,
One might be led to call it downright stupid.
Eight thousand horsemen. Yes, yes. Very good.
I see it coming.

QUESTENBERG: No deceit is meant here.
Prudence commends, necessity demands it.

WALLENSTEIN: How, my Lord Deputy? I am supposed
Not to perceive that they are tired of seeing   1240
The sword's grip and the power in my hands,
And that they seize this pretext greedily
And use the Spanish name to undercut
My troop strength, introduce into the Empire
New forces not subordinate to me?
But I am still too powerful for you   1

To cast aside that way. My contract states
That all Imperial armies shall obey me
As far and wide as German speech is spoken.
Of Spanish troops, however, and Infantes   1250
Who go as guests a-roaming through the realm,
There is no mention in the contract.—So
They sneak their way around that point in silence,
Make me first weaker, then dispensable,
Until they can make shorter work of me.
—Why these devious ways, Lord Minister?
Say what you mean! The Emperor wants to break
His pact with me. He'd like my resignation.
I shall oblige him with that favor. That was
A thing decided, Sir, before you came.   1260

(*There is a commotion among the Generals that
increases more and more.*)

I can't help feeling sorry for my Generals.
I still can't see how they, with all the sums advanced by them
Will ever get their well-deserved rewards.
A new regime will introduce new men
And former service quickly is forgotten.
Many foreigners serve in this army,
And if a man was able otherwise,
I simply did not use to ask too closely
About his ancestry or catechism.
Henceforward that will be a different story!   1270
Well—that's no more of my concern.
                    (*He sits down.*)

MAX: Now God
Forbid that it should come to that!—The army
Will rise up to a man in frightful wrath.—
The Emperor is misled, this must not be!
ISOLANI: It must not be, else all will go to ruin.
WALLENSTEIN: That it will, my loyal Isolan.
To ruin, everything we've built with care.
For all of that, a General will be found

However, and an army will assemble
Around the Emperor when the drum roll sounds.   1280
MAX (*going busily, urgently from one to the other and pacifying them*):
O hear me, General! Hear me, you Commanders!
Let us implore you, Prince! Make no decision
Till we have taken counsel and presented
Considerations to you.—Come, my friends!
I hope that all may yet be set to rights.
COUNT TERZKY: Come! In the lobby we will meet the others.

(*Exeunt most of the Generals.*)

BUTTLER (*to Questenberg*):
If good advice may find an ear with you,
Avoid, at least these first few hours, showing
Yourself in public. Possibly that golden key
Might not protect you wholly from mistreatment.   1290

(*Loud commotion outside.*)

WALLENSTEIN: The advice is sound.—Octavio, you will
Vouch to me for the safety of our guest.
I bid you now farewell, von Questenberg.

(*As the latter is about to speak.*)

No, nothing further on this hateful subject!
You have performed your duty. I am able
To see the man as separate from his office.

(*As Questenberg is about to leave with Octavio,
enter Götz, Tiefenbach, Kolalto, followed by
still other Commanders.*)

GÖTZ: Where is the man who wanted to depose—
TIEFENBACH (*simultaneously*):
What's this we hear? You want to leave us and—
KOLALTO (*simultaneously*):
We mean to live with you and die with you.
WALLENSTEIN (*with dignity, as he points to Illo*):
Here the Field Marshal knows of my intentions.   1300

(*Exit.*)

ACT III

Scene : A room.
Enter Illo and Terzky.

COUNT TERZKY: Now tell me, how do you intend to manage
  This evening at the banquet with the Generals?
ILLO: Listen to me. We will draw up a form
  In which we pledge ourselves collectively
  To be all for the Duke with soul and body
  And not deny our final blood for him,—
  Short of the obligations of our oath
  Which we owe to the Emperor. Mark this well!
  These we will set down in a special clause
  Explicitly and save our consciences.   1310
  Now note! The document so drawn will be
  Tendered to them before the dinner. No one
  Will take offense at it.—Now listen further!
  When, after table, the dull spirit of
  The wine has opened hearts and closed up eyes,
  We'll circulate a different version for
  Their signature, from which the clause is missing.
COUNT TERZKY: What! Do you think that they will feel them-
    selves
  Bound by an oath which we have treacherously
  Elicited from them by sleight-of-hand?   1320
ILLO: We'll have them caught, no matter what.—Then let them
  Scream fraudulence as loud as they can scream.
  At court their signatures will be believed
  Far sooner than their solemnest avowals.
  They're traitors once for all, they have to be;
  They'll make a virtue of necessity.

COUNT TERZKY: Well, I'm content, so long as *something* happens
   And we move from the rut that we are stuck in.
ILLO: And then—it does not matter much how well
   We manage as far as the Generals go;   1330
   Suffice it if we can persuade the master
   That they *are* with him;—for, if he once acts
   In earnest, as if he already had them,
   He *will* have them and sweep them onward with him.
COUNT TERZKY: Sometimes I cannot make him out at all.
   He lends the foe his ear, has me write Thurn
   And Arnheim, speaks against Sesina freely
   In sharpest terms, for hours at a time
   Discusses plans with us, and just when I
   Think that I have him—all at once away   1340
   He slips, and then it seems as if he had
   No thought except to stay right where he is.
ILLO: He give up his old plans! I tell you he
   Has nothing else upon his mind, asleep
   Or waking, and that that is why he asks
   The planets day by day—
COUNT TERZKY: Yes, did you know
   This very night now coming on he will
   Be shut up in the astrological tower
   Observing with the Doctor? This, I hear,
   Is an important night, and something great   1350
   And long-awaited is to happen in
   The skies.
ILLO: If only it will happen here below.
   The Generals are all full of eagerness
   Right now and can be brought to anything
   In order not to lose their chief. You see!
   We have the opportunity at hand
   For close alliance now against the court.
   Its name is harmless. We shall simply claim
   We merely want to keep him in command.
   But as you know, when the pursuit is hot   1360
   They will lose sight of how the thing began.

I plan to play the cards so that the Duke
Shall find them willing—or shall *think* them willing
For any daring venture. Then occasion
Shall lure him onward. Once the major step
Is taken, for which they will not forgive him in
Vienna, then the force of circumstances
Will lead him further, ever further; only
The choice is hard for him; when need is pressing,
His strength will come to him, and his clear vision.   1370

COUNT TERZKY: That's what the enemy is waiting for
    To bring their army over to us.

ILLO: Come!
These next few days we must advance the work still further
Than it has gone in years.—And once things stand
Propitious here below, then you will see,
The proper stars will shine on high as well.
Come to the Generals. Now the iron must
Be struck while it is hot.

COUNT TERZKY: Go in there to them, Illo.
I must await the Countess Terzky here.
You may be sure we are not idle either.—   1380
If one strand breaks, another will be ready.

ILLO: Yes, your wife smiled in such a knowing way.
    What's up?

COUNT TERZKY: A secret. Quiet! She is coming.
            (Exit Illo. Enter Countess Terzky
                from a side room.)
Well, is she coming? I can't hold him back
Much longer.

COUNTESS TERZKY: She is coming. Send him in.

COUNT TERZKY: I do not feel entirely sure that we
    Shall win the master's thanks with this. Upon this point,
    You know, he never has expressed himself.
    You have persuaded me and you must know
    How far you dare to go.

COUNTESS TERZKY: I'll answer for it.   1390
                (to herself)

I need no authorization here.—With no word spoken
We understand each other, brother-in-law.—
Do I not guess why you have brought your daughter
And why just *he* was chosen to escort her?
For this alleged betrothal to a bridegroom
Whom no one knows, may possibly deceive
Some people. I can see right through you. But
It is not fitting you should show your hand
In such a game. No! To my subtlety
All is entrusted. Very well! —You shall   1400
No wise be disappointed in your sister.

(Enter a servant.)

THE SERVANT: The Generals!
COUNT TERZKY *(to the Countess)*:
                              Now see to it that you set
His brain on fire and give him food for thought
When he comes to the banquet so he won't
Dwell long upon the signature.
COUNTESS TERZKY: You take care of your guests. Go, send him
    in.
COUNT TERZKY: For everything depends upon his signing.
COUNTESS TERZKY: Look to your guests, now. Go!

(Reenter Illo.)

ILLO: Where *are* you, Terzky?
    The house is full, and they are waiting for you.
COUNT TERZKY: I'm coming!
                (to the Countess)
                    And he should not stay too long.— 1410
    The old one otherwise might get suspicious—
COUNTESS TERZKY: A needless worry!

(Enter Max Piccolomini.)

MAX *(looking around shyly)*:   Cousin Terzky! May I?
        *(He walks to the middle of the room and
                looks around uneasily.)*
    She isn't here! Where is she?

COUNTESS TERZKY: Take a good look then
  In yonder corner, see if she is hiding
  Behind the screen perhaps—
MAX: Here lie her gloves!
  (He starts to pick them up quickly.
  The Countess takes them herself.)
  Unkindly aunt! Would you deny me this—
  You take a pleasure in tormenting me.
COUNTESS TERZKY: Such thanks for all my pains!
MAX: O, if you could
  But feel as I feel now!—Since we have been here—
  Contain myself like this, weigh words and glances!   1420
  I am not used to it.
COUNTESS TERZKY: You will get used
  To many things, my handsome friend! But now
  I must insist upon one proof of your
  Obedience, for upon this one condition only
  Can I have any part at all in this.
MAX: But where is she? Why doesn't she come in?
COUNTESS TERZKY: You must entrust it to my hands entirely.
  And who could wish you well so much as I?
  No one must know about it, not your father,
  He least of all!
MAX: No need for that. There is   1430
  No living soul to whom I would think of
  Confiding what stirs my enraptured heart.
  —O dear aunt Terzky, have all things here changed,
  Or is it only I? I seem to find myself
  As if among mere strangers. Not a trace
  Of all my former wishes and my joys.
  Where have these things all vanished? In this world
  I was not formerly dissatisfied.
  How shallow it now seems to be, how tawdry!
  My comrades are unbearable to me,   1440
  And even to my father I have nothing
  To say. The service, arms, seem merest trash.
  So must a blessed spirit feel who has

Returned from mansions of eternal joy
To childhood games and to pursuits of childhood,
To preferences and to companioncies,
And to the race of human kind entire.
COUNTESS TERZKY: Yet I must beg of you to cast a glance
   Or so yet on this very tawdry world
   Where things of much importance are in progress.   1450
MAX: Yes, something is afoot around me; I know
   By the uncommon, urgent agitation.
   When it is ripe, it will touch me as well
   Undoubtedly. Where do you think I've been, aunt?
   Now do not mock! The thronging camp oppressed me,
   The flood of intimate acquaintances,
   The stupid jokes, the pointless conversations,
   I felt confined, I had to get away,
   Find silent solitude for this full heart
   And some pure haven for my happiness.   1460
   No smiles, now, Countess! I have been to church.
   There is a cloister here, The Heavens' Gate,
   And there I went, and there I was alone.
   Above the altar hung a Blessed Virgin,
   A wretched painting, but it was the friend
   Whom I was searching for just at that moment.
   How often I have seen the Glorious One
   In all her splendor, ardor of adorers,—
   Yet went myself untouched; now suddenly
   I sensed their piety, as I sensed love.   1470
COUNTESS TERZKY: Enjoy your happiness. Forget the world
   Around you. Meanwhile friendship shall take care
   Of you and act for you with vigilance.
   Only be pliable in turn when people
   Point out to you your path to happiness.
MAX: But what is keeping her!—O golden time
   Upon that journey when each new sun brought us
   Together and the late night parted us!
   Then no sands ran, no clock was heard to strike.
   Time in its everlasting course then seemed   1480

To have stopped still for me, the more-than-blessed.
Oh, that man has already fallen from
His heaven who must think of cycling hours.
No clock strikes for a happy man.
COUNTESS TERZKY: How long since you revealed your heart to
    her?
MAX: I ventured my first word this morning.
COUNTESS TERZKY: What! Not until today in twenty days?
MAX: There at that hunting lodge it was, between
    This camp and Nepomuk, the place where you
    Rejoined us, and the final stop of all   1490
    The journey. We were standing at a window,
    Our mute gaze fixed upon the dreary fields.
    Before us the dragoons were riding up,
    The escort which the Duke had sent for us.
    Heavy upon me lay the grief of parting.
    At last with trembling I made bold to say:
    "All this reminds me, Lady, that today
        I must part from my happiness. You will
        Discover in a few hours' time a father
        And see yourself surrounded by new friends.   1500
        For you I shall be but a stranger lost
        Amid the crowd—" — "Speak to my cousin Terzky!"
    She interrupted suddenly, and as
    She said it her voice trembled and I saw
    A burning flush spread over her fair cheeks,
    And slowly rising from the ground her glance
    Met mine,—and then I could control myself
    No longer—
            *(The Princess appears in the doorway and
            stops there, observed by the Countess
            but not by Piccolomini.)*
                —boldly in my arms I clasped her,
    My lips touched hers—there was a sudden sound
    From the next room. We parted.—It was *you*.   1510
    What happened after that, you know.

COUNTESS TERZKY *(after a pause and with a stolen glance toward Thekla)*:

Are you so modest, then, or do you have
So little curiosity as not
To ask about *my* secret now?

MAX:　　　　　　　　　　　　Your secret?

COUNTESS TERZKY: Why, yes! When I stepped in that room directly

After, how I found my niece, and what
She said in that first moment when her heart
Was fresh from its surprise—

MAX *(eagerly)*:　　　　　　Well?

(Enter Thekla swiftly.)

THEKLA:　　　　　　　　　　　Spare yourself that
　　　　　　　　　　　　　　　trouble, aunt,

He'll hear that better from my lips.

MAX *(stepping back)*:　　　　My Lady!—

The things that you have let me say, aunt Terzky!　　1520

THEKLA: But has he been here long?

COUNTESS TERZKY: He has indeed, and soon his time is up.

Where have you been so long?

THEKLA: Mother was weeping so again. I see her suffer
—And cannot help it that I am so happy.

MAX *(lost in gazing at her)*:

Now I again have courage to behold you.
Today I could not. All that radiance
Of jewels surrounding you hid my Beloved.

THEKLA: Then your eye saw alone, and not your heart.

MAX: O, when this morning I discovered you　　　　　1530
Amid your family, in your father's arms,
And saw myself a stranger in that circle,—
How urgently the longing seized me at
That moment to embrace him and to call
Him *Father!* But his stern eye bade my flood
Of vehement emotions to be still,
And all those diamonds frightened me away

Which like a starry garland wreathed you round.
Why did he have to cast a spell about you
As soon as he received you, deck the angel   1540
As though for sacrifice, and on the heart
Of joy unload the burden of his rank!
For love may be a suitor unto love,
But only kings may draw near to such splendor.

THEKLA: O silence on that mummery! You see
How quickly cast aside the burden was.
   (To the Countess)
He is not light of heart. Why isn't he?
You, aunt, have turned his spirit heavy for me!
He was quite otherwise upon the journey.
So softly clear, so gladly full of talk.   1550
I'd have you ever so and never different.

MAX: Within your father's arms you found yourself
In a new world that pays you homage, charms
Your eye, if only by its novelty.

THEKLA: Yes, much intrigues me here, I won't deny it,
The many-colored stage of war delights me,
Renewing manifold a cherished image,
Attaching for me life and truth to that
Which merely had appeared a lovely dream.

MAX: For me it has made my real happiness   1560
A dream. I have these past few days dwelt on
An island in the aether's upper heights;
Now it has settled downward to the earth,
And this transition which returns me to
My former life, divides me from my heaven.

THEKLA: The game of life is cheerful to behold
When one holds treasure safely in his heart,
And I return more gladly to my finer
Possessions after having now surveyed it.—
   *(interrupting herself, and in a
      jesting tone)*
What new things and unheard of I have seen   1570
In my brief time of being here. And yet

All this must yield before the miracle
Mysteriously contained within this palace.

COUNTESS TERZKY (*pondering*):
What thing is that? I am myself acquainted
With all the sombre corners of this house.

THEKLA (*smiling*):
The way to it is guarded by the spirits.
Two griffons keep the watch beside the doors.

COUNTESS TERZKY (*laughing*):
Oh that! The astrological tower! But
How came that sanctuary, usually
So closely guarded, to open for you in   1580
Your first few hours here?

THEKLA: A little man,
Old, with white hair, and friendly face, who showed me
His favor right away, unbarred the door.

MAX: That is the Duke's astrologer, named Seni.

THEKLA: He questioned me on many things, when I
Was born, on which day and which month, and whether
My birth occurred in daytime or by night,—

COUNTESS TERZKY: He wished to cast your horoscope for you.

THEKLA: He also looked into my hand, and shook
His head with dubiousness at what he saw;   1590
The lines seemed not to please him over-much.

COUNTESS TERZKY: How did you find the room? I always have
Glanced only hastily around myself.

THEKLA: I felt an odd sensation when I entered,
Coming so quickly from the full daylight,
For suddenly dark night surrounded me
Made faintly clear by strange illumination.
Half-circle-wise were ranged around me six
Of seven mighty effigies of kings
With scepters in their hands, and on their heads   1600
Each wore a star, and all light in the tower
Seemed to be coming solely from those stars.
Those were the planets, so my guide explained,
And they controlled the course of destiny,

Hence they were represented there as kings.
The furthest one, a peevish, grim old man
With star of murky yellow, that was Saturn;
He of the ruddy glow just opposite
And clad in warlike armor, that was Mars,
And both bring little happiness to men.   1610
But at his side a lovely lady stood,
A softly shimmering star upon her head,
And that was Venus, the star-form of joy.
Upon the left stood wingèd Mercury;
And in the middle, clear as silver, gleamed
A cheerful man and with a royal mien,
And that was Jupiter, my father's star,
And at his side there stood the moon and sun.
MAX: O I will never criticize his trust
In stars and in the power of the spirits.   1620
It is not merely *pride* of man that fills
Up space with spirits and mysterious forces,
But likewise for a loving heart the common
Nature is too narrow. Deeper meaning
Lies in the fairy tales of childhood years
Than in the truth which later life imparts.
The happy world of miracles alone
Provides an answer to the heart's delight,
And opens its eternal realms to me,
Extending toward me all its thousand branches   1630
Wherein the rapt soul blissfully is cradled.
The fable is the homeland-world of love;
She loves to dwell with fays and talismans,
Believes in gods because she comes from gods.
The ancient fable creatures are no more,
The lovely race has emigrated; yet
The heart requires some form of speech; the ancient
Impulse brings us back the ancient names.
And now amid the starry skies they walk
Who once bore us companionship in life.   1640
From thence they beckon downward to a lover

And Jupiter today brings every greatness
To us, as Venus brings all things of beauty.
THEKLA: If that is what the star lore is, I'll gladly
Become converted to that cheerful faith.
It is a lovely thought and comforting
That over us, at heights immeasurable
The wreath of love already had been woven
Of glittering stars before we ever were.
COUNTESS TERZKY: The sky has thorns, not roses merely. Happy
Are you if they do not impair your wreath.   [1650
What Venus, Fortune's harbinger, has woven,
Can soon be rent by Mars, Misfortune's star.
MAX: His dismal reign will soon come to its close!
O blessed be the Duke's high-purposed zeal
To intertwine the olive with the laurel
And furnish peace for the delighted world.
Then his great heart will have no more to wish for,
He has performed enough toward fame, and now
He can live for himself and for his own.   1660
He will retire to his estates. At Gitschin
He has a handsome seat, and Reichenberg
And Castle Friedland lie delightfully;—
Up to the Riesenberge foothills stretch
The hunting ranges of his forest lands.
To his great impulse toward superb construction
He can give free indulgence unimpeded.
There he can lend encouragement to all
The arts in princely fashion, give protection
To all things noble, build, and plant, and watch   1670
The stars, and if his bold strength cannot rest,
Then he can battle with the elements,
Divert a river or blow up a cliff
And thereby pave an easy path for commerce.
Then all our histories of war will be
Tales to be told on lengthy winter nights—
COUNTESS TERZKY: I should, however, like to counsel, cousin,
Not to put away your sword too soon,

For such a bride as this one is well worth
The wooing by the wielding of the sword.   1680
MAX: O if she could be won by dint of weapons!
COUNTESS TERZKY: What was that? Did you hear? I thought I
    heard
Loud noise and quarrelling in the banquet hall.

(She goes out.)

THEKLA *(as soon as the Countess is gone, quickly and softly to*
    Piccolomini):
Don't trust them. They are not sincere.
MAX: Could they—
THEKLA: Trust no one here but me. I saw at once
    They're up to something.
MAX: Up to something! What?
What could they gain by getting up our hopes—
THEKLA: That I don't know. Believe me, though, they do
    Not mean to make us happy or unite us.
MAX: Why trust these Terzkys anyway? Do we   1690
    Not have your mother? Yes, that kindly soul
Deserves that we confide in her like children.
THEKLA: She loves you and esteems you far beyond
    All others; but she never would have courage
To keep a secret like this from my father;
Just for her peace of mind it must remain
A secret.
MAX: But why must there be a secret
At all? Do you know what I'm going to do?
I'll throw myself before your father's feet,
He shall decide my fortunes, he is loyal,   1700
He knows no guile, he hates a crooked path,
He is so good, so noble,—
THEKLA: Such are *you!*
MAX: You've only known him since today. But I
Have lived ten years already in his sight.
Will this then be the first time he has done
Unusual things, unhoped-for things? It's like him

To take one, godlike, by surprise; he always
Must be delighting and astonishing.
Who knows but what this very moment he
Is just expecting my and your confession,   1710
To make us one—You do not speak? You look
With doubt at me? What do you have against your father?
THEKLA: I? Nothing—only that he is too busy
    To have the time and leisure necessary
    To think about our happiness.
        (taking his hand tenderly)
                        Come with me!
    Let us not trust too much in human beings.
    We shall be grateful to these Terzkys for
    Their every favor, but we shall not put
    More faith in them than they deserve, and for
    The rest, we shall rely upon our hearts.   1720
MAX: O shall we ever come to happiness!
THEKLA: Are we not happy now? Are you not mine?
    Am I not yours? There lives within my soul
    A lofty courage given me by love.—
    I ought to be less open and conceal
    My heart more from you; custom so requires.
    But where would any truth be for you here
    If you were not to find it on my lips?
    We now have found each other, hold each other
    In close embrace forever. O, believe me   1730
    That is a great deal more than they intended.
    Hence let us keep it in our inmost hearts
    As if it were a sacred captured prize.
    It fell from Heaven's heights, and we shall pay
    Our thanks for it to Heaven alone. It can
    Perform a miracle for us.

            (Reenter the Countess Terzky.)

COUNTESS TERZKY (hurriedly):
    My husband says it is high time that he
    Should come to dinner.

(When they pay no attention to her,
she steps between them.)
                    Separate!
THEKLA: Oh, no!
  A minute scarcely has gone by.
COUNTESS TERZKY: Time passes quickly for you, Princess Niece.
MAX: There is no hurry, cousin.   [1740
COUNTESS TERZKY: Come! They've marked
  Your absence. Twice her father has inquired.
THEKLA: Oh, well, my father!
COUNTESS TERZKY: You don't know him, Niece!
THEKLA: Why should he be among that company
  At all? It is no place for him. They may
  Be worthy and distinguished men, but he is
  Too young for them, does not belong among them.
COUNTESS TERZKY: You'd rather keep him wholly to yourself?
THEKLA *(quickly)*:
  You've hit upon it. That is just my meaning.
  Yes, leave him here, and tell the gentlemen—   1750
COUNTESS TERZKY: Niece, have you lost your wits entirely?—
  Count!
  You are aware of the conditions.
MAX: I must obey, my Lady. And so, farewell.
  (as Thekla turns quickly away from him)
  Will you not speak?
THEKLA *(without looking at him)*:
                    No, nothing. Go.
MAX: How can I
  If you are angry—

      (He approaches her. Their eyes meet. They stand silent for
      a moment, then she throws herself into his arms and he
      clasps her tight to his bosom.)

COUNTESS TERZKY: Go! What if someone
  Came in! I hear some noise—strange voices coming—

      (Max tears himself from her arms and leaves, accompanied
      by the Countess. At first Thekla follows him with her

eyes, then walks restlessly up and down the room.
Then she stops, lost in thought. A guitar is lying on the
table. She picks it up, and after she has preluded upon it
in melancholy strains for a time, she begins to sing,
accompanying herself as she does so.)

THEKLA: The forest rushes, the clouds go by,
  The maiden walks by the shore and sky,
  The wave, it is shattered with might, with might,
  And she sings far out to the sombre night,   1760
  Her eyes all bedimmed with her weeping.

  Her heart has expired, the world is still,
  Naught further has she to wish or to will.
  Thou Holy One, summon thy child to its own,
  Of earthly delight my share I have known,
  My full share of living and loving.

              (Reenter the Countess Terzky.)

COUNTESS TERZKY: What's this, my Lady Niece? Fie! You are
    throwing
  Yourself at him. Why, I should think you might
  Be just a little choicer of your person.

THEKLA *(rising)*:
  What do you mean, Aunt?

COUNTESS TERZKY: You should not forget   1770
  Who you are, and who *he* is. I suppose
  The thought has not occurred to you.

THEKLA: What thought?

COUNTESS TERZKY: That you are daughter to the Duke of
  Friedland.

THEKLA: Indeed? What if I am?

COUNTESS TERZKY: What? What a question!

THEKLA: What we have come to be, *he* was by birth.
  He is of ancient Lombard lineage,
  Son of a Princess.

COUNTESS TERZKY: Are you in a dream?
  Of course he will be courteously requested
  To honor Europe's richest heiress with his hand.

THEKLA: That will not be required.

COUNTESS TERZKY: You will do well   1780
Not to expose yourself to a refusal.

THEKLA: His father loves him; Count Octavio
Will surely not oppose it—

COUNTESS TERZKY: His father! His! And what of yours, my
Niece?

THEKLA: Yes! You're afraid, I fancy, of *his* father,
Since you're so very secretive from him,
I mean, the father.

COUNTESS TERZKY (*looking at her searchingly*):
Niece, you are dissembling.

THEKLA: Are you so touchy, Aunt? O don't be angry!

COUNTESS TERZKY: You think you have already won your
game—
O do not gloat so soon!

THEKLA: Please don't be angry!   1790

COUNTESS TERZKY: It has not come to that.

THEKLA: I can believe it.

COUNTESS TERZKY: Can you imagine that he has expended
His life of high design in warrior's labors,
Renounced all tranquil earthly happinesses,
Expelled sleep from his couch, to Care surrendered
His noble head, for no more purpose than
To make a happy pair of you? than bring
You from your convent school at last so he
In triumph may present you with a husband
Who happens to delight your eyes?—That much   1800
He could have had at cheaper price. This seed
Was not sown so that you with girlish hand
Might pick the posy and upon your bosom
Wear it for coy effect.

THEKLA: What he did not plant for me, may still bear
The fairest fruits for me of its own will.
And if my kindly fate will have it so,
That from his awesome mighty being should
Emerge the happiness of my whole life—

COUNTESS TERZKY: You look upon things like a girl in love. 1810
   Just look around. Remember where you are.—
   You have not stepped into a house of joys,
   You do not see the walls decked for a wedding
   Nor heads of guests bedecked with garlands. Here
   Is no resplendency except of weapons.
   Or do you think these thousands were assembled
   To make up dances for your bridal feast?
   You see your father's brow is ridged with thought,
   Your mother's eyes in tears, while in the balance hangs
   Our house with all its mighty destiny.   1820
   Leave now the childish wishes of a girl
   Behind you, leave your petty feelings. Prove
   Yourself the extraordinary man's own daughter.
   A woman may not live unto herself,
   She is fast bound unto the fate of others,
   And best of all is she who can by choice
   Take interests of others to her heart
   And cherish them with tenderness and love.
THEKLA: That's what they always told me at the convent.
   I had no wishes, knew myself but as   1830
   His daughter only, as the great man's daughter.
   Such echoes of his life as reached me there
   Gave me this single thought: I was predestined
   To sacrifice myself in sorrow for him.
COUNTESS TERZKY: That is your fate. Accept it willingly.
   I and your mother set you the example.
THEKLA: He for whom I shall sacrifice myself
   Fate has revealed. I gladly follow him.
COUNTESS TERZKY: Your heart, my child, revealed it. Fate did
   not.
THEKLA: The heart's impulses are the voice of Fate.   1840
   I now am his! His gift alone is this
   New life which I am living now. He has
   Rights over his creation. What was I
   Until his love breathed new life into me?
   I will not set a lesser price upon

Myself than my Beloved sets. He who
Possesses priceless things cannot be poor.
I feel strength given me with happiness.
An earnest thing is life to earnest souls.
That I belong unto myself, I know now,   1850
I have become aware of the firm will
Within my heart, will that is proof against
Coercion, and I may now dare the utmost.
COUNTESS TERZKY: Would you risk contradiction of your father
If he determined otherwise for you?
—You dream of forcing him? Child, grasp this fact:
His name is Friedland!
THEKLA: So is my name also.
In me he shall discern his own true daughter.
COUNTESS TERZKY: What's this! His king, his Emperor cannot
    force him,
And you, his daughter, dare to cross his will?   1860
THEKLA: What no one dares, his daughter may attempt.
COUNTESS TERZKY: I must say! He is not prepared for this.
To overcome all obstacles to find
New opposition rising up against him
Out of the self-will of his daughter! Child!
Till now you have beheld your father's smile
Alone, but not the anger of his eye.
Your voice of opposition, your faltering voice,
Will it be bold enough to brave his presence?
You may perhaps, when by yourself, propose great things, 1870
May well weave wreaths of lovely rhetoric,
And arm your dove-like mind with lion's courage.
But try it! Step before his countenance
Directed full upon you, and say No!
Before him you will wither like the tender petal
Of blossoms in the fire gaze of the sun.
—I do not seek to frighten you, dear child!
To such extremes it will not come, I trust.—
Besides, I do not know his will. Perhaps
His purposes are in agreement with   1880

Your wishes. But it cannot be his will
That you, proud daughter of his fortunes, should
Act like a lovesick girl and throw yourself
Away upon the man who, if the high
Reward is destined for him, must still earn the prize by
The highest sacrifice that love can make!

(Exit.)

THEKLA *(alone)*:

I thank you for the hint! It makes
My evil premonition certainty.
So it is true? We have here neither friend
Nor loyal soul—nor anything besides   1890
Ourselves. Fierce battles threatening await us.
Do thou, O Love, lend us the strength, divine one!
Oh, she is right! These are not happy signs
That shine upon this union of our hearts.
This is no theatre where hope may dwell.
Here rattles only muffled noise of war,
And even Love appears—as if in armor
And girded for a struggle to the death.

   A lowering spirit stalks our family's line,
   And Fate will swiftly bring us to our doom.   1900
   It drives me from that tranquil home of mine,
   My soul is dazzled by enchanting bloom.
   With form angelic it entices me,
   I see that form draw nearer with each hour,
   It leads me on with godlike potency
   To the abyss. I cannot stay its power.
     (Dinner music is heard in the distance.)
O! when a house is destined to destruction
By fire, then Heaven gathers dense its clouds,
The lightning downward shoots from heights serene,
From subterranean gulfs flames upward burst,   1910
The god of joy himself with fury blind
Hurls pitch-pine wreaths into the burning building!   [1912]

(Exit.)

ACT IV

*Scene : A large hall, festively illuminated, in the middle of which
a richly set table stands endwise toward the audience. At it are
seated eight Generals, among them Octavio Piccolomini, Terzky,
and Marádas. To right and left and further toward the rear are
two other tables with six guests each. Forward stands the sideboard. The very front section of the stage remains open for
attendant pages and servants. There is movement everywhere.
Musicians from Terzky's regiment move across the stage and
around the banquet table. Before they have quite disappeared
Max Piccolomini comes in. Terzky approaches him with a document, Isolani with a goblet.*

ISOLANI : Well, Brother, here's to those we love! Where have
  You been? Quick to your seat! Our Terzky offers
  His mother's choicest wines to us, and things
  Are going on as at the Heidelberger Castle.
  You've missed the best already. At the table
  There they are handing out the princely hats
  Of Eggenberg, Slawata, Lichtenstein,
  And Sternberg's lands are on the block for bids   1920
  With all the other big Bohemian fiefs.
  If you act promptly you will get a slice.
  Go on! Sit down!

KOLALTO AND GÖTZ *(calling from the second table)*:
                  Count Piccolomini!

TERZKY:
  He'll be right with you!—Read this draft form of the oath
  See if you like the way we've drawn it up.
  They all have had their turns at reading it

107

And each man will subscribe his name to it.

MAX (*reading*):

"Ingratis servire nefas."

ISOLANI: That sounds like some old Latin motto.—Brother,
What's that in German?   1930

TERZKY: No honest man serves an ungrateful one.

MAX: "Whereas our exalted Commander, his Serene Highness the Duke of Friedland, because of divers offenses sustained,
has been of a mind to quit the service of the Emperor, but at
our unanimous request has allowed himself to be swayed to
remain with the Army and not to remove himself from us
without our sanction: we hereby collectively assume the obligation, and each man particularly in lieu of a corporeal oath,—
also to remain honorably and loyally with him, in no wise to
remove ourselves from him, and for the same to risk all things
ours, even to the last drop of ur blood, *insofar as the oath
which we have sworn to the Emperor will permit.*

(*The last words are repeated by Isolani.*)

               And moreover, if one or the other of us,
contrary to this obligation, should desert the common cause,
we declare him a fugitive from the alliance and a traitor and
pledge ourselves to take revenge therefor upon his goods and
property, life and limb. This same we attest with subscription
of our names."

TERZKY: Well, are you willing to subscribe this paper?

ISOLANI: Why should he *not* sign? Every officer
Of honor can—and must.—Bring pen and ink.

TERZKY: Leave it till after dinner.

ISOLANI (*drawing Max away*):   Come, then! Come!

(*Max and Isolani go up to the table. Terzky
motions to Neumann, who has been waiting by
the sideboard, and comes downstage with him.*)

TERZKY: You brought the copy, Neumann? Let me have it.
It's drawn so it can be mistaken for
The other?

NEUMANN: Imitated line for line,

With nothing but the part about the oath
Omitted as your Excellency commanded.   1940
TERZKY: Good! Lay it there, and straight into the fire
With this. This has accomplished what was wanted.

*(Neuman lays the copy on the table and walks to
the sideboard. Enter Illo from the adjoining room.)*

ILLO: How do things stand with Piccolomini?
TERZKY: All right, I think. He offered no objections.
ILLO: He is the only one I don't quite trust,
He and his father.—Keep your eye on both
Of them.
TERZKY: How do thinks look where you are sitting?
You're keeping your guests warm, I hope?
ILLO: They are
Quite cordial. I believe we have them. And,
As I predicted to you,—now already   1950
The talk no longer is of merely keeping
The Duke in charge. As long as they are all
Together now, thinks Montecuculi,
They should impose conditions on the Emperor
Right in his own Vienna. Oh, believe me,
Were it not for these Piccolominis
We could have spared ourselves the whole deception.
TERZKY: Now what does Buttler want? Be quiet!

(Buttler comes up to them from the second table.)

BUTTLER: Don't
Let me disturb you. I quite grasp your meaning,
Lord Marshal. May good luck attend the venture.   1960
—For my part,
     (mysteriously)
               you may count on me.
ILLO *(quickly):*   We may?
BUTTLER: With or without the clause, I do not care.
Let us be clear on this. The Duke may put
My loyalty to any test, inform him.
I am the Emperor's officer as long as

He pleases to remain the Emperor's General,
And I am Friedland's slave as soon as he
Is pleased to be his independent master.

TERZKY: An excellent exchange. This is no miser,
No Ferdinand, to whom you pledge yourself.   1970

BUTTLER: I do not cheaply sell my loyalty,
Count Terzky, and I would not have advised you
A year ago to bargain with me for
What I now offer of my own free will.
Yes, to the Duke I bring myself and my
Whole regiment. I fancy my example
Will not remain without its consequences.

ILLO: To whom is it unknown that Colonel Buttler
Shines as a paragon for the whole army!

BUTTLER: You think so, Marshal? Well, then I do not   1980
Regret my loyalty of forty years
If at age sixty my good name, preserved
So carefully, will buy such full revenge.—
You gentlemen must not be scandalized
By what I say. It makes no difference *how*
You have me, and I trust that you will not
Expect your game to warp my level judgment,—
Or think unstable mind or blood too soon
Stirred up or any other silly motive
Swerves the old man from his accustomed path   1990
Of honor. Come! I am no less determined
Because I clearly see what I am leaving.

ILLO: Well, tell us fair and square just what we are
To take you for—

BUTTLER: A friend. Here is my hand
On that. I'm yours with everything I have.
The Duke needs not just men, but money also.
I've earned a little something in his service,
I'll lend it to him, and if he survives me,
It's long since willed to him; he is my heir.
I stand alone amid the world and have   2000
No knowledge of the feeling that attaches

A man to loving wife and cherished children.
My name dies with me, my existence ends.
ILLO: Your money is not needed,—such a heart
As yours outweighs whole tuns of gold and millions.
BUTTLER: I came, a lowly horseman's groom, from Ireland
To Prague in service of a master whom
I buried. From base service in the stall
I rose through fate of war to this high peak
Of dignity, the toy of changeful luck.   2010
And Wallenstein is also Fortune's child.
I love a path the runs the same as mine.
ILLO: Strong personalities are all akin.
BUTTLER: This is a mighty moment of our times,
Propitious to decisive men and brave.
Like coins that go from hand to hand, the towns
And castles shift and swap their transient owners;
Ancient houses' scions emigrate;
New coats-of-arms, new names rise to the top;
On German soil a northern folk unwelcome   2020
Attempts to fix itself in permanency;
The Prince of Weimar girds himself with strength
To found a mighty princedom by the Main;
A longer life was all that Mansfeld lacked,
The Halberstädter likewise, to acquire
Lands of their own by bravery of their swords.
And which of these could equal our own Friedland?
There's nothing so exalted but the strong
Is warranted to set his ladder to it.
TERZKY: Ah, that is spoken like a man!   2030
BUTTLER: Be sure you have the Spaniards and Italians.
The Scotsman Lessly I will answer for.
Come, join the company!
TERZKY: Where is the cellar master?
Bring all the stock you have. The finest wines!
Today's the day. Our affairs are thriving.

(*They go to their various tables.*)
(*The cellar master and Neumann advance*

downstage. Servants pass back and forth.)

CELLAR MASTER: The noble wines! Oh if my former mistress,
His late mama, could see this saucy life,
She would turn over in her grave! —Oh yes,
Lieutenant, things are going downhill with
This noble house.—No limit or restraint.   2040
And this exalted intermarriage with
This Duke has brought us little blessing.

NEUMANN: God
Forbid! The palmy days are just beginning.

CELLAR MASTER: You think so? Much could yet be said on that
    score.

(Enter a servant.)

THE SERVANT: Some Burgundy for table four!

CELLAR MASTER: That is
Their seventieth bottle now, Lieutenant.

THE SERVANT: The German gentleman, that Tiefenbach,
Is sitting there, that's why.

(Exit.)

CELLAR MASTER: They're aiming way too high.
They want to match the splendor of Electors
And kings and where the Duke once dares to go, the Count
My noble Lord will not lag far behind.   [2050
    (to the servants)
Why stand and eavesdrop? I'll put legs on you!
Look to your tables, to the bottles! There!
Count Palfy has an empty glass before him!

(A second servant comes up.)

SECOND SERVANT: They want the golden chalice, Cellar master,
The one with the Bohemian coat-of-arms;
You know the one, the gentleman assured me.

CELLAR MASTER: You mean the one that Master Wilhelm
    wrought
For Frederick at his royal coronation,
The showpiece taken with the loot from Prague?   2060

SECOND SERVANT: Yes, *that* one. They will pass it round for toasts.

CELLAR MASTER (*shaking his head as he brings out the cup and rinses it out*):
There's one more thing to tattle to Vienna.

NEUMANN: Let's see; That is a beauty of a cup!
Of massive gold and on it clever things
Are neatly pictured in embossed relief.
Right here on this first panel: let me see:
On horseback here the haughty Amazon
Agallop over bishop's hats and croziers,
She's carrying a hat upon a staff
Beside a flag on which a chalice stands.   2070
Can you tell me what that all signifies?

CELLAR MASTER: The woman that you see on horseback there
Is the Bohemian crown's Electoral Right,
So much is signified by the round hat
And by the wild horse she is riding there.
The hat is man's adornment, for whoever
In kings' and emperors' presence may not leave
His hat upon his head, is no free man.

NEUMANN: But what about the chalice on the flag?

CELLAR MASTER: The chalice signifies Bohemian freedom   2080
Of church, as it was in their fathers' time.
Their fathers in the Hussite wars fought for
And won this privilege above the Pope,
Who will not grant the laity the chalice.
There's nothing more important than the chalice
For Utraquists, it is their precious symbol
Which cost Bohemian blood in many battles.

NEUMANN: What does the scroll say unrolled there above it?

CELLAR MASTER: It indicates Bohemia's royal charter
Which we exacted from the Emperor Rudolph,   2090
A precious parchment dear beyond all price,
Which guarantees free ringing of the bells
And public singing for the new faith and
The old. But since this Grätzer is our ruler
All that has ended now, and since the Battle

Of Prague, where Frederick Palatine lost kingdom
And crown, our church has lost its pulpit and
Its altar, and our brothers with their backs
Behold their homeland, while the Emperor clipped
Himself the royal charter with his shears.　　　2100
NEUMANN: How much you know! You are well posted on
The annals of your country, Cellar master.
CELLAR MASTER: My ancestors were Taborites, you see,
In service under Ziska and Prokóp.
Now peace be to their ashes, for they fought
In worthy cause.—Well, carry it away.
NEUMANN: First let me see this second panel here.
Just look, we have the Emperor's councillors,
Martinitz and Slawata, at the Palace
In Prague, heads down and falling from the window.　　2110
Just so! Here stands Count Thurn who ordered it.

(The servant carries the cup away.)

CELLAR MASTER: Do not recall that day. It was in May,
The twenty-third, when we were writing sixteen-
Hundred-and-eighteeen. To me it seems
Like yesterday. On that unhappy day
It all began, the great heart's sorrow of
My country. Sixteen years have passed since then
With never any peace upon the earth.—
A SHOUT FROM THE SECOND TABLE: The Duke of Weimar! Hail!
THIRD AND FOURTH TABLES:　　　　Long live Duke Bernhard!

(Music strikes up.)

FIRST SERVANT: Just hear the uproar!
SECOND SERVANT *(running up)*: Have you heard? They're toasting
Weimar!　　　　　　　　　　　　　　　2120
THIRD SERVANT:　　　　Austria's enemy!
FIRST SERVANT:　　　　　　　　The Lutheran!
SECOND SERVANT: Before, when Deodat proposed for toast
The Emperor's health, you could have heard a mouse.
CELLAR MASTER: With men at drink one overlooks a lot.
A proper servant should not hear such things.

THIRD SERVANT *(aside to the fourth servant)*:
Now keep your eye peeled, Johann, for to Father
Quiroga we'll have lots of things to tell.
He'll give us plenty of indulgences
For this.
FOURTH SERVANT: That's why I'm going to find as much
To do as possible near Illo's chair.   2130
The talk he's making there is mighty queer.
          (The servants return to their tables.)
CELLAR MASTER *(to Neumann)*:
Who is that swarthy man there with the cross
So close in conversation with Count Palffy?
NEUMANN: Oh that's another one they trust too far.
He calls himself Marádas. He's a Spaniard.
CELLAR MASTER: These Spaniards don't amount to much, I tell
     you.
Those Latin peoples are no good.
NEUMANN: Ah, ah,
You shouldn't talk that way, now, Cellar master.
Among them are the foremost Generals, just
The ones by whom the Duke sets greatest store.   2140
          (Terzky comes and picks up the paper.
          Movement begins at the tables.)
CELLAR MASTER *(to the servants)*:
There's the Lieutenant General getting up.
Look sharp! They're breaking up. Go move the chairs.
          (The servants hurry toward the rear of the
          stage. Some of the guests come forward.)
     (Octavio Piccolomini comes in conversation with Marádas
     and both stand well downstage at one end of the pros-
     cenium. To the other end comes Max Piccolomini. He
     stands alone, absorbed in thought, taking no part in the
     action of the others. The middle space between them
     and a few steps back is occupied by Buttler, Isolani,
     Götz, Tiefenbach, Kolalto, and presently Count Terzky.)
ISOLANI *(as the company come forward)*:

Good night! Good night, Kolalto.—Good night, General,
Good night! I should more rightly say: Good morning.
GÖTZ *(to Tiefenbach)*:
Well, Brother: Prosit Mahlzeit!
TIEFENBACH: That was a dinner fit for kings!
GÖTZ: Ah, yes, the Countess
Knows how. She learned it from her mother-in-law.
God rest her soul. Yes, she was quite a hostess!
ISOLANI *(starting to leave)*:
Lights! Lights!
TERZKY *(bringing the document to Isolani)*:
Wait, Brother, just a minute longer. Here   2150
Is something yet to sign.
ISOLANI: I'll sign whatever
You want me to, but just don't make me read.
TERZKY: I will not burden you. It is the oath
You know already. Just a few pen strokes.
        (as Isolani hands the paper to Octavio)
Just as it comes. Whoever gets it. Rank's
No matter.

        *(Octavio runs through the document with
        apparent indifference. Terzky watches him
        from a distance.)*

GÖTZ *(to Terzky)*: Count permit me to excuse
Myself.
TERZKY: Don't hurry off.—A nightcap?—
        (to the servants)   Hey!
GÖTZ: I couldn't!
TERZKY: Just a little game?
GÖTZ: Excuse me.
TIEFENBACH *(sitting down)*:
Forgive me, gentlemen. This standing gets me.
TERZKY: Go right ahead, be comfortable there, General!   2160
TIEFENBACH: My head is clear, my stomach is all right,
My legs somehow just will not carry me.
ISOLANI *(pointing to his corpulence)*:

You've simply taken on too big a load.

(Octavio has signed and now hands the paper to Terzky, who passes it to Isolani. The latter walks up to the table to sign.)

TIEFENBACH: The war in Pomerania brought it on.
We had to go out in the snow and sleet;
I won't get over it in all my days.

GÖTZ: The Swedes would not fight by the calendar.

(Terzky hands the paper to Don Marádas. The latter walks up to the table to sign.)

OCTAVIO *(approaching Buttler):*
You're not particularly fond of revels
Of Bacchus, are you General? I have noticed
The fact. You would enjoy yourself much better   2170
In noise of battle than in noise of feasts.

BUTTLER: I must confess it's not my sort of thing.

OCTAVIO *(coming nearer, confidentially):*
Nor is it mine, of that I can assure you.
I am delighted, worthy General Buttler,
That we agree so fully in our thinking.
A half a dozen good old friends at most
Around a cozy little table, with
A spot of good Tokay, frank hearts, and talk
That's sensible,—yes, that's the way I like it.

BUTTLER: Yes, I agree,—if one can have it that way.   2180

(The paper goes to Buttler, who walks to the table to sign. The proscenium is empty now so that the two Piccolominis are standing alone, each on his own side.)

OCTAVIO *(after observing his son from a distance for a long time, draws a little nearer to him):*
You stayed away unusually long, my friend.

MAX *(turning around quickly, embarrassed):*
I went—I was detained by urgent business.

OCTAVIO: I see you still are not entirely here?

MAX: You know confusion always makes me quiet.

OCTAVIO *(moving closer to him)*:
  I can't be told what kept you out so long?
        (with cunning)
  —Yet Terzky knows.
MAX: And what does Terzky know?
OCTAVIO *(meaningfully)*:
  He was the only one who did not miss you.
ISOLANI *(who has been watching from afar, steps up)*:
  That's right, old father! Give it to him hot!
  Pile on the coals! There's something wrong with him.
TERZKY *(coming up with the paper)*:
  Do I have all your signatures? None missing?   2190
OCTAVIO: They all have signed.
TERZKY *(shouting)*:   Now who has yet to sign?
BUTTLER *(to Terzky)*:
  Count up the names. There ought to be just thirty.
TERZKY: Here is an X.
TIEFENBACH: I am the X.
ISOLANI: He does not know his letters, but his X
  Is good, Christian and Jew will honor it.
OCTAVIO *(urgently to Max)*:
  Let's go now, both of us. It's getting late.
TERZKY: There's only *one* Piccolomini signed here.
ISOLANI *(pointing to Max)*:
  I tell you this stone guest is the missing one,
  He's not been worth his salt all evening long.

        *(Max takes the paper from Terzky's hands and
        looks at it abstractedly.)*
        *(Enter Illo from the rear room. He has the gold
        cup in his hands and is very drunk. Behind
        him are Götz and Buttler who are trying
        to hold him back.)*

ILLO: What is this? Let me go!
GÖTZ AND BUTTLER: Illo, you've had   2200
  Enough to drink!
ILLO *(going up to Octavio, putting his arm around him, and*

drinking) :
Octavio, to you!
We'll drown all grudges in this drink of friendship!
I know you've never liked me—nor I you—
God punish me for that! But now let bygones
Be bygones! I esteem you infinitely,
> *(kissing him repeatedly)*

I am your closest friend, I'll have you know!
Whoever calls you a deceitful cat
Will deal with me.

TERZKY *(softly)* :   Are you out of your mind?
Remember, Illo, where you are!

ILLO *(naively)* :
Why, what's the matter, we are all good friends.   2210
> *(with a satisfied look on his face he gazes around the entire circle)*

There's not a scoundrel here, I'm glad to say.

TERZKY *(to Buttler, urgently)* :
Take him away with you, I beg you Buttler.

> *(Buttler leads him to the sideboard.)*

ISOLANI *(to Max, who meanwhile has been staring at the paper uninterruptedly but absent-mindedly)* :
You've got it studied out? All straight now, Brother?

MAX *(as if waking from a dream)* :
But what am I supposed to do here?

TERZKY AND ISOLANI :   Sign it!

> *(Octavio is seen to fix his gaze anxiously on him.)*

MAX *(handing it back)* :
Leave it till tomorrow. It is *business*.
My wits are not about me. Send it to me
Tomorrow.

TERZKY :   But you realize—!

ISOLANI :   Here! Sign it!
You are the youngest of the entire table,
You don't claim surely to be smarter than
The lot of us together. Look! Your father   2220

Has signed it, all of us have signed it too.

TERZKY *(to Octavio)*:
Use your authority and make him sign.

OCTAVIO: My son's of age.

ILLO *(setting the cup down on the sideboard)*:
                    What's all this talk about?

TERZKY: He has refused to sign the document.

MAX: I tell you it can wait until tomorrow.

ILLO: It cannot wait till then. We all have signed it,
And you must sign it too, you've got to sign it.

MAX: Illo, sleep well.

ILLO: You can't get out of it
Like this. The Duke shall find out who his friends are.

(All the guests gather about the two of them.)

MAX: The Duke knows how I am disposed toward him,   2230
So do you all. This fuss is not required.

ILLO: That's all the gratitude the Duke can claim
For always having put these Latins first.

TERZKY *(in extreme embarrassment, to the Commanders, who
are in an uproar)*:
The wine in him is talking. Please ignore him.

ISOLANI *(laughing)*:
The wine is not inventing. He's just blabbing.

ILLO: Who isn't *with* me is *against* me. Oh,
These touchy consciences! If they cannot
Work out some loophole for themselves, some clause—

TERZKY *(quickly interrupting him)*:
He's absolutely mad, pay no attention!

ILLO *(screaming louder)*:
Some clause to save their skins. Now what's the use   2240
Of clauses? May the Devil take that clause—

MAX *(becomes attentive and looks at the paper again)*:
What can there be so dangerous in this?
You make me curious to investigate.

TERZKY *(aside to Illo)*:
What are you doing, Illo? You'll destroy us!

TIEFENBACH *(to Kolalto)*:
I saw it read a different way before.

GÖTZ: I thought so too.

ISOLANI: What are you boggling at?
Where other men's names stand, mine too can stand.

TIEFENBACH: Before the meal there was some reservation,
Some clause about our service to the Emperor.

BUTTLER *(to one of the Commanders)*:
Shame, gentlemen! Consider what it is   2250
That is at stake. The question now is this:
Shall we retain the General, or are we
To let him go? You can't split hairs so fine.

ISOLANI *(to one of the Generals)*:
And did the Duke so hedge himself with clauses
When he assigned your regiment to you?

TERZKY *(to Götz)*:
Or when you got those contracts for supplies
That net you thousands in a single year?

ILLO: A pack of scoundrels, making rascals of us!
Who is dissatisfied, speak up! I'm here!

TIEFENBACH: Well, this is only talk.

MAX *(having read, returns the paper)*:
Until tomorrow.   2260

ILLO *(stuttering with rage and losing control of himself, holds
the paper toward him with one hand and his dagger with
the other)*:
Write—Judas!

ISOLANI: Shame, Illo!

BUTTLER ⎫
OCTAVIO ⎬ Take his dagger!
TERZKY ⎭

MAX *(seizing his arm suddenly and disarming him, to Terzky)*:
Get him to bed!   [2262]

(Exit.)

*(Illo, shouting curses and abuse, is held by
several of the Commanders. On the scene of
general departure the curtain falls.*

ACT V

Scene: A room in Piccolomini's dwelling. It is night.
Enter Octavio Piccolomini. A servant holds a lamp for him.

OCTAVIO: Show my son in to me as soon as he
    Arrives.—What time is it?
THE SERVANT: It's nearly morning.
OCTAVIO: Set here your lamp.—We shall not go to bed
    Tonight at this late hour. You may retire.

> *(Exit the servant.)*
> *(Octavio walks pensively through the room.*
> *Enter Max Piccolomini, not immediately*
> *noticed by him. Max watches him silently*
> *for a few minutes.)*

MAX: Are you displeased with me, Octavio?
    God knows that for that ugly quarrel I
    Was not to blame.—I saw that you had signed;
    What you approved should have been good enough   2270
    For me,—and yet it seemed—you know—I can
    In such things only follow my own light,
    Not that of others.
OCTAVIO *(going up to him and embracing him)*:
               Follow it still further,
    My best of sons! It gave you truer guidance
    Tonight than the example of your father.
MAX: Explain yourself more clearly.
OCTAVIO: I shall do so.
    For after what has happened here this evening
    No further secrets must exist between us.

> *(after both have sat down)*

Max, tell me what you think about this oath
Which was submitted for our signature.   2280
MAX: I take it for some harmless thing, although
  I have no love for such formalities.
OCTAVIO: No other reason led you to refuse
  The signature they sought to force from you?
MAX: It was a serious thing,—my mind was elsewhere,—
  The issue in itself seemed not so urgent—
OCTAVIO: Be open, Max. Did you have no suspicion?
MAX: What was I to suspect? Not in the least.
OCTAVIO: Thank your good angel, Piccolomini!
  He held you unaware from the abyss.   2290
MAX: I don't know what you mean.
OCTAVIO: Then I will tell you.
  It was intended you should lend your name
  To back a scoundrel's trick, and that you should
  By stroke of pen renounce your oath and duty.
MAX (standing up):
  Octavio!
OCTAVIO: Pray keep your seat. You have
  Much more to hear from me, my friend. For years
  You have lived on in dazzlement outstripping
  Belief. The blackest plot is being spun
  Before your eyes, a power out of hell
  Beclouds the vivid daylight of your senses.—   2300
  I can no longer keep my silence. I
  Must take the blindfold from your eyes.
MAX: Before
  You speak, consider well! If nothing but
  Suspicion is your subject,—and I almost
  Fear it is nothing further,—spare me! I
  Am in no mood to hear you out in silence.
OCTAVIO: Though you may have sound cause to flee from this
  Enlightenment, I have more urgent cause
  To bring it to you. I could safely leave
  You to your innocence of heart and your   2310
  Own judgment. But I now perceive the net

Laid out to catch your heart itself.—The secret
    (fixing him sharply with his eye)
That you conceal from me, wrests *mine* from me.

MAX *(tries to answer but stops and casts his eyes to the floor
    with embarrassment.)*

OCTAVIO *(after a pause):*
  Know then, they are deceiving you—and playing
  Most shamefully with you and with us all.
  The Duke pretends he is about to leave
  The army; at this juncture they propose
  A plan—to steal the army from the Emperor
  And lead it over to the enemy.

MAX: That priest-hatched tale I've heard before, but I   2320
  Did not expect to hear it from your mouth.

OCTAVIO: The mouth from which you hear it at this moment
  Will guarantee it is no priest-hatched tale.

MAX: How mad would they make out the Duke to be!
  They fancy he could plot to gather up
  Some thirty thousand troops of proven honor,
  More than a thousand noblemen among them,
  Lure them away from oath and code and duty
  And then unite them for a scoundrel's action?

OCTAVIO: O he desires by no means anything   2330
  So vilely shameless.—What he wants of us
  Will bear a name more innocent by far.
  He simply wants to bring peace to the Empire,
  And since *this* peace is hateful to the Emperor,
  He wants to—well, he wants to *force* it on him.
  He wants to satisfy all factions, and,
  As price for all his efforts, keep Bohemia,
  Which he controls already, for himself.

MAX: Does he deserve, Octavio, that we—
  That we should think of him in such base terms?   2340

OCTAVIO: There is no question here of how we think.
  The case speaks for itself with clearest proofs.
  My son, you are not unaware how ill

We stand at court.—And yet you have no notion
Of all the machinations and deceits
That have been set in motion to besow
The camp with mutiny. All bonds are severed
That linked an officer together with
His Emperor, linked the soldier trustfully
Together with the lives of citizens.   2350
Devoid of duty and devoid of law
He stands embattled toward the state he should
Protect and threatens to reverse his sword
Against it. Things have gone so far that at
This moment now the Emperor has to tremble
At his own army,—has to fear the daggers
Of traitors in his capital,—his fortress,
Yes, is about to hide his tender grandsons
Away, not from the Swedes, not from the Lutherans,
—No, but hide them away from his own troops.   2360
MAX: O stop! You frighten me, you stagger me.
   I know that empty terrors set one trembling,
   But false illusions bring the real disaster.
OCTAVIO: This is no false illusion. Civil war,
   Of all wars most unnatural, will flare
   Unless we counter it with sudden rescue.
   Many Generals have long since been bought,
   Subalterns' loyalty is wavering,
   Likewise whole regiments and garrisons.
   The forts are in the trust of foreigners.   2370
   To dubious Schafgotsch they have given over
   Silesia's total force of arms; to Terzky
   Five regiments of horse and infantry;
   To Illo, Kinsky, Buttler, Isolan,
   The best equipped and mounted of the troops.
MAX: And to us too.
OCTAVIO: Because they think they have us.
   Think they can lure us with fair promises.
   To me he has assigned the duchies Glatz
   And Sagan, and I clearly see the hook

On which they plan to fetch you in.

MAX: No! No!   2380
  I tell you, No!

OCTAVIO: O open up your eyes!
  Why do you think that we were ordered up
  To Pilsen? To consult us for advice?
  Now when has Friedland asked for our advice?
  No, we were called to sell ourselves to him,
  And if we balk,—to be his hostages.
  And that is why Count Gallas stayed away.
  Nor would you see your father here, if higher
  Responsibility did not detain him.

MAX: He makes no secret of the fact that we   2390
  Were summoned here for his sake.—And you must
  Admit he needs our arms to back him up.
  When he has done so much for us, our duty
  Bids us do something now for him.

OCTAVIO: Do you
  Know what this is that we should do for him?
  That Illo's drunken boastfulness revealed it.
  Consider what it was you heard and saw.
  That paper falsified, that all-important
  Omitted clause, do these things not bear witness
  We were to be involved in nothing good?   2400

MAX: What happened with that document tonight,
  As far as I'm concerned, was nothing but
  A stupid trick played by that fellow Illo.
  This tribe of meddlers drives things to extremes.
  They see the Duke has had a falling out
  With those at court, and wrongly think they serve him
  By widening the breach beyond all cure.
  Of all of this, be sure, the Duke knows nothing.

OCTAVIO: It pains me to destroy faith in a man
  Which seems to you to be so rightly founded.   2410
  But here I cannot spare you.—Here you must
  Take steps, and quickly too, here you must act.
  —I therefore will confess—that everything

That I confided to you now, which seems
Incredible to you—I have it from
His own—the Duke's own lips.

MAX *(with vehement emotion):*   O do not say that!

OCTAVIO: Yes, he himself confided to me—what
  I had long since found out through other channels:
  That he intends to link up with the Swedes
  And at the head of that united army   2420
  Intends to force the Emperor—

MAX: He is quick
  To anger, and the court has given sharp
  Offense; at some ill-humored moment, yes,
  He may perhaps have once let slip his tongue.

OCTAVIO: It was in all cold blood that he avowed
  This to me. Then, since he took my amazement
  For fear, he confidentially produced
  Some correspondence with the Swedes and Saxons
  That gave him hope of tangible assistance.

MAX: It can not be! can *not* be! *can* not be!   2430
  You see it cannot be! Inevitably
  You must have shown the signs of your revulsion,
  He would have taken your advice, or you
  —Would not stand here alive beside me now!

OCTAVIO: Of course I did express my doubts to him.
  I warned him urgently and earnestly
  Against it.—But my inner feeling, my
  Revulsion I hid deep within me.

MAX: Could you
  Have been so false? That is not like my father!
  I could not quite believe your words when you   2440
  Spoke evil things of *him;* I can believe
  Still less when you speak slander of yourself.

OCTAVIO: It was not I who pried into his secrets.

MAX: His confidence deserved sincerity.

OCTAVIO: He was no longer worthy of the truth.

MAX: Less worthy still of you was your deceit.

OCTAVIO: My son, it is not always possible

In life to keep such childlike purity
As promptings of the inner voice would bid us.
On constant guard against sly treachery,   2450
Not even honest spirits can remain
Quite frank.—This is the curse of evil deeds:
That they spawn further deeds and always evil ones.
I split no hairs, I only do my duty.
The Emperor has prescribed my conduct for me.
It would be better possibly to follow
The heart in every case; but in so doing,
Many worthy ends would be rejected.
The need here is, my son, to serve the Emperor.
To that the heart may say what it may say.   2460

MAX: Today I do seem bound to miss your meaning.
    The Duke, you say, disclosed his heart to you in frankness:
    It was bent on an evil end: now *you*
    Claim you deceived him for a worthy end.
    I beg you: Stop! You will not rob me of
    My friend,—but do not let me lose my father!

OCTAVIO *(suppressing his irritation)*:
    You still are not aware of everything,
    My son. There's more yet to reveal.
        (after a pause)   Duke Friedland
    Has made his preparations. He relies
    Upon his stars. He plans to take us unawares.   2470
    He fancies that his sure hand grasps already
    The golden circlet of Bohemia.—But—
    He is in error.—We have acted also.—
    He grasps his own mysterious evil fate.

MAX: Do nothing sudden, father! Oh, by all
    Things good I conjure you. No over-haste!

OCTAVIO: With stealthy tread he crept along his evil way;
    And just as soft and slyly Vengeance followed him.
    She stands already grim and unperceived behind him;
    Just one step more, and he will touch her, shuddering.   2480
    —You have seen Questenberg with me. Till now
    You have observed his public errand only.

He brought along a secret one as well
Known to me only.
MAX: May I know it?
OCTAVIO: Max!
—In saying this I place the Emperor's welfare,
Your father's life as well, into your hands.
This Wallenstein is precious to your heart,
A hardy tie of love and veneration
Has bound you to him from your early childhood;—
You cherish the desire—Let me again   2490
Anticipate your hesitant confiding—
You cherish hopes of being closer to him
Than ever.
MAX: Father!
OCTAVIO: I can trust your heart, I know,
But can I be sure of your self-control?
Will you be able to confront this man
With tranquil countenance if I commit
His total destiny to you?
MAX: You mean
When you commit to me his total guilt?
OCTAVIO (takes a paper out of the casket and hands it to him.)
MAX: What? What? An open letter from the Emperor?
OCTAVIO: Read it.
MAX (after casting a glance at it):
                    The Duke proscribed, condemned to death! 2500
OCTAVIO: Just so.
MAX: O this is harsh. O wretched error!
OCTAVIO: Read on. Control yourself.
MAX (after reading on, with a look of astonishment at his father):
                          What? You? You are—
OCTAVIO: Just for the moment—and until the King
Of Hungary can come up to the army—
Am I invested with command.
MAX: And do you think that you could wrest it from him?
Don't ever dream it! —Father! Father! Father!
A wretched office has devolved upon you.

This paper—this! You plan to activate it?
Disarm that mighty man amid his very   2510
Army and surrounded by his thousands?
You—you are lost—and we are all lost with you!

OCTAVIO: I know what risks I run in doing this.
I stand in the Almighty's hand; He will
Raise up His shield before the good Imperial
House and He will confound the works of Darkness.
The Emperor still has loyal servants; even
In camp there are brave men enough who will
Fight cheerfully for the good cause. Those who
Are loyal have been warned, the rest are watched.   2520
I simply wait for his first step; as soon—

MAX: Would you act hastily on mere suspicion?

OCTAVIO: Far be the tyrant's methods from the Emperor!
He punishes the deed, not the intention.
The Duke still holds his fate within his hands.—
If he leaves unfulfilled his criminal action,
He will be quietly relieved of his
Command, he will yield to his Emperor's son.
Exile with honor to his castles will
Be more a blessing than a punishment   2530
For him. However, his first overt step—

MAX: In what would such a step consist? He never
Will take an evil one. But you might well
—You have already done so—misinterpret
His noblest one.

OCTAVIO: Blameworthy as the Duke's
Ends may have been, his steps overtly taken
Will still admit a lenient construction.
I do not plan to use this document
Short of a deed as will attest high treason
Incontrovertibly and thus condemn him.   2540

MAX: And who will be the judge of that?

OCTAVIO: Yourself.

MAX: O then this paper never will be needed.
I have your word you will not act before

You have brought me myself to full conviction.
OCTAVIO: Can it be possible? Still, after all
You know, you can believe him innocent?
MAX: Your judgment can be wrong, but not my heart.
   (continuing with more composure)
His thought cannot be grasped like other thoughts.
Just as he links his destiny to stars,
He bears a likeness to them in their wondrous,   2550
Profound, eternally unfathomed paths.
They wrong him, be assured. All this will be
Resolved. We shall behold his purity
Emerge in radiance from this black suspicion.
OCTAVIO: I long to see it.
                (Enter a servant.)
   What is it?
THE SERVANT: Sir, a courier waits outside.
OCTAVIO: So early in the day! Who is it then?
   From where?
THE SERVANT: He would not tell me.
OCTAVIO: Admit him. Let no hint of this be known.
     (Exit the servant. Enter a Cornet.)
   It's you, Cornet? You bring word from Count Gallas?   2560
   Give me the letter.
THE CORNET: My report is oral.
   The General did not trust a letter.
OCTAVIO: Speak, then.
THE CORNET: He said to tell you—May I speak here freely?
OCTAVIO: My son knows everything.
THE CORNET: We have him.
OCTAVIO: Whom?
THE CORNET: The go-between, Sesina.
OCTAVIO *(quickly):*   Do you now?
THE CORNET: Caught in the Böhmerwald by Captain Mohrbrand
   Two days ago, en route to Regenspurg
   And carrying despatches to the Swedes.
OCTAVIO: And the despatches—
THE CORNET: In Vienna where

The General sent them with the prisoner   2570
At once.

OCTAVIO: At last! At last! This is great news!
For us this man is a most precious vessel
Containing weighty things.—Did they find much?

THE CORNET: Six packets with Count Terzky's coat-of-arms.

OCTAVIO: None in the Duke's own hand?

THE CORNET: Not that I know of.

OCTAVIO: What of Sesina?

THE CORNET: He seemed very frightened
When he was told he was bound for Vienna.
Count Altring bade him have no fear, however,
If he would only make a full confession.

OCTAVIO: Is Altring with your master now? I heard   2580
That he lay ill in Linz.

THE CORNET: He has been with
The General for three days in Frauenberg;
They have assembled sixty companies
Already, chosen men, and send you word
That they are waiting only for your orders.

OCTAVIO: Much can occur within a few days' time.
When must you leave?

THE CORNET: I wait for your command.

OCTAVIO: Stay till this evening.

THE CORNET: Yes, Sir.

(He starts to go.)

OCTAVIO: No one saw you?

THE CORNET: No one. The Capuchins admitted me
As usual through the cloister postern gate.   2590

OCTAVIO: Go get some rest and keep well out of sight.
I mean to send you back before this nightfall.
Things now lie close to their unfolding, and
Before the day declines, that fatefully
Is breaking forth across the heavens now,
The lot of last decision must be cast.

(Exit the Cornet.)

What now, my son? It all will soon be clear,
—For everything, I know, went through Sesina.

MAX *(who has stood in vehement inner conflict through the
whole of the foregoing scene, decisively):*
I shall find clarity a shorter way.
Farewell.

OCTAVIO: Where are you going?

MAX: To the Duke. 2600

OCTAVIO *(aghast):*
What?

MAX *(returning):*
If you thought that I would play a part
Within this game of yours, you woefully
Miscalculated. My path must be straight.
I cannot be sincere of tongue and false
Of heart—nor countenance a man's relying
Upon me as a friend and salve my conscience
By thinking he does so at his own risk
And that my lips have never lied to him.

I must be worth the price that I am bought for.
—I go now to the Duke. And I intend 2610
Before the day is out to challenge him
To clear his name before the world and by
A forthright step to rip your artful web.

OCTAVIO: Would you do that?

MAX: Make no mistake: I shall.

OCTAVIO: In you I have miscalculated, yes.
I thought that I would find a wise son who
Would bless the hands of my beneficence
In drawing him away from the abyss;—
I find one blinded, whom a pair of eyes
Have made a fool, whom passion shrouds in mist, 2620
Whom even day's full light will not make sane.
Go ask him! Go! Be rash to the degree
Of giving out your father's secret and
Your Emperor's. Go, compel me prematurely
To make a violent break with him. And now,

When one of Heaven's miracles has shed
Protection on my secret till today
And lulled to sleep suspicion's clear-eyed gaze,
I live to see my very son destroy
By senseless, reckless conduct all the work   2630
Diplomacy achieved by such great toil.

MAX: O this diplomacy, how I abhor it!
By your diplomacy you will yet force him
To take a step—Yes, you would go so far as *make*
Him guilty just because you *want* him guilty.
O this can have none but an evil end.—
Let it resolve itself whichever way
It may, I sense disaster looming near.—
For when he falls, this kingly man will pull
A world to its destruction down with him,   2640
And like a ship which in the middle ocean
All of a sudden catches fire and bursts
Aloft and instantaneously casts all
The crew it bore out into sea and sky
So we, who in his fortunes are involved,
Shall all be carried down in his collapse.

You may proceed as you see fit; grant *me*,
However, leave to act in my own fashion.
Between this man and me all must be pure,
And I must learn before this hard day's end   2650
Whom I must sacrifice, my father or my friend.   [2651]

(As he walks away, the curtain falls.)

THE DEATH OF WALLENSTEIN

A Tragedy in Five Acts

CHARACTERS

WALLENSTEN
OCTAVIO PICCOLOMINI
MAX PICCOLOMINI
TERZKY
ILLO
ISOLANI
BUTTLER
CAVALRY CAPTAIN NEUMANN
AN ADJUTANT
COLONEL WRANGEL, an envoy from the Swedes
GORDON, Commandant of Eger
MAJOR GERALDIN
MACDONALD ⎰ Captains in Wallenstein's army
DEVEROUX ⎱
A SWEDISH CAPTAIN
An embassy of Cuirassiers
THE BURGOMASTER OF EGER
SENI
THE DUCHESS OF FRIEDLAND
COUNTESS TERZKY
THEKLA
FRÄULEIN NEUBRUNN, Lady in waiting to the Princess
VON ROSENBERG, Equerry to the Princess
Dragoons, servants, pages, members of the retinue

Time: February 1634, immediately subsequent to the action of
The Piccolominis.

Place: During the first three acts, at Pilsen; during the last two
acts, at Eger, another town in Bohemia.

ACT I

A room arranged for astrological operations and equipped with spheres, maps, quadrants, and other astronomical instruments. The curtain is raised in front of an observatory in which may be seen the seven images of the planets, each in a niche and weirdly lighted. Seni is observing the stars, Wallenstein is standing before a large black chart on which the aspect of the planets is figured.

WALLENSTEIN: Enough now, Seni. Come, let us go down.
The day dawns and the hour belongs to Mars.
Now we can operate no further. Come,
We know enough.
SENI: Allow me one more view
Of Venus, Highness. She is rising now.
Her light is like a sun against the east.
WALLENSTEIN: Yes, she is in her earth-close phase just now
And sheds her influence down in all its force.
    (Examining the figure on the chart.)
Good-omened aspect! Thus the mighty triad
Conjoins at last portentously together,   10
And both the stars of blessing, *Jupiter*
And *Venus*, take the sly and ruinous Mars
Squarely between them and compel that ancient
Mischief-maker to perform my service.
For he was long of hostile mind toward me
And with his vertical or biased shining,
In quartile or in counterphase, directed
Red lightnings at my stars, thereby impairing
Their virtuous properties. Now they have
Prevailed above this enemy of old   20

137

And bring him to me captive in the sky.
SENI: With no Maleficus disturbing either
  Of these great Lumina! And *Saturn* harmless
  And impotent there in *cadente domo.*
WALLENSTEIN: Saturnus' reign is ended, which controlled
  The birth of things within the womb of earth
  And in the depths of human minds and held
  Its sway above all things that shun the light.
  It is no longer time to brood and plot,
  For Jupiter, the radiant god, prevails   30
  And draws the darkly meditated work
  With might into the realm of light.—Now action
  Is called for, suddenly, before the aspect
  Of favor once again flees from my head,
  For changeful ever is the heaven's arch.
          (*A knocking is heard at the door.*)
  A knock. See who it is.
TERZKY (*outside*):   Unlock the door!
WALLENSTEIN: It's Terzky.
  What is so urgent? We are occupied.
TERZKY (*outside*):
  Put everything aside for now, I beg you.
  This cannot be put off.
WALLENSTEIN: Then open, Seni.

          (*As the latter opens the door for Terzky, Wallenstein
          draws the curtain before the images.*)
                    (*Enter Terzky.*)

TERZKY: You've heard the news? He's captured and already 40
  Delivered to the Emperor by Gallas.
WALLENSTEIN (*to Terzky*):
  Who is captured? Who has been delivered?
TERZKY: The man who knows our entire secret, who
  Knows all transactions with the Swedes and Saxons,
  Through whom all business has been carried on—
WALLENSTEIN (*falling back*):
  O not Sesina? Tell me No, I beg you!

TERZKY: Right on his way to Regenspurg and the Swedes
  Agents of Gallas seized him, who has long
  Been spying out his movements. On his person
  Was my whole packet to Count Kinsky, to   50
  Matthias Thurn, to Oxenstirn, to Arnheim.
  All that is in their hands, now they have knowledge
  Of everything that has been going on.

                    (Enter Illo.)

ILLO *(to Terzky):*
  He knows?
TERZKY: He knows.
ILLO *(to Wallenstein):* Do you still think that you
  Can make peace with the Emperor and revive
  His trust in you? Yes, granting even that
  You now were willing to renounce your plans?
  They know what you intended. Now you must
  Go forward, for you can retreat no longer.
TERZKY: They now have documents at hand against us   60
  That testify incontrovertibly—
WALLENSTEIN: But nothing from my hand. That I deny.
ILLO: So? Do you fancy that what was transacted
  In your name by this man, your brother-in-law,
  Will not be charged against *your* reckoning?
  His word should pass as yours to Swedes but not
  To enemies down in Vienna?
TERZKY: You gave no written papers.—But consider
  How far you went in speech with this Sesina.
  Will he keep still? If he can save himself   70
  By publishing your secret, will he keep it?
ILLO: Not even you think that! And now that they
  Have been apprised of just how far you've gone,
  What are you waiting for? You can retain
  Command no longer, and if you give it up,
  Then you are lost beyond all hope of rescue.
WALLENSTEIN: The Army is my guarantee. The Army
  Will not desert me. Whatever they may know,
  The power is mine. They've got to swallow that.

—And if I give my pledge of loyalty,   80
They'll have to be quite satisfied with that.
ILLO: You have the Army. For the moment now
It's yours. Beware, however, of the slow
And silent power of time. The soldiers' favor
Will shield you yet today and yet tomorrow
From open force. But if you give them time,
Unnoticed they will undermine the good
Opinion which now forms your solid footing,
Filch one and then the other slyly from you,—
Until, when finally the earthquake comes,   90
The faithless rotten structure will collapse.
WALLENSTEIN: It is a luckless business!
ILLO: Oh, I will call it lucky rather, if
It has the effect upon you that it should,
And goads you on to act.—The Swedish Colonel—
WALLENSTEIN: Has he arrived? Do you know what he brings?
ILLO: He will declare himself to you alone.
WALLENSTEIN: A luckless, luckless chance! —Ah, yes! Sesina,
He knows too much and will not hold his tongue.
TERZKY: He's a Bohemian rebel-fugitive,   100
A price is on his head. If he can save
Himself at your expense, will he hold back?
And if they question him upon the rack,
Will he, the coward, have sufficient strength?
WALLENSTEIN (lost in thought):
There's no restoring trust now any more.
And now no matter how I act, I shall
Forever be a traitor in their eyes.
If I, however honorably, return
To duty, it will be of no avail.
ILLO: It would mean ruin. They will not ascribe it   110
To loyalty but to your impotence.
WALLENSTEIN (pacing up and down in vehement agitation):
What? Must I now fulfill my plan in earnest
Because I toyed too freely with the thought?
He's damned that trifles with the Devil!

ILLO: If you have only played a game, believe me,
   You'll have to pay for it in solemn earnest.
WALLENSTEIN: And if I must fulfill my plan, it must
   Be now, right now, while still the power is mine.
ILLO: If possible, before their shock wears off,
   Before they can anticipate your action—   120
WALLENSTEIN *(looking at the signatures)*:
   I have the generals' word in writing here—
   Max Piccolomini is not here. Why not?
TERZKY: He was—he thought—
ILLO: Some notion that he had
   It was not needed between you and him.
WALLENSTEIN: He is quite right, it is not needed—
   The regiments refuse to go to Flanders,
   They have submitted me a document
   Protesting opposition to the order.
   The first step has been taken toward rebellion.
ILLO: Believe me, you will lead them sooner to   130
   The enemy than to the Spaniards now.
WALLENSTEIN: I want to hear, however, what the Swede
   May have to offer.
ILLO *(hurriedly)*:   Will you call him, Terzky?
   He's standing there outside.
WALLENSTEIN: Wait just a bit.
   This has surprised me so—it came so fast—
   I am not used to having Chance sweep me
   Blindly along with darkling mastery.
ILLO: For now, hear what he says; appraise it later.

                (Exeunt Terzky and Illo.)

WALLENSTEIN *(speaking to himself)*:
   Can it be possible? Can I no longer
   Act as I wish? No more retreat, if I   140
   So choose? Must I act out the deed because
   I thought of it and did not shun temptation—
   Fed my heart on this dream, saved up the means
   On the uncertain chance of realization,

And only kept approaches to it open?—
By Heaven's mighty God! I never meant it
In earnest, never fixed it as decided.
I did no more than to enjoy the thought;
The freedom and the capability
Engrossed my fancy. Was it wrong to take   150
Delight in visions of the royal hope?
Was not my will still free within my bosom,
Did I not still behold the good path at
The side that kept return still open to me?
Where do I see myself led suddenly?
Pathless the space behind me, and a wall
Of my own building towers up ahead
To block reversal of my course.
      (He stops, deep in thought.)
Guilty I stand, and I can not shake off
This guilt no matter how I try. The mere   160
Ambiguousness of life accuses me,
And even pure deeds from a blameless source
Will be misread and poisoned by suspicion.
Were I the traitor that they take me for,
I would have kept up fair appearances,
I would have drawn concealment tight about me
And not lent voice to temper. Conscious of
The innocence of unperverted will,
I gave vent to my bile and to my passion—
The words were bold because the deed was not.   170
And now, farseeing, they will fit to plan
What happened totally without a plan,
And what my joyous spirit and my anger
Led me to say from excess of emotion
They will knit in an artful web against me
And make of it a fearful accusation
Which I must face in silence. Thus I have
Spun my own net about me to my ruin
And only violence can rip it free.
      (again standing still)

How different! when the free impulse of courage   180
Drew me to that bold act to which distress and
Self-preservation harshly now compel me.
Grave are the features of Necessity.
Not without shuddering awe may human hand
Dip into Destiny's mysterious urn.
My deed belonged to me while it was yet
Within my bosom. Once released from that
Safe corner of my heart, its mother ground,
And sent into the alien fields of life,
It passes to the hands of those sly powers   190
Which skill of man can not make fit for trust.
          (He paces vehemently through the room,
               then stops again in thought.)
What is this thing that you would venture? Have you
Acknowledged it before yourself with fairness?
You seek to overturn the tranquil power
Throned in possession hallowed by the years
And resting on the solid base of custom,
Attached to pious childhood faith of nations
By virtue of a thousand rugged roots.
This will not be a war of strength with strength:
Of such I have no fear. Such I would chance   200
With any foe whom I can see and look
Into the eye, who, being full of courage,
May fire my courage too. The foe unseen
I fear, who in men's hearts opposes me,
Fearsome by coward fear alone.—Not what
Proclaims itself as full of life and force
Is fearsome to the point of peril. It is
The humdrum and eternal yesterday,
What always was and always comes anew,
What holds good for tomorrow just because   210
It held good for today. For man is made
Of humdrum stuff and Habit is his nurse.
Woe to disturbers of his venerable
Old trash, the heirlooms from his ancestors.

The *year* exerts a sanctifying force;
A thing that's grey with age is sacred to him.
Be in possession, and the right is yours,
And holily the mob will guard it for you.
          (*to the page who comes in*)
Is it the Swedish Colonel? Show him in.
          (*Exit the page.—Wallenstein fixes his
          gaze at the door.*)
It is still clean—yet! Crime has not yet passed   220
Across that threshold.—Just so narrow is
The borderline between two roads of life!

          (*Enter Colonel Wrangel.*)

WALLENSTEIN (*after fixing a mustering glance upon him*):
     Your name is Wrangel?
WRANGEL: Gustav Wrangel, Colonel
     Of the blue Südermannland Regiment.
WALLENSTEIN: It was a Wrangel who before Stralsund
     Did me much mischief and by brave defense
     Was cause for that sea-town's resisting me.
WRANGEL: The doing of the element with which
     You fought, not my desert, Lord Duke. The Baltic
     By might of storm did battle for its freedom   230
     Lest sea and land should serve a single man.
WALLENSTEIN: You snatched the Admiral's Hat from off my head.
WRANGEL: I come to place a crown upon it now.
WALLENSTEIN (*motions him to be seated and sits down himself*):
     Now your credentials. Do you have full powers?
WRANGEL (*dubiously*):
     There are so many doubts to be resolved—
WALLENSTEIN (*after reading*):
     This letter makes a lot of sense. It is
     A wise and clever chief you serve, Lord Wrangel.
     The Chancellor writes he is but carrying out
     The very notion of the deceased king
     In helping me to the Bohemian crown.   240
WRANGEL: He speaks quite truly. The illustrious deceased

Thought always very highly of Your Grace's
Preeminent mind and military gifts.
The man best qualified to rule, he pleased
To say, should always be the king and ruler.
WALLENSTEIN: Well might he say it.
      (taking his hand confidentially)
Now quite sincerely, Colonel Wrangel, I
Was ever a good Swede at heart.—Ah, that
You found out in Silesia and at Nürnberg.
I often had you in my power, yet always   250
Let you slip out by some back door. It's that
That they cannot forgive me in Vienna,
It's that that drives me to this present step.—
And now since our advantages agree,
Let us develop perfect confidence
In one another.
WRANGEL: Confidence will come
When each of us first has his guarantee.
WALLENSTEIN: The Chancellor, I observe, does not yet trust me
Entirely. I confess—the game does not
Stand wholly in my favor. His Grace opines,   260
If I can trifle this way with the Emperor
Who is my master, I could do the same
With enemies, and *one* could sooner be
Forgiven me than could the *other* one.
Is that not your opinion too, Lord Wrangel?
WRANGEL: I have a function merely, no opinion.
WALLENSTEIN: The Emperor now has forced me to the last
Extreme. I can no longer honorably
Serve him. For safety's sake, as last resort,
I take this hard step which my conscience must   270
Condemn.
WRANGEL: There I believe you. No one goes
This far who does not have to.
      (after a pause)
                       What it is
That moves your princely Highness thus to treat

Your lord and Emperor may not properly
Be judged by us. The Swede is fighting for
His own just cause with his good sword and conscience.
The opportunity and circumstances
Are in our favor. All is fair in war.
We take whatever comes and do not scruple.
And if all this is just as you maintain—   280

WALLENSTEIN: What can there be to doubt of? Not my will?
Or strength? My promise to the Chancellor was,
If he entrusted sixteen thousand men
To me, I would add to them from the Emperor's
Army eighteen thousand more—

WRANGEL: Your Grace
Is known as an exalted warrior prince,
A second Attila and Pyrrhus, and with
Amazement people speak of how some years
Ago, against all human expectation,
You conjured up an army out of nothing.   290
However—

WALLENSTEIN: Yes, however?

WRANGEL: His Grace feels
To conjure sixty thousand men from nothing
And put them in the field might be more easy
Than that the sixtieth part of them should be—

WALLENSTEIN: Well, what? Speak out!

WRANGEL: Misled to mutiny.

WALLENSTEIN: Does he? He judges like a Swede and like
A Protestant. You Lutherans battle for
Your Bible. You are fighting for a cause.
You march behind your banners with your hearts.—
When one of you deserts and goes to join   300
The enemy he breaks bond with two masters
At once. With us that is no wise the case—

WRANGEL: Good Lord in Heaven! Have they in this country
No homeland then, no hearthside, and no church?

WALLENSTEIN: I'll tell you how these matters stand here.—Yes,
The Austrian has a fatherland, and loves it,

And has, what's more, a reason for so loving.
But *these* armed men, that call themselves Imperials,
That house here in Bohemia, they have none.
They are the dregs of foreign countries, that   310
Abandoned part of peoples to whom nothing
Belongs at all except the common sunlight.
And this Bohemian land for which we fight
Has no heart for its master, whom the fortune
Of weapons has imposed, not its own choice.
Ill-willed it bears religion's tyranny,
Brute force has cowed but has not pacified it.
There lives a burning memory for revenge
Of horrors perpetrated on this soil.
And can a son forget how once his father   320
Was hounded into Mass by packs of dogs?
A people that has suffered *that* is frightful,
Avenging or enduring such abuse.
WRANGEL: But the nobility, the officers?
Such criminal defection, my Lord Duke,
Is without parallel in history.
WALLENSTEIN: They stand with me, and unconditionally.
You may believe your own eyes, if not me.
          (*He hands him the formula of oath. Wrangel reads
          it over and after reading lays it silently on the
          table.*)
Well, do you grasp me now?
WRANGEL: Grasp it who can!
Lord Duke! I drop the mask.—Yes, I do have   330
Authority to come to terms. The Rhinegrave
Stands only four days' march from here with fifteen
Thousand men and only waits for orders
To join your troops. These orders I shall issue
Just as soon as we agree on terms.
WALLENSTEIN: What does the Chancellor want?
WRANGEL (*dubiously*):
This makes twelve regiments, all Swedish troops,
My head must be their guarantee. This could

Prove nothing but a trap—
WALLENSTEIN (*starting up*):   Swede! Have a care!
WRANGEL: I must
    Therefore insist Duke Friedland sever ties   340
    Irrevocably and finally with the Emperor,
    Or else no Swedish troops will be committed
    To him.
WALLENSTEIN: Speak plainly. What is your requirement?
WRANGEL: First to disarm the Spanish regiments
    Pledged to the Emperor, then seize Prague and cede
    That town, together with the border fortress
    Of Eger, to the Swedes.
WALLENSTEIN: Your price is high!
    Prague! Eger, yes! But Prague? That will not do.
    I'll give you every guarantee that you
    Can reasonably demand of me. But Prague—   350
    Bohemia—these I can protect myself.
WRANGEL: That no one doubts. But we are not concerned
    About the mere protection. We wish not
    To have our men and money spent for nothing.
WALLENSTEIN: Quite proper.
WRANGEL: And, till we are compensated,
    Prague stands our pledge.
WALLENSTEIN: Do you trust us so little?
WRANGEL (*rising*):
    The Swede must be upon his guard with Germans.
    We have been summoned here across the Baltic.
    We have preserved the Empire from destruction—
    Sealed with our blood the freedom of religion,   360
    The sacred teaching of the Gospel.—But
    Already this is felt as benefit
    No longer, only as a burden; people
    Eye foreigners askance within the realm
    And gladly would dismiss us with a handful
    Of money to our native forests. No!
    We have not lost our king upon the field
    For Judas' price, for ringing gold and silver!

The noble lifeblood of so many Swedes
Has not been shed for gold and silver's sake.   370
And not for meager laurels shall we hoist
Our sails again to seek our fatherland.
We mean to stay as citizens here on
This soil that our king conquered with his death.
WALLENSTEIN: Help me hold down our common enemy,
    And that fine borderland cannot escape you.
WRANGEL: And when the common enemy is down,
    Who will knit up new ties of friendship then?
    We are aware, Lord Duke,—although the Swede
    Is not supposed to see,—that you have secret   370
    Negotiations with the Saxons. Who will
    Assure us *we* are not the scapegoats for decisions
    Considered properly concealed from us?
WALLENSTEIN: Well did the Chancellor select his man,
    He could not send me one more obdurate.
        (rising)
    Devise a better plan then, Gustav Wrangel.
    No more of Prague.
WRANGEL: My powers go no further.
WALLENSTEIN: Cede you my capital? I would sooner go
    Back—to my Emperor.
WRANGEL: If there still is time.
WALLENSTEIN: That still is mine to do, at any moment.   390
WRANGEL: Perhaps some days ago it was. But not
    Today—not since Sesin was taken captive.
        (as Wallenstein, struck, remains silent)
    Lord Duke! We think your offer is quite honest,
    Since *yesterday* we have felt certain of it.
    Now that this paper certifies the *troops,*
    There would seem nothing in the way of trust.
    Prague shall not come between us. My Lord Chancellor
    Will be content to have the older quarter,
    He leaves your Grace the Hradschin and the suburb.
    But Eger must be opened to us first   400
    Before a junction can be contemplated.

WALLENSTEIN: I must then trust in *you,* but you need not
Trust *me?* I shall consider your proposal.
WRANGEL: Not for too long, I beg. Negotiations
Have now dragged on into their second year.
If nothing comes of them this time, the Chancellor
Will take them for concluded permanently.
WALLENSTEIN: You press me hard. A step like this must be
Reflected on.
WRANGEL: No need to think at all,
Lord Duke, swift action only brings success.   410

(Exit Wrangel; reenter Terzky and Illo.)

ILLO: Is it all right?
TERZKY: Are you agreed?
ILLO: That Swede
Left here quite pleased. So then did you agree?
WALLENSTEIN: Listen, nothing has occured as yet.
And—having thought it over, I would rather
Not do it.
TERZKY: What! What's this?
WALLENSTEIN: To live dependent
Upon these haughty Swedes? I could not stand it.
ILLO: Do you come as a fugitive to beg
Their help? You bring more than you would receive.
WALLENSTEIN: What happened with that royal Bourbon who
Sold himself to his people's enemy   420
And on his fatherland inflicted wounds?
A curse was his reward and human loathing
Avenged his impious and unnatural deed.
ILLO: Is that *your* case?
WALLENSTEIN: I tell you, loyalty
To every man is like a close bloodbrother,
Each man feels himself born as its avenger.
The enmity of sects, the rage of parties,
Old jealousy and envy make their peace;
Whoever fought with fury to destroy
Each other will compact and come to terms   430

To hunt the common foe of man, the wild
Beast that breaks ravening in among the flock
Where man abides in safety,—for his own
Astuteness cannot shield him absolutely.
Upon his forehead only Nature placed
The light of eyesight, faithful loyalty
Is meant to guard his unprotected back.
TERZKY: Think no worse of yourself than does the foe
   Who to this action offers eager hands.
   Charles V, the uncle and the forebear of   440
   This Emperor, did not have such tender conscience,
   He took that Bourbon in with open arms.
   Self-interest alone controls the world.

(Enter the Countess Terzky.)

WALLENSTEIN: Who called you? This is no affair for women.
COUNTESS TERZKY: I come to offer my congratulations.—
   Have I perhaps arrived too soon? I hope not.
WALLENSTEIN: Exert your rights here, Terzky. Bid her leave.
COUNTESS TERZKY: I gave a king to the Bohemians once
   Before.
WALLENSTEIN: He acted like it.
COUNTESS TERZKY *(to the others):*   Well, where do
   Things stand?
TERZKY: The Duke won't do it.
COUNTESS TERZKY: Won't? He must!   450
ILLO: It's up to you now. Try it. I give up
   When people talk of loyalty and conscience.
COUNTESS TERZKY: When everything still lay in far-off distance
   And paths stretched infinitely ahead of you,
   Then you had courage and decisiveness,—
   And now when out of dream reality
   Emerges, with fulfillment near, success
   Assured, now you begin to falter? Are you
   Brave only in the planning, cowardly
   In action? Good! Prove to your enemies   460
   That they are right. That's just what they expect!

Your purpose they believe; you may be sure
That they will prove it to you, signed and sealed!
But no one thinks the act is possible;
They would then have to fear you and respect you.
How can it be? When you have gone this far,
And when the worst is known, and when the deed
Is reckoned as already carried out,
You would pull back and lose the fruit of labor?
Planned merely, this is but a vulgar crime;   470
Once done, it is immortal enterprise;
Once done successfully, it will be pardoned,
For every outcome is an act of God.

(Enter a servant.)

THE SERVANT: Commander Piccolomini.
COUNTESS TERZKY *(quickly):*   Must wait.
WALLENSTEIN: I cannot see him now. Some other time.
THE SERVANT: Two minutes' time is all that he requests.
    He says he has an urgent matter—
WALLENSTEIN: Who knows what he may bring us? I will see him.
COUNTESS TERZKY *(laughing):*
    For *him* it may be urgent. You can let
    It wait.
WALLENSTEIN: What is it?
COUNTESS TERZKY: You shall learn that later.   480
    I am concerned with settling Wrangel's business.

(Exit the servant.)

WALLENSTEIN: If only I still had a choice—if some
    Less drastic course could yet be found—I still
    Would take it now and shun these far extremes.
COUNTESS TERZKY: If that is all you want, just such a course
    Lies close ahead of you. Dismiss this Wrangel.
    Renounce your hopes of old and cast away
    Your former life, make up your mind to start
    A new one. Virtue has its heroes too,
    As Fame has, and as Fortune. Journey down   490
    This minute to Vienna and the Emperor,

Take well-filled treasure chests along, declare
You merely sought to test your servants' trust
And merely play a hoax upon the Swedes.

ILLO: For that it's too late too. Too much is known.
He would just go to lay his head upon the block.

COUNTESS TERZKY: I have no fear of that. There are no proofs
To try him legally. They will shun force.
They'll quietly allow the Duke to leave.
I see how everything will come about: 500
The King of Hungary will come, and it
Will be self-understood the Duke should go;
No explanations will be necessary.
The King will have the troops sworn in, and all
Will be right where it was, in proper order.
And one fine day the Duke will have departed.
On his estates things will wax lively then:
There he will hunt, construct, maintain his studs,
Create himself a court, award gold keys,
Show hospitality at splendid tables,   510
In short, be a great king—in miniature!
And since he shrewdly has resigned himself
To have in fact no more significance,
They let him seem what he is pleased to seem;
A great prince he will seem until he dies.
Ah, well! the Duke is after all just one
Of those new men whom war brought to the top,
An over-night creation of court favor
Which with a like experience of effort
Makes Barons and makes Princes.   520

WALLENSTEIN (rising, in vehement agitation):
Show me a way of issue from this press,
Ye powers of succor, show me such a one
As I can walk! For I can not draw warmth
From my own will and thoughts like one of those
Glib champions at words, those virtue-praters,—
Nor loftily tell Fortune as she turns
Her back on me: "Go, then, I need you not!"

If I can act no more I am undone.
I shall not shy from sacrifice or perils
To hold back from the final, extreme step.   530
But yet before I sink to nothingness
And end so small, who once began so great,
Before the world confuses me with those
Low creatures which one day creates and crushes,
Let world and future times pronounce my name
With loathing and let Friedland be the by-word
For every damnable vile deed.

COUNTESS TERZKY: What is there here so all at odds with
     Nature?
     I cannot see it. Tell me what it is.
     —O do not let dark ghosts of superstition   540
     Become the masters over your bright spirit!
     You stand accused of treason, whether wrongly
     Or properly is not the question now.—
     But you are lost if you do not make quick use of
     The power you have.—Does there exist a creature
     So peaceable that it would not defend
     Itself with all its vital force? What is there
     So daring urgency will not excuse it?

WALLENSTEIN: This Ferdinand was once so well disposed
     Toward me, he loved me, held me in esteem,   550
     I stood the nearest to his heart. What prince
     Did he revere like me?—And now end thus!

COUNTESS TERZKY: You treasure every little favor dearly
     And have no recollection of the injuries?
     Must I recall for you how he rewarded
     Your loyal services at Regenspurg?
     You had offended all the classes of
     The realm; to make him great, you had assumed
     The whole world's hatred and the whole world's curses;
     In all of Germany you had no friend   560
     Because you had lived only for your Emperor.
     To him alone you clung amid the storm
     That gathered head against you at the Diet

In Regenspurg.—And there he sold you out!
Yes, sold you out! to that Bavarian, you,
As victim for that high-and-mighty man.
And do not say the dignities restored
Made up for that outrageous first injustice.
Good will did not restore you really, no,
The law of harsh necessity restored   570
The office which they gladly would deny you.

WALLENSTEIN: I do not owe this office that I hold
   To his good will, I grant, nor to his favor.
   If I abuse it, I abuse no trust.

COUNTESS TERZKY: His trust? His favor?—He had need of you!
   Necessity, that vehement compeller,
   Whose service is not done with hollow names
   And figureheads, who asks for deeds, not tokens,
   Who always seeks the highest and the best
   And puts him at the helm though she must snatch   580
   Him from among the human dregs,—she gave you
   This post and wrote out your commission for it.
   As long as possible this generation
   Will get along with purchased souls of slaves
   And with the string-moved puppets of their skill;—
   But when the final showdown moves upon them
   And hollow sham no longer works, the whole
   Thing falls into the mighty hands of Nature,
   The Titan that obeys itself alone,
   Knows naught of compromises, and deals with them   590
   On *its* own terms alone, and not on *theirs*.

WALLENSTEIN: That's true! They always saw me as I am,
   Never did I deceive them in their bargain,
   I never thought it worth the trouble to
   Conceal my bold aggressive turn of mind.

COUNTESS TERZKY: You always showed yourself as fearsome,
      rather.
   Not *you*, who always were true to yourself,
   But *they* are wrong who stood in fear of you

And yet entrusted power to your hands.
For every personality is right   600
That lives in true agreement with itself.
There is no sin but inconsistency.
Were you some other man eight years ago
When you crossed Germany with fire and sword
And cracked the whip above the various states,
Scorned all the Empire's ordered ways, invoked
The awesome right of Might, and rode roughshod
Over every local princeling's power
Establishing your Sultan's mastery?
Then was the time to break your haughty will,   610
To call you then to order. But the Emperor
Deigned to be pleased with what was useful to him
And silently put his imperial seal
Upon those impious acts. What then was just
Because you did it *for* him then, today
Is shameful suddenly because it is
Now aimed *against* him?

WALLENSTEIN (*rising*):
    I never saw it in this light.—Yes! It
    Is really so. This Emperor perpetrated
    Acts in this realm by virtue of my arm   620
    That never rightfully should have been done.
    This prince's cloak itself which I now wear
    I owe to services which are sheer crimes.

COUNTESS TERZKY: Confess then that between the two of you
    There can be no concern with right and duty,
    Only with power and *opportunity!*
    The moment has arrived when you must strike
    The balance of this mighty life account.
    Triumphant stand the starry signs above you,
    The planets beckon prosperous fortune down   630
    And cry: "Now is the time!" Have you for nothing
    Been measuring out the courses of the stars
    A lifetime long?—Have you applied the quadrant

And circle, duplicated on these walls
The zodiac and globe of heaven, grouped
Around in mute prophetic images
The seven overlords of fate,
Solely to play a futile game with them?
Does all this preparation come to nothing,
Is there no substance to this hollow art,   640
That it is meaningless, without effect
Upon you at this moment of decision?

WALLENSTEIN *(has been pacing up and down in violently agitated
state during the last speech. He stops suddenly and interrupts
the Countess.)*
Call Wrangel here, and have three messengers
Mounted immediately.

ILLO: Praise be to God!

(He hurries away.)

WALLENSTEIN: It is the evil genius, his and mine.
It strikes at him through me, his tool to power,
And I foresee the steel of vengeance is
Already whetted keen for *my* breast also.
Whoever sows the dragon's teeth, let him
Not hope for cheerful harvest. Each misdeed   650
Bears its avenging angel, hope for evil,
Beneath its heart.
                    He can no longer trust me.
And I, on my side, can no more return.
Come then what must. Fate is forever in
The right, because the heart within us is
Its most obedient executive.
        (to Terzky)
Show Wrangel to my study. I shall give
Instructions to the messengers myself.
Send for Octavio.
        *(to the Countess, who wears a triumphant
            expression)*
                O do not gloat

Too soon! The powers of Fate are jealous powers.   660
Their rights sustain a harm from joy of ours.
Within their hands we lay the seeds: the end
Will teach us whether they will mar or mend.   [663]

(As he walks away, the curtain falls.)

ACT II

A room. Wallenstein and Octavio Piccolomini.

WALLENSTEIN: He sends me word from Linz that he is ill,
But I have sure reports he is in hiding
In Frauenberg together with Count Gallas.
Seize both of them and send them here to me.
The Spanish regiments you will take over,
Make constant preparations, never finish
And if they press you hard to march against me,   670
You will say Yes, but all the same stay put.
I know the task will be congenial to you,
Just doing nothing in this game. You like
To save appearances as long as you
Are able; drastic steps are not for you,
And so I have picked out this role for you,
This time your sloth to move will render you
Most useful.—And, if Fortune should meanwhile
Declare for me, then you know what to do.
                    (Enter Max Piccolomini.)
Go now, old man. You must get started yet   680
Tonight. Take my own horses.—This chap here
I'll keep with me.—And make your farewells short!
We shall, I think, meet all again together
With joy and happiness.
OCTAVIO *(to his son)*:   We shall speak further.

            (Exit Octavio Piccolomini.)

MAX *(approaching Wallenstein)*:
My General—

WALLENSTEIN: That I no longer am
If you are still the Emperor's officer.
MAX: So it still stands; you mean to leave the Army?
WALLENSTEIN: I have renounced the Emperor's service.
MAX: And mean to leave the Army?
WALLENSTEIN: I rather hope
To bind it closer to me and more firmly.   690
        (He sits down.)
Yes, Max. I did not want to tell you this
Before the hour had struck for taking action.
The happy temperament of youth will grasp
Right things with ease, and it is a delight
To test one's judgment in an exercise
Where the example may be simply solved.
But when from two sure evils one must be
Selected, when the heart can not return
Quite whole out of the clash of duties, then
It is a blessing not to have a choice,   700
And then necessity becomes a favor.
—Such is the present case. Do not look back.
It cannot help you any more. Look forward!
Do not pass judgment, just prepare to act!
—The court has fixed resolve for my destruction.
I have made up my mind to head them off.
—We shall make an alliance with the Swedes,
They're splendid people and good friends of ours.
        (He pauses waiting for Piccolomini's answer.)
—I've startled you. Dont' answer me just now.
I'll give you time to gather up your thoughts.   710

        (He rises, walks toward the back. Max stands
        for a long time motionless, lost in the most
        vehement anguish. When he makes a move-
        ment, Wallenstein comes back and stands in
        front of him.)

MAX: My General!—You have brought me to adulthood
Today. Till now I have been spared the task

Of finding my direction and my way.
I followed you unquestioningly. I needed
But look to you alone and know my way
Was right. Today now for the first time you
Refer me to myself, compelling me
To make a choice between my heart and you.

WALLENSTEIN: Fate gently cradled you until today.
  You could perform your duties like mere child's play,   720
  Indulging every gracious impulse, acting
  Forever with an undivided heart.
  Things can be thus no longer. Hostilely
  The paths diverge and duties clash with duties.
  You must opt for a party in the war
  Now breaking into kindled flame between
  Your Emperor and your friend.

MAX: Is *war* the word?
  But war is horrible, like Heaven's plagues,
  Yet good sometimes, like them, a dispensation.
  Is this a good war you are undertaking   730
  Against the Emperor with the Emperor's army?
  O God in Heaven! what a change this is!
  Is speech like this unseemly used by me
  To you, who like the steady polar star
  Have seemed to me the guiding rule of life!
  O what a rift you open in my heart!
  The deep-worn habit of a lifelong awe
  And sacred custom of obedience to
  Your name, must I unlearn these things? Oh, no,
  Do not direct your countenance upon me!   740
  Those always were for me the features of
  A god, they cannot lose their power so soon.
  My senses even now are in your thrall
  Although my bleeding soul has been wrenched free.

WALLENSTEIN: Max, hear me.

MAX: Do not do it! Do not do it!
  Oh, see, your pure and noble features still
  Reveal no sign of this unholy act.

Its taint is yet upon your fancy merely
And innocence will not allow itself
To be expelled from your exalted mien.   750
O cast this black stain out, this enemy.
Then it will only be an evil dream
Sent to bear warning to each sturdy virtue.
Mankind are subject to such moments; but
The good emotions must emerge triumphant.
You will not come to such an end. It would
Discredit every lofty nature in
The human breed and every mighty force,
It would substantiate the crass illusion
That freedom will allow of nothing noble   760
And that constraint alone is to be trusted.

WALLENSTEIN: The world will judge me harshly; I expect that.
Whatever you can say, I have already
Said to myself. Who would not shun extremes
If he could circumvent them! But I have
No choice. I must use force or else endure it.—
Things stand thus. Nothing else remains for me.

MAX: So be it then! Maintain yourself by force
In your command, defy the Emperor, and,
If need be, push to open mutiny: 770
I cannot praise it but I can forgive it.
I'll share with you what I do not approve.
But just do not become—a traitor! Now
I have pronounced the word,—O not a traitor!
That is no overstepping of the limits,
No error caused by sheer excess of spirit.
O that is something different—that is black,
As black as hell.

WALLENSTEIN (frowning darkly yet speaking calmly):
O youth is quick and ready with advice
That proves as hard to handle as a knife blade.   780
In their hot heads they smartly take the measure
Of things that can be only self-directed.
To them all things are either fine or vile,

Evil or good, straight off, and what their fancy
Conceives as crowded under those vague captions
They load upon affairs and lives of men.
The world is narrow and the brain is broad;
Thoughts dwell together side by side with ease,
But things in space clash harshly with each other;
Where one has room the other must give way;   790
Lest one should be expelled, he must expel;
Strife is the rule and only strength prevails.
—Whoever walks in life without a wish,
Denies himself all purpose, he may live
In careless fire along with salamanders,
Taintless in the taintless element.
But nature fashioned me of grosser matter
And my desires attract me to the earth.
The earth belongs unto the evil spirit,
Not to the good one. What the gods send from   800
On high to us are only common goods;
Their light gives joy but it enriches no one,
And none achieves possessions in their state;
The precious stones, the gold that all men prize,
These must be wrested from the tricky powers
That house ill-humored underneath the day.
Without a sacrifice their favor is
Not won, and no man lives who ever brought
His soul back pure, returning from their service.
MAX *(with emphasis):*
    Distrust, distrust those tricky powers! They do   810
    Not keep their word! They are deceitful spirits
    Who are beguiling you toward the abyss.
    Do not put faith in them! I warn you.—Oh,
    Return to duty! Surely you can do so!
    Send me down to Vienna. Yes, do that.
    Let me make peace between you and the Emperor
    He does not know you, I, however, know you,
    Through my pure eyes he shall behold you, I
    Shall bring you back his confidence in you.

WALLENSTEIN: It is too late. You don't know what has happened.
MAX: And even if too late—if so far gone   [820
  That only crime will save you from a fall,
  Then fall! Fall worthily, as you have stood.
  Lose your command. And leave the stage. This you
  Can do with glory; do it also guiltless.
  —You have lived much for others; live then once
  Just for yourself! I will accompany you,
  I never will divide my fate from yours.—
WALLENSTEIN: It is too late. While you are wasting words
  My messengers are putting milestone after   830
  Milestone far behind them as they hasten
  To carry my commands to Prague and Eger.
  —Resign yourself. We act as we must act.
  So let us with firm step and dignity
  Perform the inevitable.—What am I doing
  Worse than that Caesar did whose name today
  Still signifies the world's supreme achievement?
  He led into attack on Rome the legions
  Rome had entrusted to him for protection.
  Had he laid down his sword he would have been   840
  Destroyed, as I would be if I disarmed.
  I sense his spirit somewhat in myself.
  Give me his luck! The rest I will endure.

       (*Max, who up till now has stood in painful
       struggle, suddenly walks away. Wallenstein,
       struck with amazement, watches him as he
       goes, and remains behind lost in profound
       thought.*)
                                   (*Enter Terzky.*)

TERZKY: Max Piccolomini left you just now?
WALLENSTEIN: Where is that Wrangel?
TERZKY: He has gone.
WALLENSTEIN: So soon?
TERZKY: He seemed as if the earth had swallowed him.
  He had just left you when I looked for him,—

I had more things to say to him,—but he
Was gone and no one knew a thing about him.
I think he was the Evil One himself,   850
No man could vanish quite so suddenly.

(Enter Illo.)

ILLO: It can't be true you're sending the old man?
TERZKY: Octavio! What! What are you thinking of?
WALLENSTEIN: He's going to Frauenberg to bring up here
    The Spanish and Italian regiments.
TERZKY: Now God forbid you should do such a thing!
ILLO: Do you intend to trust that sneak with soldiers?
    And let him get beyond your sight, right now,
    Right at this very moment of decision?
TERZKY: You won't do that. No, not for anything!   860
WALLENSTEIN: What curious men you are.
ILLO: Oh just this once
    Observe our warning. Do not let him go.
WALLENSTEIN: And why should I not trust him this *one time*
    When I have always done so? What has happened to
    Deprive him of my good opinion of him?
    To suit your whim, not mine, am I to change
    My old and tested judgment? Do not think
    I am a woman. Just because I trusted
    Him *till* today, I mean to trust him *now*.
TERZKY: Must he be just the one? Send someone else!   870
WALLENSTEIN: It has to be the one whom I have chosen.
    He fits the errand, so I gave it to him.
ILLO: He suits you just because he is a Latin.
WALLENSTEIN: I know you never cared for either one
    Of them; because I love them and esteem them,
    Prefer them openly to you and others,
    As they deserve, you find them thorns within
    Your flesh! What is your jealousy to me
    Or to my errand? That you hate them, makes them
    No worse to me. Love as you will or hate,   880
    I leave to each his own mind and affections,

But I know what each one of you is worth.

ILLO: He shall not go—not if I have to have them smash
His carriage wheels.

WALLENSTEIN: Restrain yourself, Illo!

TERZKY: That Questenberg, what's more, was always hanging
Around with him the whole time he was here.

WALLENSTEIN: That happened with my knowledge and
permission.

TERZKY: And I know too that secret messengers
From Gallas come to him.

WALLENSTEIN: That is not true.

ILLO: O you are blind with your wide-open eyes!   890

WALLENSTEIN: You will not shake my faith which is erected
Upon foundations of profoundest knowledge.
If he is lying, the whole star-science lies.
For be advised, I have a pledge from Fate
Itself he is the truest of my friends.

ILLO: Have you another pledge that this pledge is
Not lying?

WALLENSTEIN: Moments come in life when one
Is closer to the world-soul than is usual,
And then one has a chance to question Fate.
One of those moments came the night preceding   900
The action of the Lützen battle, when,
Leaning against a tree and full of thoughts,
I stood there gazing at the plain. The camp-fires
Were burning murkily across the mist,
The muffled sounds of arms, the sentinels
On rounds monotonously broke through the stillness.
My life in its entirety, both past
And future, at that moment crossed before
The inner vision of my mind, and my
Prophetic spirit linked the furthest future   910
To that next morning's course of destiny.
     Then to myself I said: "Here you command
So many! They are followers of your stars,
They wager, as upon a lucky number,

Their all upon your head alone, they are
Aboard your ship of Fortune here with you.
And yet the day will come when Fate will strew
All these again far, far asunder. Only
A few will loyally remain with you.
Now I should like to know which one, of all   920
This Camp encompasses, will be to me
Most faithful. Fate, give me a sign; It shall
Be he who on the coming morning first
Approaches me with tokens of affection."
And pensive with that thought, I fell asleep.
Then to the thick of battle I was guided
In spirit. Mighty was the press. My horse
Was shot from under me, I sank, and over
Me rode indifferently the steeds and riders,
And I lay gasping like a dying man   930
Mangled beneath the beating of their hooves.
Then suddenly an arm braced me with help,
It was Octavio's,—and quickly I awoke.
The day had come—Octavio stood before me.
"My brother, do not ride today," he said,
"Your dappled horse as usual. Rather mount
"This safer beast that I have chosen for you.
"Do me this favor, for a dream has warned me."
The swiftness of that beast gave me escape
From the pursuit of Bannier's dragoons.   940
My cousin rode the dappled horse that day,
I never saw again the steed or rider.

ILLO: That was coincidence.

WALLENSTEIN (positively):   Coincidence
Does not exist. What seems blind chance to us,
Is just what rises from the deepest springs.
I have it under oath and seal that he
Is my good angel. So, not one word more!

(He walks away.)

TERZKY: My comfort is that Max remains as hostage.

ILLO: And he shan't get away from here alive.

WALLENSTEIN *(stopping and turning around)*:
O do not be like women who come back   950
Invariably to what they said at first
When one has spoken reason hours on end!
—The deeds and thoughts of human kind,—learn this,—
Are not like blindly tumbling waves at sea.
The inner world, its microcosm, is
The deep shaft out of which they well forever.
They are inevitable, as fruit to tree,
Chance cannot juggle them in transformations.
Once I have probed the heart's core of a man
I know his wishes and his actions also.   960

(Exeunt.)

SCENE 2

A room in Piccolomini's residence.
Enter Octavio Piccolomini, dressed for travelling, and an
Adjutant.

OCTAVIO: Is the detachment here?
THE ADJUTANT: Waiting below.
OCTAVIO: These men can be relied on, Adjutant?
Out of which regiment did you select them?
THE ADJUTANT: From Tiefenbach's.
OCTAVIO: That regiment is loyal.
Have them wait quietly down in the rear court,
Let no one see them till you hear me ring.
The house will then be closed and sharply watched,
And anyone you meet will be arrested.

(Exit the Adjutant.)

I trust their services will not be needed,
For I am certain of my calculations.   970
But stakes are high, the Emperor's very service,

And better too much foresight than too little.

(Enter Isolani.)

ISOLANI: Here am I.—Well, what other ones are coming?
OCTAVIO *(mysteriously):*
  First, just a word with you, Count Isolani.
ISOLANI *(mysteriously):*
  Is this the start? The Duke is planning something?
  You can rely on me. Just test me out.
OCTAVIO: I may do that.
ISOLANI: Well, Brother, I am not
  One of those people who are brave with words
  But when it comes to deeds are shamefully
  Not there. The Duke has been a friend to me.   980
  It's true, God knows, I owe him everything.
  He can count on my loyalty.
OCTAVIO: That we shall see.
ISOLANI: Be on your guard. Not everyone thinks thus.
  There are a lot of people here who still
  Side with the court and think those signatures
  Tricked from us lately are not binding on them.
OCTAVIO: They do? Name me the gentlemen who think so.
ISOLANI: Damnation! All the Germans talk that way.
  And Esterhazy, Kaunitz, Deodat
  Are saying now they must obey the court.   990
OCTAVIO: That pleases me.
ISOLANI: You're pleased?
OCTAVIO: To hear the Emperor
  Still has such good friends and devoted servants.
ISOLANI: Don't joke about it. They are not bad men.
OCTAVIO: Of course not. God forbid I should be joking.
  Quite seriously. I joy to see the good cause
  So strong.
ISOLANI: Now what the Devil? What is this?
  Are you then not—? What am I here for then?
OCTAVIO *(with dignity):*
  To state now fair and square which you prefer

To be: the Emperor's friend or enemy!

ISOLANI (*defiantly*):

I shall make such a statement to the man   1000
Who has the right to ask me such a question.

OCTAVIO: This document shows if I have that right.

ISOLANI: Wha— What? This is the Emperor's hand and seal.
    (*He reads.*)
"Hence all commanders of Our army will
"Obey the orders of Our cherished, loyal
"Lieutenant General Piccolomini
"As if they were Our own. . . ." Hm—yes—yes—so—yes!
I—offer my congratulations, General.

OCTAVIO: Then you submit to this command?

ISOLANI: I—but—
You take me by such quick surprise—I shall,   1010
I trust, be given time to think—

OCTAVIO: Two minutes.

ISOLANI: My God this is a matter—

OCTAVIO: Clear and simple.
You are to state which thing you mean to do:
Serve faithfully your master or betray him.

ISOLANI: Betray—My God! —Who even mentioned treason?

OCTAVIO: Such is the case. The Duke is now a traitor.
He means to give the army to the foe.
Make your stand clear. Shall you abjure the Emperor?
Sell yourself to the enemy? Shall you?

ISOLANI: What? I? Abjure the Emperor's Majesty?   1020
Did I say such a thing? When could I have
Said that?

OCTAVIO: You have not said that yet. Not yet.
I'm waiting now to see if you will say it.

ISOLANI: Well, that is kind of you, now, testifying
Yourself that I did not say such a thing.

OCTAVIO: You do, therefore, renounce the Duke?

ISOLANI: If he
Is plotting treason.—Treason cuts all ties.

OCTAVIO: And you are quite resolved to fight against him?

ISOLANI: He has been kind to me,—but if he is
  A scoundrel, strike him God! the score is cancelled.   1030
OCTAVIO: It pleases me that you should yield with such
  Good grace. You will leave secretly tonight
  With all the light-armed troops; it must appear
  That this command came from the Duke himself.
  In Frauenberg is the assembly point,
  There Gallas will give you your further orders.
ISOLANI: It shall be done. Would you remind the Emperor
  As well about how ready you have found me?
OCTAVIO: I'll praise your action.
              (Exit Isolani; enter a servant.)
                        Colonel Buttler? Good.

              (Isolani comes back in.)

ISOLANI: Forgive my brusque behaviour too, old man.   1040
  Lord! how was I to know before how great
  A person I was standing!
OCTAVIO: That's quite all right.
ISOLANI: I am a great old prankster, and if I
  Have let slip some rash words about the court
  At times amid the merriment of wine,
  You realize I meant no harm.

                (Exit Isolani.)

OCTAVIO: Have no
  Concern on that score!—That one was successful.
  Fortune, show equal favor with the others!

              (Enter Buttler.)

BUTTLER: I am at your command, Lieutenant General.
OCTAVIO: Welcome as a worthy friend and guest.   1050
BUTTLER: You do me too much honor.
OCTAVIO *(after both are seated)*:
  The friendliness which yesterday
  I offered as we met you left unanswered,
  Indeed mistook it for an empty phrase.
  That wish proceeded from my heart, I meant it

Quite seriously, for this is now a time
When good men ought to join in close alliance.
BUTTLER: Men of like minds alone can be allies.
OCTAVIO: All good men I would term like-minded men.
I take into a man's account such actions   1060
As only character will urge him to.
For force of blind misunderstandings often
Will drive the best man from his proper path.
You passed through Frauenberg. Count Gallas trusted
No words to you? Tell me. He is my friend.
BUTTLER: He only wasted words in speaking to me.
OCTAVIO: That I regret, for his advice was good,
And I would give you similar advice.
BUTTLER: Spare your exertion—and spare me the shame
Of meriting so ill your good opinion.   1070
OCTAVIO: Let us speak frankly, time is precious now.
You are aware how matters stand. The Duke
Is planning treason. I can tell you further:
He has accomplished it. Some hours ago
The pact was settled with the enemy.
Toward Prague and Eger ride the messengers,
Tomorrow he will take us to the foe.
But he betrays himself, for Shrewdness watches,
Friends loyal to the Emperor still remain here,
Invisible but mighty is their league.   1080
This manifesto lays the ban upon him,
Declares the army free of its allegiance,
And calls upon all men of good intentions
To rally to my leadership. Choose, then:
Will you share our good cause with us or share
With him the evil lot of evil men?
BUTTLER (rising):
His lot is mine.
OCTAVIO: Is that decision final
With you?
BUTTLER: It is.
OCTAVIO: Consider, Colonel Buttler.

You still have time. Your rashly spoken words
Shall lie deep buried in my loyal bosom.   1090
Withdraw them. Make a better choice. You have
Not hit upon the good one.

BUTTLER: Have you any
More orders for me now, Lieutenant General?

OCTAVIO: Consider your white hair! Take back those words.

BUTTLER: Farewell.

OCTAVIO: What? Would you draw your good brave sword
In such a quarrel? Would you change to curses
The thanks which you have earned from Austria
By all your forty years of loyalty?

BUTTLER (laughing bitterly):
Thanks from the House of Austria?

(He starts to leave.)

OCTAVIO (allows him to get as far as the door, then calls out.)
                                Buttler!

BUTTLER: Sir?

OCTAVIO: And what about that Count?

BUTTLER: What Count?

OCTAVIO: I mean   1100
That title of a Count.

BUTTLER (breaking forth violently):
                        Death and damnation!

OCTAVIO (coldly):
You did apply for it. They turned you down.

BUTTLER: This insult shall not pass unpunished. Draw!

OCTAVIO: Put up your sword. State calmly how that matter went.
Then I shall not deny you satisfaction.

BUTTLER: Let all the world be told about that weakness
For which I never can forgive myself.
—Lieutenant General, I possess ambition,
Contempt was something I could never bear.
It wounded me to see that birth and titles   1110
Had more weight in the army than true merit.
I did not wish to be less than my equals,

Thus in a luckless hour I let myself
Be led to that misstep.—It was sheer folly!
But I did not deserve to pay so dear
A price for it.—Rejection was their privilege.—
Why make rejection sharper with contempt
That hurt, why strike the old man down, their servant
Who kept his trust, and crush him with their scorn
By rude reminder of his shameful birth,   1120
Because in one weak moment he forgot
Himself! But Nature gave the worm a sting
That reckless arrogance has trodden on—

OCTAVIO: You must have been the victim of a slander.
Have you no notion what foe did you this
Disservice?

BUTTLER: Be it who it may! It must
Be some unprincipled base knave, a courtier,
A Spaniard, scion of some ancient house
Whose upward way I blocked, a jealous scoundrel
Hurt by my self-accomplished dignity.   1130

OCTAVIO: Now tell me, did the Duke approve that step?

BUTTLER: He urged me to it, interceded for me
Himself with all his noble warmth of friendship.

OCTAVIO: So? Are you sure of that?.

BUTTLER: I read the letter.

OCTAVIO (pointedly):
And so did I.—its contents were quite different.
            (Buttler is struck.)
By chance I happen to possess that letter
And can convince you with your very eyes.

            (He gives him the letter.)

BUTTLER: Ha! What is this?

OCTAVIO: I fear, now, Colonel Buttler,
Some one has played a nasty trick on you.
The Duke, you say, urged you to take this step?   1140
He speaks about you in this letter with
Contempt, suggests the Minister chastise

What he describes as your conceit.

> *(Buttler has read the letter. His knees tremble,*
> *he gropes for a chair and sits down.)*

No foe is persecuting you, and no one
Desires your harm. The hurt you have sustained
Comes from the Duke alone. His aim is clear.
He sought to alienate you from your Emperor.--
From your revenge he hoped to gain what your
Staunch loyalty would never let him count on
So long as you remained in tranquil spirits.   1150
He meant contemptuously to use you as
A lifeless tool, a means to vicious ends.
He gained his goal, succeeded all too well in
Enticing you away from that good path
Which you have trodden now for forty years.

BUTTLER *(his voice trembling)*:
   Can His Imperial Majesty forgive me?

OCTAVIO: He does still better. He makes good the harm
   Done to a worthy man gratuitously.
   He freely reconfirms your old commission
   Obtained you by the Duke for evil reasons.   1160
   The regiment which you command is yours.

BUTTLER *(tries to get up, sinks back. His mind works vehemently,*
   he tries to speak and cannot. Finally he takes his sword from
   his sword-belt and hands it to Piccolomini.)

OCTAVIO: What's this? Control yourself!

BUTTLER: Take it!

OCTAVIO: What for?
   Reflect!

BUTTLER: Take it. I am not worthy of
   This sword.

OCTAVIO: Receive it from my hand anew
   And wield it ever for the Right with honor.

BUTTLER: And I broke faith with such a gracious Emperor!

OCTAVIO: Then make that good again. Break with the Duke.

BUTTLER: I, break with him!

OCTAVIO: What's this? You change your mind?
BUTTLER *(in a fearful outburst):*
No more than break with him? He shall not live!
OCTAVIO: Accompany me to Frauenberg where all   1170
The loyal ones are joining Altringer
And Gallas. Many others I have brought
Back to their duty; they are fleeing Pilsen
Tonight.
BUTTLER *(after pacing back and forth in violent agitation, steps*
up to Octavio with a look of determination):
Count Piccolomini! May I,
The man who broke his trust, now speak of honor?
OCTAVIO: You may, who now repent so earnestly.
BUTTLER: Then leave me here on pledge of honor.
OCTAVIO: **What**
Is in your mind?
BUTTLER: And with my regiment,
Let me remain.
OCTAVIO: I trust you. Tell me, though,
With what design?
BUTTLER: Events will show that. Ask me   1180
No further now! Trust me. You can. By God!
You won't be leaving him to his good angel!
Farewell!
                    (Exit Buttler.)
          (Enter a servant with a note.)

THE SERVANT: A stranger brought this and was off
At once. The horses of the Duke are waiting
Below.
                    (Exit the servant.)

OCTAVIO *(reading):*
     "Be off at once. Your trusty Isolan."
—Oh, if this city only were behind me!
So close to port and must the ship yet founder?
Away, away! There's no more safety here
For me.—But what about my son?

*(Enter Max Piccolomini in a state of utmost
agitation, his eyes rolling wildly, his gait un-
steady. He does not seem to notice his father
who stands some distance away and looks at
him pityingly. With long strides he crosses
the room, stops again, and finally throws
himself into a chair, staring straight ahead.)*

OCTAVIO *(approaching him)*:
I'm going away, my son.
*(When he receives no answer he takes him by
the hand.)*
       My son, farewell.   1190

MAX: Farewell.

OCTAVIO: You will come soon?

MAX *(without looking at him)*:   I come with you?
Your way is crooked, it is not my way.
  (Octavio drops his hand, startled.)
O, if you had been honest and straightforward
It never would have come to this, all would
Be different. He would not have done this awful
Thing. Good men would have kept their hold on him,
The toils of evil ones would not have snared him.
Why all this soft tiptoeing like a thief
And like thieves' henchmen slyly lurking? Wretched
Dissimulation, mother of all evil,   1200
Bringer of woe, who ruins us!
Pure frankness, world-sustaining frankness,
Would have proved the salvation of us all.
Father! I can not, can not forgive you.
The Duke has played me false, most horribly,
But you yourself have acted not much better.

OCTAVIO: My son, I make allowance for your grief.

MAX *(rises, surveys him with a dubious glance)*:
Father? Father, can it be? Could you
Have meant deliberately to force things to
This pass? You profit by his fall. Octavio, 1210
I cannot find that good.

OCTAVIO: My God in Heaven!
MAX: Alas for me! I have confounded Nature.
  How did suspicion enter my free soul?
  Belief and trust and hope have all departed,
  For everyone that I esteemed deceived me.
  No! No! Not everyone! I still have her,
  And she is true and taintless like the sky.
  On all sides is false semblance, and betrayal,
  And murder, poison, perjury, and treason.
  The single pure, undesecrated spot   1220
  In all humanity is in our love.
OCTAVIO: Max, come with me at once, that will be best.
MAX: What? Come before I take farewell of her?
  My last farewell?—O never!
OCTAVIO: Spare yourself
  The anguish of a parting which must be.
  Come with me. Come, my son.
            (He tries to draw him away.)
MAX: No! By God who lives!
OCTAVIO (more urgently):
  Come with me! I, your father, order you.
MAX: Order what is human. I shall stay.
OCTAVIO: Max, in the Emperor's name, go with me now!
MAX: No Emperor can ordain laws for the heart.   1230
  And would you rob me of the only thing
  Misfortune leaves to me, her sympathy?
  Must what is cruel now be cruelly
  Performed? Must I ignobly do what is
  Inevitable? In secret coward's flight
  Like one unworthy, steal away from her?
  She shall behold my grief and suffering,
  And she shall hear my anguished soul's lament
  And shed her tears for me.— Oh, human beings
  Are cruel, ah, but she is like an angel.   1240
  From hideous frenzy of despair she will
  Preserve my soul, she will absolve my pain
  Of death with tears and gentle words of comfort.

OCTAVIO: You will not break away, you cannot do so.
  Oh, come, my son, and save your innocence!
MAX: O do not squander words for nothing. I
  Go my heart's way, in that I can have faith.
OCTAVIO *(beside himself, trembling):*
  Max! Max! If this horrendous thing befalls me,
  If you—my son—my very blood—I dare
  Not think it!—sell yourself to that bad man   1250
  And brand our family's honor with disgrace,
  The world shall witness the extreme of horror
  And from the sword-point of a son shall drip
  His father's blood poured out in ghastly combat.
MAX: O if you had thought better of mankind
  You would have acted in a better way.
  O damnable suspicion! Wretched doubt!
  For it there is no firm, no steady ground,
  All is unstable where belief is wanting.
OCTAVIO: And if I trust your heart, will it be always   1260
  Within your power to follow where it leads?
MAX: You have not forced my heart's election now,
  Nor will the Duke be able so to do.
OCTAVIO: O Max, I never will see you come back.
MAX: You shall not see me come unworthy of you.
OCTAVIO: I go to Frauenberg. The Pappenheimers
  I leave here with you. Tuscany, Lorraine,
  And Tiefenbach will also stay to shield you.
  They love you and are loyal to their oath,
  And they would rather bravely die in battle   1270
  Than ever quit their leader and their honor.
MAX: Of this you may be sure: I shall die here
  Fighting, or I shall lead them out of Pilsen.
OCTAVIO *(on the point of leaving):*
  My son, farewell!
MAX: Farewell!
OCTAVIO: What? Not one glance
  Of love? No clasp of hands as we take leave?
  It is a bloody war to which we go

And hidden and uncertain is the outcome.
We did not use to part thus from each other.
Then it is true? I have a son no longer?   [1279]

    (Max falls into his arms. They hold each other
      in a long silent embrace, then withdraw in
      opposite directions.)

ACT III

A room in the quarters of the Duchess of Friedland. Countess Terzky, Thekla, and Fräulein von Neubrunn, the latter two both occupied with needlework. [It is the following morning.]

COUNTESS TERZKY: You have no question for me, Thekla?
    Nothing?   1280
I have long waited for a word from you.
Can you endure to go this length of time
Without so much as mentioning his name?
Or am I now superfluous already
And are there other channels than through me?–
Confess, niece. Have you seen him?
THEKLA: I have not
Seen him today or yesterday.
COUNTESS TERZKY: Nor heard
From him? Hide nothing from me.
THEKLA: Not a word.
COUNTESS TERZKY: And you can be so calm?
THEKLA: I am quite calm.
COUNTESS TERZKY: Leave us, Neubrunn.

(Fräulein von Neubrunn withdraws.)

                   I dislike the fact   1290
That he should keep so still at just this time.
THEKLA: At just this time!
COUNTESS TERZKY: When he knows everything!
For now should be the time for him to speak.
THEKLA: Speak plainer if I am to understand.
COUNTESS TERZKY: For just that reason I dismissed her. Thekla,
You are a child no longer. Your heart has

181

Attained majority. You are in love.
A bold heart goes with love. That you have shown.
Your spirit has more of your father in it
Than of your mother. For that reason you can hear   1300
What *she* could not endure to hear.

THEKLA: I beg you, bring this preface to an end.
Let it be what it may. Speak out. It cannot
Distress me more than all this introduction.
What is it you would say? Come to the point.

COUNTESS TERZKY: But you must not be frightened—

THEKLA: Name it! Please!

COUNTESS TERZKY: It lies with you to do your father a great
service.

THEKLA: A thing like that could lie with *me?* What can—

COUNTESS TERZKY: Max Piccolomini loves you. You can
Inseparably unite him with your father.   1310

THEKLA: Does that need me? Is he not so already?

COUNTESS TERZKY: He was.

THEKLA: And why should he no longer be?
And always be?

COUNTESS TERZKY: He's also for the Emperor.

THEKLA: No more than duty asks of him, and honor.

COUNTESS TERZKY: Proofs of his love are what is now required,
Not of his honor.—Honor! Duty! Those
Are terms ambiguous with many meanings.
You may construe them for him, but his love
Should make his honor clear to him.

THEKLA: How so?

COUNTESS TERZKY: He must renounce the Emperor or you.   1320

THEKLA: He will be glad to go with Father into
Private life. You heard him say himself
How much he wished to lay his weapons down.

COUNTESS TERZKY: He must not lay them down, that is the
point,
But rather use them for your father's sake.

THEKLA: He would with joy pour forth his blood, his life,
For Father if injustice should befall him.

COUNTESS TERZKY: You seem to miss my meaning.—Listen, then.
Your father has just broken with the Emperor
And is about to join the enemy   1330
And all the army with him—
THEKLA: O my mother!
COUNTESS TERZKY: We need a good example so the Army
Will follow him. The Piccolominis
Enjoy a high distinction; they control
Opinion, what they do will be decisive.
The father will be guaranteed us through
The son.—Hence much is in your hands.
THEKLA: O poor unhappy mother! What a mortal blow
Impends above you!—She will not survive it.
COUNTESS TERZKY: She will submit to the inevitable.   1340
I know her.—Distant, future things distress
Her fearful heart; but what unalterably
Confronts her she will bear with resignation.
THEKLA: O my prophetic soul! —I feel it now,
The icy hand of horror clutches now
Around my joyous hopes and makes me shudder.
I knew it.—As I entered here, at once
An anxious premonition warned me that
Ill-fortuned stars were hanging over me.—
But why do I first think about myself?—   1350
O Mother! Mother mine!
COUNTESS TERZKY: Control yourself.
Do not burst forth in idle lamentations.
Secure your father's friend and your beloved,
Then everything can yet be for the best.
THEKLA: The best! What? We shall be forever parted!
Of that there can no more be any question.
COUNTESS TERZKY: He cannot give you up. He will not leave you.
THEKLA: O the unhappy man!
COUNTESS TERZKY: But if he really loves you, his decision
Will swiftly follow.
THEKLA: His decision will   1360
Soon follow, have no doubt of that. Decision!

Is there one yet to make?

COUNTESS TERZKY: Control yourself.
I hear your mother coming.

THEKLA: How shall I
Endure her sight?

COUNTESS TERZKY: Control yourself.

(Enter the Duchess.)

THE DUCHESS *(to the Countess)*:   I heard
Loud talking, sister. Who was here?

COUNTESS TERZKY: No one
Was here.

THE DUCHESS: I am so fearful. Every noise announces
The tread of some misfortune's messenger.
Can you inform me, sister, how things stand?
Will he do as the Emperor wishes, send
The Cardinal the mounted troops? And tell me,   1370
Was his reply to Questenberg a good one
When he dismissed him?

COUNTESS TERZKY: No. That it was not.

THE DUCHESS: Then all is over! I foresee the worst.
They will depose him; everything will once again
Be as it was at Regenspurg.

COUNTESS TERZKY: It will
Not be that way. Not this time. Have no fears.

*(Thekla, strongly moved, rushes to her mother
and, weeping, clasps her in her arms.)*

THE DUCHESS: O this inflexible and untamed man!
What have I not endured and suffered in
The trouble-crowded union of this marriage!
As if bound fast upon a fiery wheel   1380
That madly spins with restless, ceaseless whirling,
I have lived out an anguished life with him,
And always at the brink of an abyss,
Half toppling to the plunge, he swept me on.
—No, do not weep, my child. Let not my grieving
Become an omen of ill luck for you

Or poison the position which awaits you.
There lives no second Friedland; you, my child,
Need not fear you will meet your mother's fate.
THEKLA: O let us flee from here, dear Mother. Quickly!   1390
Quickly! There is no place here for us.
Here each successive hour produces some
New, monstrous offspring in a line of terrors.
THE DUCHESS: A lot more tranquil will be yours.—We, too,
I and your father, once knew happy days.
The early years I still recall with joy.
He then was still the man of cheerful striving,
Ambition was his fire of gentle warmth,
Not yet the flame that rages and devours.
The Emperor loved him, put his faith in him,   1400
And what he did invariably succeeded.
But since that day of woe at Regenspurg
That sent him plunging downward from the heights,
A restive, uncompanionable spirit,
Suspicious and morose, has come upon him.
Tranquillity deserted him, and, trusting
No more his former fortune or his strength,
He turned his heart to those dark skills which never
Blessed any man who cultivated them.
COUNTESS TERZKY: You see things through your eyes.—Is this,
    however,   1410
The kind of talk with which to wait his coming?
You know that he will soon be here. Shall he
Find *her* in this condition?
THE DUCHESS: Come, my child.
Wipe away your tears, and show your father
A cheerful face.—See, here's a bow all loose—
This strand of hair must be pinned up again.
Come, dry your tears. They will disfigure your
Dear eyes.—What was it I was going to say?
Oh yes, this Piccolomini is quite
A worthy gentleman and full of merit.   1420
COUNTESS TERZKY: Precisely, sister.

THEKLA *(to the Countess, with anxiety):*

Aunt, would you excuse me?

(She starts to leave.)

COUNTESS TERZKY: Where are you going? Your father will be
coming.

THEKLA: I cannot see him now.

COUNTESS TERZKY: But he will miss you,
He will be asking for you.

THE DUCHESS: Why is she leaving?

THEKLA: I cannot bear to see him now.

COUNTESS TERZKY *(to the Duchess):*   She is
Not well.

THE DUCHESS *(with concern):*
But what can ail the darling child?

*(Both follow the young lady and try to prevent
her from leaving.)*
(Enter Wallenstein, in conversation with Illo.)

WALLENSTEIN: Is all still quiet in the camp?

ILLO: All quiet.

WALLENSTEIN: Not many hours, and then the news must come
From Prague to say that capital is ours.
Then we can throw away the mask and to   1430
The local troops proclaim the action taken
Together with the news of our success.
Example counts for everything in cases
Like this. Man is an imitative creature,
The forwardmost will always lead the herd.
The troops in Prague do not know otherwise
Than that the Pilsen people side with us,
And here in Pilsen they will swear for us
Because in Prague they have set the example.
—Buttler, you say, has now declared for us?   1440

ILLO: Of his own will, quite unsolicited,
He came to offer you his regiment.

WALLENSTEIN: Not every voice, I find, is to be trusted
Which sounds its warning note within the heart.

The lying spirit often will, to cheat us,
Assume the simulated voice of truth
And spread deceiving oracles abroad.
Thus from this brave and worthy man, this Buttler,
I need to ask forgiveness for mute wrong.
A feeling which I am not master of,—   1450
I will not call it fear,—comes over me
And in his presence makes my senses shudder
And checks the joyous impulse of my love.
And now this honest man the spirit warns
Against presents me my first pledge of luck.

ILLO: And his esteemed example, do not doubt,
Will win the best men in the army to you.

WALLENSTEIN: Go now and send me Isolani here
At once. I put him under obligation
Lately. I will make a start with him.   1460

*(Exit Illo.—The others meanwhile have come
forward again.)*

Just look, the mother with her lovely daughter!
Let us for once let business matters rest.—
Come! I should like to pass a pleasant hour
In the beloved circle of my own.

COUNTESS TERZKY: It is long since that we were thus together,
Brother.

WALLENSTEIN *(aside to the Countess)*:
            Can she be told? Is she prepared?

COUNTESS TERZKY: Not yet.

WALLENSTEIN: Come here, my daughter, sit beside me.
There is a blessed spirit on your lips.
Your mother has much praised to me your skill
At music, and she claims a gentle voice   1470
Of harmony dwells in you which enchants
The soul. I feel the need of such a voice
Just now to drive away the evil demon
That fans his swarthy wings about my head.

THE DUCHESS: Where have you put your zither, Thekla? Come

And let your father hear a sample of
Your skill.

THEKLA: :   O Mother, Mother! Lord in Heaven!

THE DUCHESS: Come, Thekla, come and entertain your father.

THEKLA: I cannot, Mother—

COUNTESS TERZKY: What? What is this, Niece?

THEKLA *(to the Countess)*:
   O spare me—Sing!—now in the anguish of   1480
My heavy-burdened heart—to sing for him
Who drives my mother to her grave!

THE DUCHESS: What, Thekla, temperamental moods? Must your
Kind father have expressed a wish in vain?

COUNTESS TERZKY: Here is the zither.

THEKLA: O dear Lord—how can I—

      (She holds the instrument with trembling
      hands; her spirit is torn by vehement struggle,
      and just at the moment when she is about
      to start singing she is seized by a convulsive
      shudder, throws the instrument aside, and
      walks rapidly away.)

THE DUCHESS: My child—Oh, she is ill!

WALLENSTEIN: What ails the girl? Is this her usual way?

COUNTESS TERZKY: Well, since she herself betrayed it, I
Shall not keep silent either.

WALLENSTEIN: What?

COUNTESS TERZKY: She loves him.

WALLENSTEIN: Loves! Whom?

COUNTESS TERZKY: She loves young Piccolomini. 1490
Have you not noticed it? My sister either?

THE DUCHESS: Oh, was it that that weighed upon her heart!
God bless you now, my child! You need not
Blush for the choice which you have made.

COUNTESS TERZKY: This journey—
If this was not what you intended, then
You have yourself to blame. You should have chosen
Some other escort for her!

WALLENSTEIN: He knows of this?
COUNTESS TERZKY: He hopes to marry her.
WALLENSTEIN: He hopes to marry—Is the youngster mad?
COUNTESS TERZKY: Let her hear this herself!
WALLENSTEIN: He hopes to carry off
  The Duke of Friedland's daughter? Well, the notion   [1500
  Pleases me. His thoughts are by no means so base.
COUNTESS TERZKY: Because you always favored him so much,
  Why,—
WALLENSTEIN: He intends to be my heir at last.
  Well, yes. I love him and esteem him, but
  What has all that to do with marrying
  My daughter? Does one show one's favors with
  One's daughters, with one's only children?
THE DUCHESS: His high-born cast of mind and his demeanor—
WALLENSTEIN: May well win him my heart but not my daughter.
THE DUCHESS: His rank and lineage —   [1510
WALLENSTEIN: His lineage!
  He is a vassal, and my son-in-law
  I will select among the thrones of Europe.
THE DUCHESS: O my beloved Duke, let us not climb
  Too high lest we should fall again too low.
WALLENSTEIN: Should I have paid so high a price to reach
  This height, to range above the common heads
  Of human beings only to conclude
  At last my life role with such common
  Relationships? Was it for this that I—   1520
      (*He checks himself suddenly and gets control*
              of himself.)
  She is the only thing of mine that will
  Survive me on the earth; I want to see
  A crown upon her head or else not live.
  I will risk everything—yes, everything—
  To make her great—yes, at this very moment
  As we are speaking—
      (*He reflects.*)
            I am now supposed,

Like some soft-hearted father, burgher-fashion,
To join a pair of lovers in a match?
Am I supposed to do this now, right now,
Just when I mean to crown my finished work?—   1530
Oh no, she is a jewel I have hoarded,
The last coin and most precious of my treasure.
I shall surrender her for nothing less
Indeed than for the scepter of a king—

THE DUCHESS: You go on building, building to the clouds,
My husband, building on and ever on,
And do not think of how the narrow base
May not support the towering construction.

WALLENSTEIN (to the Countess):
Have you announced to her where I have chosen
For her to live?

THE COUNTESS: Not yet. Tell her yourself.   1540

THE DUCHESS: What? Are we not returning to Carinthia?

WALLENSTEIN: No.

THE DUCHESS: Nor to any one of your estates?

WALLENSTEIN: There it would not be safe for you.

THE DUCHESS: Not safe
In lands the Emperor owns, with his protection?

WALLENSTEIN: For that the spouse of Friedland may not hope.

THE DUCHESS: O God, have you pressed things as far as that?

WALLENSTEIN: In Holland you will find protection.

THE DUCHESS: What?
You send us into Lutheran domain?

WALLENSTEIN: His Grace, Duke Franz von Lauenburg will be
Your escort to that country.

THE DUCHESS: Lauenburg?   1550
The friend of Swedes, the Emperor's enemy?

WALLENSTEIN: The Emperor's enemies are mine no more.

THE DUCHESS (looking in terror at the Duke and at the
    Countess):
Then it is true? It is? You are deposed?
You are relieved of your command? O God
In Heaven!

COUNTESS TERZKY *(aside to the Duke):*
  Let us leave her with that notion.
You see that she could never bear the truth.
    (Enter Count Terzky.)
Terzky! What is wrong? What look of horror
As if he had just seen a ghost!
TERZKY *(taking Wallenstein aside, softly):*
Did you command the Croats to ride out?
WALLENSTEIN: I gave no orders.
TERZKY: Then we are betrayed.   1560
WALLENSTEIN: What's that?
TERZKY: They left last night, the infantry
As well. The villages around stand empty.
WALLENSTEIN: And Isolan?
TERZKY: Why, you sent him away.
WALLENSTEIN: I?
TERZKY: Didn't you? You didn't send him out?
Nor Deodat? They have both disappeared.

    (Enter Illo.)

ILLO: Has Terzky told you—
TERZKY: He knows all.
ILLO: And also that Maradas, Esterhazy,
 Kolalto, Götz, and Kaunitz have deserted?—
TERZKY: Damnation!
WALLENSTEIN *(motioning):* Quiet!
COUNTESS TERZKY *(having watched them anxiously from a
 distance, now steps up):*
      Terzky! What has happened?
 What is it?
WALLENSTEIN *(about to leave):*
    Nothing. Let us go.
TERZKY *(starting to follow him):*   It's nothing,   1570
 Theresa.
COUNTESS TERZKY *(holding him back):*
  Nothing? Can't I see that all
Lifeblood has left your ghost-white cheeks and that

My brother's calmness is affected merely?

(Enter a page.)

THE PAGE: An Adjutant is asking for Count Terzky.

(Exit the page with Terzky following him.)

WALLENSTEIN: See what he brings.—
(to Illo):   This could not have occurred
So secretly without some mutiny
Involved.—Who has the gate watch?

ILLO: Tiefenbach.

WALLENSTEIN: Have Tiefenbach relieved immediately
And Terzky's grenadiers mount guard.—And listen!
Have you some news of Buttler?

ILLO: I met Buttler.   1580
He will be here directly. He is loyal.

(Exit Illo. Wallenstein starts to follow him.)

COUNTESS TERZKY: Sister, stop him! Do not let him go—
There has been some disaster—

THE DUCHESS: Lord! What is it?

(She clings to him.)

WALLENSTEIN *(disengaging himself):*
Be still! Unhand me! Sister! Dearest wife,
We are in camp, and here things are this way,
Here storm and sunshine quickly alternate,
Here temperaments are hot and hard to manage,
Peace never favors a commander's head.—
If I must stay here, go away. Laments
Of women badly suit the work of men.   1590

(He starts to leave. Reenter Terzky.)

TERZKY: Stay here. This window gives a view of it.

WALLENSTEIN *(to the Countess):*
Go sister.

COUNTESS TERZKY: No!

WALLENSTEIN: I must insist.

TERZKY *(taking her aside and with a meaningful glance toward*

the Duchess):   Theresa!
THE DUCHESS: Come sister, since he so commands.

(The ladies withdraw.)

WALLENSTEIN *(stepping up to the window):*   What is it?
TERZKY: There is a scurrying and gathering
  Among the troops and no one knows the reason.
  Mysteriously and with ill-boding silence
  Each corps is falling in beneath its colors,
  The Tiefenbachs are wearing ugly looks,
  And only the Walloons are standing fast
  Down in their camp, allowing no one in,   1600
  And keeping calm as is their usual way.
WALLENSTEIN: Has Piccolomini appeared among them?
TERZKY: We looked, but could not find him anywhere.
WALLENSTEIN: What message was there from that Adjutant?
TERZKY: My regiments sent him as deputy:
  They take their oath to you anew and wait
  With warlike pleasure for the call to battle.
WALLENSTEIN: But how did all this furor reach the camp?
  The news was to have been kept from the army
  Till Fortune had declared for us in Prague.   1610
TERZKY: O if you had believed me! Yet last evening
  We begged you not to let Octavio,
  That sneak, get out beyond the gates; and you
  Yourself lent him the horses for his flight.
WALLENSTEIN: Oh, that old story! Now, once and for all,
  No more about that silly, wrong suspicion!
TERZKY: Oh yes, you trusted Isolani too,
  And yet he was the first one to desert you.
WALLENSTEIN: I plucked him only yesterday from ruin.
  Farewell! I never hoped for gratitude.   1620
TERZKY: And so they all are, one just like another.
WALLENSTEIN: Does he do wrong by leaving me this way?
  He still pursues the god whom he has served
  At gaming-tables all his life. He joined
  My luck, he breaks that bond, but not with me.

But what was *I* to him, or he to *me*?
I am the mere ship on which he embarked
His hopes and blithely sailed the open sea.
He sees it coasting dangerously past rocks
And swiftly sets to salvaging his cargo.   1630
Light as a bird up from the hospitable branch
That held its nest, he flies away from me,
No human bond is broken then between us.
Yes, he deserves to see himself betrayed
Who looked for heart within a thoughtless man.
In characters that swiftly fade life prints
Its images upon sleek brows, no thing
Will fall into a bosom's empty depths,
A cheerful mind will stir the flippant blood
But no soul makes the vital organs warm.   1640
TERZKY: Yet for my own part I prefer to trust
    Sleek brows before those deeply furrowed ones.

(Enter Illo, furious.)

ILLO: Mutiny and treason!
TERZKY: Ha! What now?
ILLO: The Tiefenbachs, when I gave them the order
    For them to be relieved—rebellious rascals! —
TERZKY: Well?
WALLENSTEIN: What, then?
ILLO: They refused obedience.
TERZKY: Then shoot them down! O give the order for it!
WALLENSTEIN: Easy there! What reason do they give?
ILLO: That no one may give orders now except
    Lieutenant General Piccolomini.   1650
WALLENSTEIN: What—How is that?
ILLO: That is the way he left it,
    He showed them in the Emperor's hand.
TERZKY: The Emperor's—
    You hear that, Duke?
ILLO: At his behest, what's more,
    The Colonels moved out yesterday from here.

TERZKY: You hear!

ILLO: And Montecuculi, Caraffa,
And six more Generals besides are missing,
And he persuaded them to follow him.
He had already had all that long since
In writing from the Emperor and arranged it
Besides just recently with Questenberg.   1660

> *(Wallenstein collapses into a chair*
> *and covers his face.)*

TERZKY: O if you only had believed me!

> *(Enter the Countess Terzky.)*

COUNTESS TERZKY: I cannot bear this anguish any longer.
In Heaven's name, tell me what is amiss.

ILLO: The regiments are now deserting us.
Count Piccolomini has proved a traitor.

COUNTESS TERZKY: My premonition!

> *(She rushes out of the room.)*

TERZKY: If you had believed me!
You see now how the stars have lied to you!

WALLENSTEIN *(straightening up)*:
The stars do not deceive, but this has happened
Against the courses of the stars and Fate.
The art is true, but that false heart has brought   1670
Lies and deceit into the very skies.
Prediction rests on trust alone; but where
Nature herself strays from her boundaries,
All science is in error. If it was
A superstition to degrade no form
Of human kind by such suspicion, then
I shall not hold this weakness as a shame!
Religion animates the very beasts,
Not even savages drink with their victim
Into whose heart they mean to run the sword.   1680
This was no hero's feat, Octavio!
Your cunning did not triumph over mine,

Your evil heart it was that gained this shameful
Victory against my honest one.
No shield broke your deathblow; relentlessly
You dealt it to my unprotected heart.
I am a child against that kind of weapons.

(Enter Buttler.)

TERZKY: O look! Buttler! He is a friend in need!

WALLENSTEIN *(goes to meet him with outstretched arms and*
cordially embraces him):
Come to my heart, you old comrade-in-arms!
The sight of sunshine in the spring is not   1690
So sweet as a friend's face at such an hour.

BUTTLER: My General—I have come here—

WALLENSTEIN *(leaning on his shoulder):*   Do you know:
The old man has betrayed me to the Emperor.
Just think of it! For thirty years we have
Lived side by side enduring all together.
We have shared sleep upon a single camp bed,
Drunk from a single glass, and shared a single
Morsel. I leaned upon him, as I lean
Upon *your* loyal shoulder now, and yet
The very moment when my bosom throbs   1700
In loving confidence against his bosom,
He spies out his advantage, drives his knife
With stealthy slyness to my heart.

(He hides his face on Buttler's breast.)

BUTTLER: Forget the traitor; Tell me, what will you
Do now?

WALLENSTEIN: Well, well advised. Farewell, Octavio!
I still have friends a-plenty,—do I not?
And Fate still loves me, for, precisely now
When this deceiver's guile has been unmasked,
She sends a loyal heart to me. No more
Of him. And do not think the loss of him   1710
Grieves me, what grieves me is his treachery.
For I held both of them in fond esteem,

And then this Max, he loved me quite sincerely,
He has not played me false, not he.—Enough,
Enough of this! This calls for swift decision.—
The mounted messenger sent by Count Kinsky
From Prague may now appear at any moment.
Whatever news he brings, he must not fall
Into the rebels' hands. So quickly now
Despatch a trusted messenger to meet him   1720
And bring him to me by a secret route.

(Illo starts to go.)

BUTTLER *(detaining him)*:
  General, whom are you expecting?
WALLENSTEIN: The mounted messenger who brings me news
  How things have gone in Prague.
BUTTLER: Hum!
WALLENSTEIN: What is wrong?
BUTTLER: You do not know, then?
WALLENSTEIN: What?
BUTTLER: What caused this furor
  In camp?
WALLENSTEIN: What did?
BUTTLER: The messenger, he—
WALLENSTEIN *(eagerly)*:   Well?
BUTTLER: He did arrive.
TERZKY AND ILLO: He did?
WALLENSTEIN: My messenger?
BUTTLER: Some hours ago.
WALLENSTEIN: And I was not informed?
BUTTLER: The sentries seized him.
ILLO *(stamping his foot)*:   Damn!
BUTTLER: His letter was
  Ripped open. It has made the rounds of camp.—   1730
WALLENSTEIN: Do you know what was in it?
BUTTLER *(reluctantly)*:   Do not ask me.
TERZKY: My God, then, Illo! Everything is lost!
WALLENSTEIN: Keep nothing from me. I can hear the worst.

Prague has been *lost?* Has it? Tell me straight out.
BUTTLER: It has been lost. And all the regiments
In Budweis, Tabor, Braunau, Königingrätz,
In Brünn and Znaym have left you and sworn new
Allegiance to the Emperor. You yourself
Are under ban with Kinsky, Terzky, Illo.

(Terzky and Illo show alarm and fury.
Wallenstein stands calm and firm.)

WALLENSTEIN *(after a pause):*
It is decided. That is well.—And I   1740
Am quickly cured of all tormenting doubts.
My heart is free again, my spirits clear,
It must be night for Friedland's stars to shine.
With hesitant decision, with uncertain mind
I drew my sword, resisting as I did so
As long as choice was still vouchsafed to me.
Necessity has come, doubt flees afar,
I fight now for my head and for my life.

(Exit Wallenstein, followed by the others.)
(Enter the Countess Terzky from a side room.)

COUNTESS TERZKY: No! I can not endure it any longer.—
Where are they? Empty everywhere. They leave me   1750
Alone—alone and in this frightful anguish.—
I have to force myself before my sister,
Seem tranquil, and hold in all torments of
A heart oppressed.—This I can not endure!
—If we should fail, if he should have to go
A fugitive and empty-handed to
The Swedes, and not as honored ally, followed
With pomp and army's might,—if we must travel
From land to land like the Count Palatine,
A scornful monument to fallen greatness—   1760
I shall not live to see that day! And if
He could himself endure to sink so low,
I could not bear to look upon him sunken.

(Enter the Duchess and Thekla.)

THEKLA *(trying to hold the Duchess back)*:
O dearest Mother, stay out here with me!
THE DUCHESS: No, there is still some awful secret here
Withheld from me.—Why does my sister shun me?
Why do I see her running aimlessly
About in fear, and you, too, terror-stricken?
And what do all these silent gestures mean
Which you keep furtively exchanging with her?   1770
THEKLA: Nothing, dear Mother!
THE DUCHESS: Sister, I must know.
COUNTESS TERZKY: What use is there to make a secret of it!
Can we conceal it? Sooner, later, you
Will have to learn of it and learn to bear it.
This is no time to yield to weakness now,
Our need is courage and a mind composed
And we must put our fortitude to practice.
Hence it is better that her fate be settled
In a few words.—We have deceived you, Sister.
You think the Duke has been deposed.—The Duke   1780
Is not deposed.—He is—
THEKLA *(going up to the Countess)*: You want to kill her?
COUNTESS TERZKY: The Duke is—
THEKLA *(throwing her arms around her mother)*:
                    O be steadfast now, my Mother!
COUNTESS TERZKY: The Duke has risen in revolt. He meant
To join the enemy. The army has
Deserted him, and everything has failed.   [1785]

*(At these words the Duchess wavers, then falls
fainting into her daughter's arms.)*

SCENE 2

*A room in the Duke of Friedland's quarters. Wallenstein in
armor.*

WALLENSTEIN: You have achieved your ends, Octavio!—Here
I stand once more abandoned, almost as

When I walked from the Diet of the Princes
At Regenspurg. Then I had just myself.—
But you have learned what *one* man can be worth.   1790
You have hacked off my branches of adornment
Until I stand a leafless trunk; the pith,
However, still retains a vital strength
Which burgeoning once bore an entire world.
I stood you in an army's stead on one
Occasion, singlehanded. There before
The Swedish strength your armies had all melted,
Beside the Lech died Tilly, your last hope,
Into Bavaria like a swollen river
Gustavus onward rushed, and in Vienna   1800
The Emperor in his castle shook for fear.
Soldiers then were costly, for the crowd
Will always follow Luck.—Then eyes were turned
To me, the help in time of need. The Emperor's pride
Bent then before the man who had been wronged.
I was to rise up with Creation's Call
And fill the hollow camps with men. I did so.
The drum-roll called recruitment, and my name
Passed like a god of war across the world.
Abandoned then were plow and workshop, all   1810
Came thronging to the well-known flag of hope.—
       I feel myself to be the same as then!
It is the mind that builds itself the body,
And Friedland will fill up the camp around him.
Lead on your thousands daringly against me,
It is their wont to triumph under me
But not against me.—When head and limbs are sundered
Then we shall see wherein the soul resided.
                (*Enter Illo and Terzky.*)
Have courage, friends, have courage! We are not
Yet down. Five Terzky regiments are still   1820
For us, and Buttler's doughty hordes.—Tomorrow
A force of sixteen thousand Swedes will join us.
I went no stronger forth nine years ago

To win the Emperor all of Germany.

(Enter Neumann, who takes Terzky aside and
talks to him.)

TERZKY *(to Neumann):*
What do they want?
WALLENSTEN: What now?
TERZKY: Ten cuirassiers
Up from the Pappenheim to see you on
Their regiment's behalf.
WALLENSTEIN *(quickly to Neumann):*   Have them come in.
                        (Exit Neumann.)
Something may come of this. Mark me, they still
Are doubtful and they still may be won over.

(Enter Illo. Ten cuirassiers, led by a Corporal,
march in and, executing commands, take up
formation before the Duke and present arms.)

WALLENSTEIN *(after scanning them for a time, to the Corporal):*
I know you well. You come from Bruges in Flanders,   1830
Your name is Mercy.
THE CORPORAL: Heinrich Mercy, yes Sir.
WALLENSTEIN: You were cut off while on the march, surrounded
By Hessians, yet fought clear of them. You were
A hundred eighty men against their thousand.
THE CORPORAL: Sir, that is true.
WALLENSTEIN: And what was given you
For that bold feat?
THE CORPORAL: The honor I requested,
Sir, to become a member of this corps.
WALLENSTEIN *(turning to another man):*
And you were one of those who answered when I called
For volunteers upon the Altenberg
To help wipe out that Swedish battery.   1840
SECOND CUIRASSIER: That's right, Sir.
WALLENSTEIN: I do not forget a man
With whom I ever once exchanged a word.

Men, state your business.

THE CORPORAL (*giving the command*):   Shoulder arms!

WALLENSTEIN (*turning to a third man*):   Your name
Is Risbeck and your birthplace is Cologne.

THIRD CUIRASSIER: Risbeck from Cologne, Sir.

WALLENSTEIN: You brought the Swedish Colonel Dübald in
As prisoner into the camp at Nürnberg.

THIRD CUIRASSIER: No, Sir, not I.

WALLENSTEIN: No! You're quite right! That was
Your older brother that did that.—You had
A younger brother, what became of him?   1850

THIRD CUIRASSIER: He is at Olmütz with the Emperor's army.

WALLENSTEIN (*to the Corporal*):
Well, state your case.

THE CORPORAL: A letter from the Emperor came into
Our hands, that said—

WALLENSTEIN (*interrupting*):   Who chose you?

THE CORPORAL: Each troop chose
Its man by lot.

WALLENSTEIN: Well, to your matter, then.

THE CORPORAL: A letter from the Emperor came into
Our hands, that said we should renounce our oath
To you because you are a foe and traitor.

WALLENSTEIN: And what conclusion have you reached?

THE CORPORAL: Our comrades
In Braunau, Budweis, Prague, and Olmütz have   1860
Complied already. Regiments Toscana
And Tiefenbach have followed their example.
—But we do not believe you are a foe
And traitor, we think that is nothing but
A pack of lies the Spaniards have made up.
     (*with naive trust*)
Tell us yourself what you are up to, Sir.
You always have been fair and square with us.
We have the highest confidence in you.
No other mouth shall shove in here between us,
The good Commander and his own good troops.   1870

WALLENSTEIN: Ah, there, I recognize my Pappenheimers.
THE CORPORAL: Your regiment sends you this message, then:
  If it is your intention only to
  Retain this warrior's scepter which befits you
  And which the Emperor trusted to your hand,
  And to be Austria's upright Field Commander,
  Then we will stand by you and be your guard,
  As is your proper right, against all comers.—
  And if the other regiments should all
  Forsake you, then we shall alone be faithful   1880
  To you and give our very lives for you.
  That is our honor code in Cavalry
  That we should die before we let you perish.
  But if things are the way the Emperor's letter
  Says, if it's true you mean to take us to
  The enemy in that unfaithful way,—
  Which God forbid,—then we will leave you too
  And do just what the letter says to do.
WALLENSTEIN: Listen, children—
THE CORPORAL: Not too many words.
  Say Yes or No, and we'll be satisfied.   1890
WALLENSTEIN: Listen: I know that you are sensible.
  You think, judge for yourselves, and do not follow
  The herd. That's why, you know, I always singled
  You out with honor from the army's mass.
  A General's rapid glance counts only flags,
  He does not notice individual faces,
  Severe and blind his iron order rules,
  For man to man can count for nothing here,—
  Such has not been, you know, my way with you.
  When you began to manage for yourselves   1900
  In this hard trade, and when I caught the gleam
  Of human thought upon your faces, then
  I treated you as independent men
  And granted you the right to speak your minds—
THE CORPORAL: Yes, you have always shown us decent treatment,
  General, honored us with trust, and shown

Us favor over other regiments.
And we do not trail with the common pack,
As you can see. We want to stick with you.
Say just one word,—your word will be enough,—   1910
Just say it is not treason you are planning,
You do not mean to lead your army to
The enemy.
WALLENSTEIN: They have betrayed me, *me*!
The Emperor has traduced me to my foes.
Unless my brave troops rescue me, I fall.
I will entrust myself to you.—Your hearts
Shall be my fortress. See, against this bosom
Their aim is fixed, against this head of grey!
That's Spanish gratitude! That's our reward
For mortal battle at that ancient fortress   1920
And on the plains of Lützen! That is what
We gain for breasts bared to the hallebards,
For making hard stones and the icy ground
Our pillows. No stream was too swift for us,
No forest too impenetrable, we followed
That Mansfeld with unflagging spirits on
Through every serpent-twist of his retreat.
A marching without rest was our whole life,
And, homeless as the sounding winds, we stormed
Our way across the war-tormented world.   1930
And now that we have done the heavy work
Of arms, the thankless, curse-beladen work,
With tireless, loyal arms heaved off the weight
Of war, here this imperial youngster comes
To claim an easy peace and to entwine
The olive branch, the hard earned trophy of
Our head into his blond and boyish locks—
THE CORPORAL: That he shall not, as long as we can stop him.
No one but you shall end this frightful war,
For it was you who led it with renown.   1940
You led us out upon the bloody field
Of death, you, no one else, and you shall lead

Us home with joy to the fair fields of peace,
And share with us the fruits of this long task—
WALLENSTEIN: What? Do you think you will enjoy those fruits
    At last in your old age? Do not believe it!
    You will not live to see the end of this
    Involvement. This war will consume us all.
    Austria wants no peace. That is the reason,
    Because I seek for peace, why I must fall.   1950
    What does Austria care if this long war
    Wears armies out and devastates the world?
    She only wants to grow, acquire more land.
    Ah, you are touched.—I see the noble anger
    Flash like the lightning in your warriors' eyes.
    O if my spirit could inspire you now
    As bold as when it led you once to battle!
    You would stand by me? would protect me in
    My rights by force of arms?—That is magnanimous!
    But do not think you will achieve that end,   1960
    You little army! You will sacrifice
    Yourselves for your Commander's sake for nothing.
        (confidentially)
    No! Let us safely tread, and look for friends.
    The Swede has promised us his help, let us
    Appear to take it, till, to both a terror,
    We hold the fate of Europe in our hands
    And from our camp lead Peace arrayed in garlands
    Of beauty forth to a rejoicing world.
THE CORPORAL: Then you are just pretending with the Swedes?
    You don't mean to betray the Emperor, or   1970
    Make Swedes of us? You see, that's just the point
    That we are anxious to find out from you.
WALLENSTEIN: What is the Swede to me? I hate him like
    The pit of Hell. God willing, I intend
    To drive him home across the Baltic soon.
    My thought is for the country as a whole.
    You see, I have a heart, the German people's misery
    Grieves me. You are just common soldiers, but

You think uncommonly, you seem to merit
More than the rest a private word from me.—   1980
Look! Fifteen years the torch of war has blazed
And still there is no peace. The Swede, the German,
The Papist and the Lutheran, none of them
Will yield before the other. Every hand
Against all others. Everything is party,
And no judge anywhere. Where will it end?
Who will unsnarl the knot which grows and keeps
On growing of itself?—It must be severed.
I feel I am that man of Destiny
And hope with your help to accomplish it.   1990

(Enter Buttler in excitement.)

BUTTLER: That was not well advised, Sir!
WALLENSTEIN: What was not?
BUTTLER: Fair-minded men will blame us for it.
WALLENSTEIN: What, then?
BUTTLER: It's open declaration of rebellion.
WALLENSTEIN: What is it, then?
BUTTLER: Count Terzky's regiments have ripped
    Off the imperial eagles from the standards
    And put your emblems on them.
THE CORPORAL *(to the cuirassiers)*:   Right face! March!
WALLENSTEIN: A curse upon this plan and him who planned it!
    (to the cuirassiers as they are marching away)
Halt, children, halt—There's some mistake—Hear me—
And I will punish it severely—Wait!
They will not listen.
            (to Illo):   Follow them, explain   2000
To them, and bring them back at any cost.
            (Illo hurries out.)
This plunges us in ruin.—Buttler! Buttler!
You are my evil genius. Why did you report
This matter in their presence? Everything
Was going well—I had them half won over.—
Those madmen, with their heedless eagerness

To be of use! O Luck plays cruelly
With me! It is the zeal of friends that ruins
Me, not the hatred of my enemies.

*(The Duchess rushes in to the room, followed by
Thekla and the Countess Terzky.)*

THE DUCHESS: O Albrecht! What is it you have done?
WALLENSTEIN: This yet!   2010
COUNTESS TERZKY: Forgive me, Brother. I just could not keep—
They now know everything.
THE DUCHESS: What have you done!
COUNTESS TERZKY *(to Terzky)*:
Is there no hope? Has everything been lost?
TERZKY: Without exception. Prague is in the Emperor's hands,
The regiments have sworn their new allegiance.
COUNTESS TERZKY: O treacherous Octavio! —Count Max
Has also left?
TERZKY: What else would you expect?
He has gone with his father to the Emperor.

*(Thekla throws herself into her mother's arms
and hides her face in her bosom.)*

THE DUCHESS *(clasping her in her arms)*:
Unhappy child! Still more unhappy mother!
WALLENSTEIN *(taking Terzky aside)*:
Go, have a travelling carriage made up quickly   2020
Down in the postern court for their departure.
(pointing to the women)
Have Scherfenberg go with them, he is loyal.
He goes to Eger with them, we'll come later.
(Reenter Illo.)
(to Illo)
You did not bring them back?
ILLO: You hear that uproar?
The whole corps of the Pappenheimers is
Advancing. They demand their Colonel back,
This Max; he is inside this castle now,

They claim, and you are holding him by force,
And if you do not give him up, they know
A way to liberate him with their swords.   2030

(Everyone stands in astonishment.)

TERZKY: What can this mean?
WALLENSTEIN: Did I not tell you so?
O my prophetic heart! He is still here.
And he has not betrayed me, was not able
To do so.—I have never doubted it.
COUNTESS TERZKY: If he is here, then everything is well.
I know what will forever keep him here!

(She embraces Thekla.)

TERZKY: It can not be! Just think! The old man has
Betrayed us and gone over to the Emperor:
Would *he* dare stay behind?
ILLO *(to Wallenstein):*   That four-in-hand
You gave him recently, I saw led through   2040
The market place not many hours ago.
COUNTESS TERZKY: He can't be far away, Niece!
THEKLA *(having fixed her eyes on the door, cries eagerly):*
                                      There he is!

(Enter Max Piccolomini.)

MAX *(advancing to the middle of the room):*
Yes, here he is! I can no longer bear
To stalk about this house with cautious tread
Awaiting the propitious moment from
Some covert place.—This biding time, this anguish
Surpasses my endurance!

        *(walking over to Thekla, who has thrown herself
            into her mother's arms)*

O look at me! Do no avert your eyes,
Sweet angel! Speak out free to all. Fear no one.
Let him who will, hear that we love each other.   2050
Why should we hide it further? Secrecy
Is for the happy, but misfortune, hopeless

Misfortune has no further need of veils
And can stand open to a thousand suns.
>   (*He catches sight of the Countess who is gazing*
>   *at Thekla with a jubilant look.*)

No, Cousin Tcrzky, do not look at me
With eager hopes! I have not come to stay,
I come to take farewell.—It is all over.
I must, I must renounce you, Thekla,—must!
But yet I cannot take your hatred with me.
Grant me a single glance of sympathy,   2060
Say that you do not hate me. Say that, Thekla.
>   (*taking her hand, deeply moved*)

My God, my God, I cannot leave this spot,
I cannot do it,—nor can I relinquish
This hand. Say, Thekla, that you pity me
And are convinced I have no other course.
>   (*Thekla, avoiding his glance, gestures toward*
>   *her father; he turns to confront the Duke of*
>   *whose presence he only now becomes aware.*)

You here?—It was not you that I was seeking.
My eyes were not meant to behold you ever
Again. I have to do with her alone.
I come for absolution from her heart,
All else is wholly without consequence.   2070

WALLENSTEIN: You think that I am fool enough to let you go,
To play a scene of magnanimity
With you? Your father has turned scoundrel on me.
In my eyes you are nothing but his son.
And have not come into my power for nothing.
Do not imagine I will honor that old friendship
Which he so ruthlessly destroyed. The times
Of love are past, the times of mild forbearance,
And now revenge and hate will have their turn.
Like him, I too can be inhuman.   2080

MAX: Deal with me as your might permits. But you
Well know that I do not defy your anger,
Nor do I fear it. What it is that keeps

Me here, you know.
          (taking Thekla by the hand)
See now! I hoped to owe you everything,
Yes, everything. The lot of saints I hoped
To have from your paternal hand. You have
Destroyed all that, and do not care. Indifferent,
You trample in the dust the happiness
Of your own kin. The god *you* serve is not   2090
A god of mercy. Like the senseless, blind,
Dire element with which no covenant
Is made, you harken to the heart's wild urge
Alone. And woe to them that trust you, building
Their hut of happiness against your slope
Confidingly, lured by your gracious shape!
Abruptly, unannounced, in silent nighttime
The treacherous volcano seethes and bursts
In raging violence, its furious torrent
Pours down and overbears with horrible   2100
Destructiveness whatever man has planted.
WALLENSTEIN: It is your father's heart which you depict.
What you describe is framed just so within
His vitals, in that black deceiver's bosom.
Oh, craft of Hell has tricked me. The abyss
Sent me the best disguised of all its spirits,
The one most skilled in lies, and stationed him
Beside me as a friend. Who can withstand
The power of Hell? I took the basilisk
And nursed it at my breast and let it feed   2110
Upon my own heart's blood; and there it sucked
Its swollen fill from my full breasts of love;
I never entertained suspicion of him,
Wide open there I left the gates of thought
And threw away the key of wise precaution.—
Amid the interplanetary spaces
Of starry skies my eyes searched for the foe
Which I had shut within my heart of hearts.
—If I had been to *Ferdinand* as this

Octavio has been to me,—I would not,—   2120
I could not—have declared a war against him.
He was my dread Lord merely, not my friend.
The Emperor never did trust my good faith,
There was already war between us when
He issued this Commander's staff to me,
For cunning and suspicion are forever
At war, and only faith and trust keep peace.
Whoever poisons trust commits the murder
Of unborn generations in the womb.

MAX: Oh, I will not defend my father. Woe   2130
  To me that I can not!
Things heavy with misfortune have occurred,
One impious action follows on another
To link a tightly locking chain of horrors.
But how came we, who have incurred no guilt,
Into this circle of unhappiness
And crime? With whom did we break faith? Why must
Our fathers' double guilt and impious deeds
Entwine us like a monstrous pair of serpents?
Why must our fathers' hatred unallayed   2140
Wrench us apart as well, who love each other?

(He embraces Thekla with vehement sorrow.)

WALLENSTEIN (who has fixed his eyes silently upon him, now
    approaches him):
  Max, stay with me.—O do not leave me, Max!
You know, in Prague, in winter quarters, once
They brought you to my tent, a tender lad
To German winters uninured; your hands
Were stiff with cold around the heavy flag
And stoutly you refused to let it go. And then
I picked you up and wrapped my cloak around you,
And was myself your nurse, and felt no shame
At little services, and tended you   2150
With that attentive care a woman gives,
Until against my heart and warmed by me

You felt young life with joy again within you.
When have I ever changed my mind since then?
I have made many thousands rich, I have
Made gifts of lands to them, rewarded them
With posts of dignity:—you I have *loved,*
Have given you my heart, my very self.
The rest were all mere strangers, you were my
Child in my house.—Max, you can not desert me now.   2160
It cannot be, it is beyond belief
That Max can be deserting me.

MAX: My God!

WALLENSTEIN: I cherished you and cared for you from childhood.
What has your father ever done for you
That I have not done also in full measure?
I have spun out a net of love around you.
Destroy it if you can.—You are bound to me
By every tender bond the soul can bind,
By every sacred ligature of Nature
Which can tie human beings to each other.   2170
Go then, desert me, serve your Emperor, let him
Reward you with his golden chain of favor
And hang his Golden Fleece about your neck
Because your friend, the father of your youth,
And holiest feelings had no value for you.

MAX *(with a fierce struggle):*
O Heaven! What else can I do? I must!
My oath—my duty—

WALLENSTEIN: Duty—ah, to whom?
Who are you? If *I* do the Emperor wrong,
The sin is mine, not yours. Do you control
Yourself? Are you the master of yourself?   2180
Do you stand free amid the world as I do
So you may be the author of your actions?
In *me* you have your roots, I am your Emperor,
Obeying me, belonging to me, that
Is where your honor lies, your law of Nature.
And if the star on which you live and dwell

Forsakes its orbit, throws itself in flames
Against a neighbor world and sets it burning,
You cannot choose to follow it or not,
It sweeps you forth in its momentum's swing   2190
Together with its ring and all its moons.
With little guilt you go into this battle,
The world will not have blame for you, but praise,
For setting highest value on your friend.

(Enter Neumann.)

What is it?
NEUMANN: The Pappenheimers are dismounted now
And coming on on foot; they are determined
To storm this castle sword in hand in order
To liberate the Count.
WALLENSTEIN *(to Terzky)*:   Go draw the chains
Across the gate and move the cannon up.   2200
I'll give them a reception made of chain shot.
     (Terzky goes out.)
Dictate to me by force of swords! Go, Neumann,
Tell them they must withdraw, immediately,
Those are my orders, and to wait in silence till
They learn what I am pleased to do.
COUNTESS TERZKY: Release him!
Release him, I implore you!
ILLO *(at the window)*:   Death and devils!
WALLENSTEIN: What is it?
ILLO: They have climbed the City Hall,
The roof is being cleared and cannon trained
Against this house—
MAX: The madmen!
ILLO: They are going
To fire on us—
THE DUCHESS AND COUNTESS TERZKY: Lord God in Heaven!
MAX: Let me   2210
Go and explain to them down . . .
WALLENSTEIN: Not one step!
MAX *(pointing to Thekla and the Duchess)*:

Their lives! And yours!

WALLENSTEIN: What do you bring me, Terzky?

(Reenter Terzky.)

TERZKY: News from our loyal regiments. Their spirits
  Are not to be contained much longer now,
  They beg you for permission to attack,
  They're masters of the Prague Gate and the Mill Gate,
  And if you only would send down the word
  They could strike at the enemy's rear lines,
  Wedge him into the town, and overpower
  Him easily inside the narrow streets.   2220

ILLO: O come! Don't let their eagerness grow cool!
  The Buttler forces will be true to us!
  We have the larger numbers and we'll beat them
  And end the insurrection here in Pilsen.

WALLENSTEIN: Is this town to become a battlefield,
  And is fraternal discord, fiery-eyed,
  To be set loose to rage about its streets?
  And must decision be entrusted to
  Deaf fury that will not hear any leader?
  There is no room for fighting, only carnage,   2230
  And once the rage of Furies is unleashed
  There is no master's voice to call them off.
  Well, let it come. I have long thought about it,
  Let it burst forth with quick and bloody force.
        (turning to Max)
  Well, now? Will you attempt a bout with me?
  You have your freedom to depart. Take up
  A stand opposed to me. Lead them to battle.
  You know the art of war, you have learned something
  From me. I need not blush for my opponent.
  You will not live to see a finer day   2240
  For paying me your schooling.

COUNTESS TERZKY: Has it come
  To this? O Cousin, Cousin, can you bear it?

MAX: The regiments entrusted to me I

Have vowed to lead in good faith to the Emperor,
And I intend to keep that vow or die.
My duty can require no more. I will
Not fight against you if I can avoid it.
As foe your head is holy to me still.

(Two shots are fired. Illo and Terzky
hurry to the window.)

WALLENSTEIN: What was that?
TERZKY: They've killed him!
WALLENSTEIN: Whom?
ILLO: The Tiefenbachers fired
   That shot.   [2250
WALLENSTEIN: At whom?
ILLO: At that same Neumann whom
   You sent to—
WALLENSTEIN: Death and devils! Then I will—

(He starts to go.)

TERZKY: Will you expose yourself to their blind fury?
THE DUCHESS AND COUNTESS TERZKY: In Heaven's name don't
   go!
ILLO: Not just now, General!
COUNTESS TERZKY: O stop him! stop him!
WALLENSTEIN: Let me go!
MAX: Don't do it,
   Not now. This rash and bloody deed has roused
   Them to a fury. Wait for their remorse—
WALLENSTEIN: Away! I have already hesitated
   Too long. They have pushed their outrageous boldness
   This far because they did not see my face.   2260
   But they shall see my face, and hear my voice.—
   Are they not still *my* troops? Am I not their
   Commander and their feared authority?
   Let's see if they no longer recognize
   The face that was their sun in battle's darkness.
   There is no need of arms. I'll show myself

Upon the balcony before these rebels,
And quickly tamed, their mutinous mind, I tell you,
Will seek its channel of obedience.

(*Exit Wallenstein, followed by Illo,*
Terzky, and Buttler.)

COUNTESS TERZKY (*to the Duchess*):
When they behold him—There is hope yet, Sister.   2270
THE DUCHESS: Hope! I have none.
MAX (*who has been undergoing a visible struggle during this last*
scene, now comes closer):   This I can not endure.
I came here with fixed purpose in my soul.
I thought that I was acting blamelessly,
Yet I must stand like one deserving hatred,
A crass inhuman brute and loaded with
The curses and contempt of all whom I
Hold dear, see loved ones heavy pressed unjustly
Whom with a single word I could make happy.
My heart rebels within me and two voices
Are raised in argument within my bosom.   2280
Night is within me, I can not discern the right.
Indeed, indeed, you spoke quite truly, Father,
I trusted far too much to my own heart.
I falter and do not know what to do.
COUNTESS TERZKY: You do not know? Does not your heart
    inform you?
Then I will tell you that!
Your father has committed shrieking treason
Against us, and against the Duke's own head,
And plunged us in disgrace. From all of this
It is quite clear what you, his son, should do: 2290
Atone for what that villain has committed,
Set an example of sound loyalty
So that the name of Piccolomini
Shall not become a byword and a curse
Forever to the House of Wallenstein.
MAX: Where is a voice of truth that I can follow?

Desires and passions move us all. O that
An angel would descend from Heaven now
To draw the right for me, unfalsified,
From springs of purest light with purest hands!   2300
     (as his eyes fall on Thekla)
What? Am I seeking for that angel still?
Do I seek any other?
    (He approaches her and puts his arm around her.)
        Here before
This heart, this holy, pure, unerring heart,
I lay the matter; I shall ask your love,
Which can confer joy on the innocent
Alone but from the guilty turns away.
Can you still love me if I do stay here?
If you declare you can, then I am yours.
COUNTESS TERZKY *(significantly)*:
Think of—
MAX *(interrupting her)*:
      No, do not think. Speak as you feel.
COUNTESS TERZKY: Think of your father—
MAX *(interrupting her)*:   I am asking you, 2310
You, my Beloved, not Duke Friedland's daughter!
There is no question of a crown to win,
That might be thought about with cunning mind;
The question *is* of your friend's peace of mind
And fortunes of a thousand heroes' hearts
Who will take up his action as their model.
Shall I renounce the Emperor's oath and service?
Shall I direct the parricidal bullet
Into Octavio's camp? For, once that bullet
Has left the barrel, it no longer is   2320
A lifeless instrument; it is alive,
A spirit enters into it, the Furies,
Avengers of impiety, seize on it
And guide it with their guile the worst of ways.
THEKLA: O Max—
MAX *(interrupting her)*:

                    No, do not speak too suddenly.
I know you. To your noble heart it might
Seem that the hardest duty were the foremost.
Not the sublime, the merely human must
Prevail. Think what the Duke has done for me.
Think too of how my father paid him for it.   2330
A hosts's spontaneous impulses, and those
Of sacred friendship also, constitute
A sacrosanct religion of the heart,
And Nature's horror will avenge them harshly
On foul barbarians who violate them.
Put everything into the balance, speak
And let your heart decide.
THELKA: O yours long since
    Made its decision. Follow your first-felt
    Emotion—
COUNTESS TERZKY: Wreched girl!
THELKA: How could it fail
    To be the right, the thing that tender heart   2340
    First seized upon and found immediately?
    Go and fulfill your obligation! I
    Would love you always, for, choose as you may,
    You always would act nobly, always would
    Be worthy of yourself.—Remorse shall not
    Disturb your fair serenity of soul.
MAX: Then I must leave you, must abandon you!
THEKLA: As you are faithful to yourself, so will
    You be to me. Fate separates us, yet
    Our hearts are joined. A bloody hatred sunders   2350
    Eternally the families of Friedland
    And Piccolomini, but we do not
    Belong among these families.—Away!
    Make haste, make haste to set your good cause clear
    Of our disastrous one. On our heads lies
    The curse of Heaven. They are marked for ruin.
    My father's guilt will draw me also to
    Destruction. Do not grieve for me. My fate

Will be decided soon.

> *(Max takes her into his arms, deeply moved.*
> *Off-stage is heard a long, wild, far-echoing*
> *cry: "Vivat Ferdinandus!" to the accompani-*
> *ment of martial instruments. Max and*
> *Thekla hold each other motionless in an*
> *embrace.)*
>
> *(Enter Terzky.)*

COUNTESS TERZKY *(going to meet him)*:
 O what was that? What was that shouting for?   2360
TERZKY: It is all over, everything is lost.
COUNTESS TERZKY: What? Did they pay no heed to his
 appearance?
TERZKY: None. Everything was useless.
THE DUCHESS: They were shouting
 "Vivat!"
TERZKY: Yes, for the Emperor.
COUNTESS TERZKY: O the traitors!
TERZKY: They would not even let him get to speak.
 When he began to talk they struck up with
 A deafening peal of military music.
 —Here he comes.

> *(Enter Wallenstein, followed by Illo*
> *and Buttler.)*

WALLENSTEIN *(as he enters)*:
 Terzky?
TERZKY: My Lord?
WALLENSTEIN: Have all our regiments
 Stand by in readiness to march today.   2370
 Before this evening we shall leave from Pilsen.
> *(Exit Terzky.)*
 Buttler!
BUTTLER: Sir!
WALLENSTEIN: The commandant at Eger is
 Your friend and countryman. Write him at once

By mounted messenger to be prepared
Tomorrow to receive us in the fortress.—
You and your regiment will follow us.

BUTTLER: It shall be done, Sir.

WALLENSTEIN (*steps between Max and Thekla, who during this time have held each other in close embrace*):

Separate!

MAX: Oh God!

(*Cuirassiers with rifles levelled enter the room and gather at the rear. Simultaneously are heard from below lively passages from the Pappenheimer March which seem to be summoning Max.*)

WALLENSTEIN (*to the cuirassiers*):
He's here. And free now. I shall not detain him.

(*He turns and stands in such a way that Max can neither approach him nor come near Thekla.*)

MAX: You hate me, drive me forth in anger from you.
The bond of our old love must rend asunder,   2380
Not loosen gently, and you seek to make
That painful rending still more painful to me!
You realize I have not learned to live
Without you yet.—Forth to a wilderness
I go, and everything, yes, everything
I prize remains behind.—O do not turn
Your eyes away from me! Show me once more
Your countenance revered and dear forever!
Do not reject me—
(*He starts to take his hand. Wallenstein withdraws it. He turns to the Countess.*)
                    Is there here no other
Eye that might pity me?—You, Cousin Terzky—   2390
(*She turns away from him. He addresses the Duchess.*)

You, mother whom I reverence—
THE DUCHESS: Go, Count, where
Your duty calls you.—Thus some day you can
Become our loyal friend and our good angel
Before the Emperor's throne.
MAX: You give me hope,
You do not drive me to complete despair.
O do not dazzle me with vain illusions.
For me disaster is a certainty.
Thank Heaven which provides the means to end it.
    (The martial music begins again. The room is
    filled with more and more armed men. He
    notices Buttler standing there.)
Ah, Colonel Buttler, you here too?—And will you
Not follow me?—Oh, very well! Be truer   2400
To your new master now than to your old one.
Come! Promise me, give me your hand upon it,
That you will guard his life, keep him from harm.
    (Buttler refuses his hand.)
The Emperor's ban hangs over him and marks
His princely head for every cutthroat villain
Who wants to win the bloody deed's reward.
A friend's devoted tending and the eye
Of loyal love are what he needs,—and those
I see around him as I go—
    (Casting ambiguous glances at Illo and Buttler.)
ILLO: Look for
The traitors in your father's camp, and Gallas'.   2410
Here only *one* is left yet. Go and spare us
The hateful sight of him. Be off with you!
    (Max tries once again to approach Thekla;
    Wallenstein prevents it. He stands undecided,
    sorrowful. Meanwhile the room is becoming
    more and more crowded and the horns sound
    ever louder challenges and at shorter and
    shorter intervals.)

MAX: Blow! Blow!—O would it were the Swedish horns,
And that the way were to the field of death,
And all these swords, yes, all these swords that I
Behold here drawn were thrust into my breast.
What do you want? Have you come here to snatch me
Away?—O do not drive me to despair!
Do not do that! You might regret it!
  (*The room is completely filled with armed men.*)
Still more and more.—Here weight is hung on weight,   2420
The ponderous mass of them will drag me down.—
Consider what it is you do. It is not well
To choose a man in full despair as leader.
You tear me from my happiness: then to
The Goddess Vengeance I devote your souls.
It is your ruin that you choose thereby:
Who goes with me, let him prepare to die!   [2427]

> (*As he turns toward the rear a sudden commotion develops among the cuirassiers, they surround him and escort him amid wild tumult. Wallenstein remains motionless. Thekla falls into her mother's arms.*)
> *The curtain falls.*

ACT IV

In the Burgomaster's house in Eger. [The following afternoon.]
Enter Buttler, who is just arriving.

BUTTLER: He has gone in. His Fate conducted him.
  The portcullis has dropped away behind him.
  And when the drawbridge swayed and lowered, bore   2430
  The weight of him, and swaying rose again,
  All avenues of rescue were cut off.
  Thus far, then, Friedland, and no further! says
  The Goddest Destiny. Your meteor
  Rose from Bohemian soil, astounding men,
  Described a gleaming path across the skies;
  Now on Bohemia's borders it must sink! —
  You have abjured the ancient flags, and trust,
  Rash blinded man, to Fortune as of old!
  To carry war into the Emperor's lands   2440
  And overturn the Lares' sacred hearth,
  You take up weapons in your impious hands.
  Beware—it is the evil spirit of
  Revenge that goads you—lest Revenge destroy you!

(Enter Gordon.)

GORDON: It's you?—O how I yearn to hear you speak.
  The Duke a traitor! O my God; and also
  A fugitive! his princely head proscribed!
  I beg you, General, tell me in detail
  How all this came about up there in Pilsen.
BUTTLER: You did receive the letter which I sent   2450
  Ahead to you by mounted messenger?

GORDON: And dutifully performed what you commanded.
Without delay I opened up the fortress
To him, for an imperial letter bade me
Comply in blind obedience with *your* orders.
But please forgive me! When I saw the Duke,
Then I began to have my doubts again.
For truly, like no man beneath the ban
Did Friedland make his entry in this city.
Upon his brow there shone as formerly   2460
The ruler's majesty that speaks to be
Obeyed, and quietly as in the days
Of order, he examined my accounts.
Guilt and misfortune make men affable
And fallen Pride will frequently defer
With flattery before the lesser man.
But sparingly, with dignity, the Duke
Weighed each word of approval, like a master
That lauds a servant who has done his duty.

BUTTLER: It all occurred exactly as I wrote you.   2470
The Duke has sold the army to the foe
And tried to open Prague and Eger to them.
At this report the regiments all left him,
All with exception of the five which Terzky
Commands and which have come here with him now.
The ban has been proclaimed against his head
And every loyal subject is required
To bring him in, dead or alive.

GORDON: O such
A gentleman,—a traitor to the Emperor!
So gifted too! O what is human greatness!   2480
I often said that that could come to no
Good end. His might and greatness and this dimly
Determined power proved a snare to him.
Mankind will always grasp for more, one dare
Not trust their moderation. Only law
Expressly clear will hold them to their limits
And the deep-trodden way of customs' usage.

The military power in this man's hands
Was of a new and quite unnatural kind,
It made him equal to the very Emperor.   2490
His haughty mind unlearned the art of bending.
But what a pity for a man like that!
None could stand firm, I fancy, where he fell.
BUTTLER: Save your laments until he needs such pity,
The mighty man is now still to be feared.
The Swedes are marching on toward Eger; soon,
Unless we stop them fast and firmly, they
Will make the junction of the troops. This must not be.
The Duke must never leave this place again
Of his free will, for I have pledged my honor   2500
And life itself to make him captive here,
And it is your support that I depend on.
GORDON: O would that I had never seen this day!
This post of honor I received from him,
This fortress he himself entrusted to me,
Which I must now transform into his prison.
We mere subalterns have no will; it is
The free, the mighty man alone who can
Obey his fine and human impulses.
But we are merely henchmen of the law,   2510
The cruel law. Obedience is the virtue
To which the man of low degree aspires.
BUTTLER: Waste no regret on these small-compassed limits
Of scope. Much freedom brings much error, but
The narrow path of duty is secure.
GORDON: So everyone, you say, has left him now?
Yet he established thousands in their fortunes,
For he was regal in his spirit and
His open hand was ever full of gifts.—
        (with a side glance at Buttler.)
He raised up more than one man from the dust   2520
And elevated him to ranks and honors.
With all of that he did not buy himself
A friend, not *one*, who would stand fast by him!

BUTTLER: He has one here for whom he scarcely hoped.
GORDON: I never have enjoyed a favor from him.
  I almost doubt that in his greatness he
  Has ever once recalled his boyhood friend.—
  My service kept me far away from him,
  His eye lost me within these fortress walls
  Where I, out of his favor's reach, maintained   2530
  My own heart's freedom in obscurity.
  For when he sent me to this castle, he
  Still took his duty seriously. I do not
  Betray his confidence by faithful guarding
  Of that which was committed to my trust.
BUTTLER: So tell me, will you carry out the ban
  And lend your help in making his arrest?
GORDON (sorrowfully, after a thoughtful silence):
  If it is so,—if things are as you say,—
  And if he has betrayed his Lord the Emperor,
  And sold the army, and proposed to open   2540
  The country's strongholds to the country's foes,
  Why, then there is no saving him.—And yet
  It's hard that of all people Fate takes me
  To be the instrument of his destruction.
  For we were pages at the court of Burgau
  Together; I however was the elder.
BUTTLER: So I have heard.
GORDON: That's thirty years ago. The daring spirit
  Already gripped that twenty-year-old youth.
  His mind was serious beyond his years,   2550
  To great things only manfully directed.
  Among our midst he passed with silent spirit,
  His own sole company. The childish pleasures
  That boys enjoy held no attraction for him.
  And yet he would some times be strangely moved
  All of a sudden; from his secret heart
  Would pour up, wise and bright, a ray of thought
  To make us stare with awe, not rightly knowing
  If madness or a god had spoken through him.

BUTTLER: Yes, it was there he once sustained a fall   2560
　Down from a window-bay two storeys high
　Where he had gone to sleep, yet he got up
　Unharmed. They say that tendencies toward madness
　Were to be seen in him from that day on.
GORDON: He brooded more, that is quite true, and he
　Turned Catholic. That preserving miracle
　Had oddly changed him. Now he felt himself
　A favored and emancipated being,
　And boldly, like a man who cannot stumble,
　He ran the swaying slack-rope of his life.   2570
　Then Destiny took us far, far apart.
　With spritely tread he went the path of greatness,—
　I felt quite giddy watching him,—became
　A Count, a Prince, a Duke, a Dictator,
　And now he finds all these too small for him,
　He reaches out to grasp a crown of kings
　And plunges into fathomless destruction!
BUTTLER: Stop. Here he comes.

*(Enter Wallenstein in conversation with the
Burgomaster of Eger.)*

WALLENSTEIN: You once were a free city? I observe
　Your coat-of-arms shows only half an eagle.   2580
　Why only half?
THE BURGOMASTER: We used to be direct
　Dependents of the Empire, but the city
　Was put in pawn two hundred years ago
　To the Bohemian crown. Hence this half eagle
　Is all we have. The lower part is cancelled
　Till such time as the Empire may redeem us.
WALLENSTEIN: You would deserve your freedom. Just stand fast.
　Give ear to no sedition. How high are
　Your taxes?
THE BURGOMASTER *(shrugging his shoulders)*:
　　　We can barely manage them.
　The garrison is on our bill besides.   2590

WALLENSTEIN: You shall have some relief. And tell me now,
Are there still Protestants within the city?

       (The Burgomaster is startled.)

O yes, I am aware that many are still hidden
Within these walls.—Yes, come right out and say it.—
You are yourself one, aren't you?

       *(He fixes him with his eyes. The Burgomaster
        is terrified.)*

                       Have no fear.

I loathe the Jesuits.—If I had my way,
They'd have been ousted from the Empire long
Ago.—Missal or Bible! I don't care.—
I've proved that to the world.—I had a church
Built for the Evangelicals myself   2600
In Glogau.—Burgomaster, what's your name?

THE BURGOMASTER: Pachhälbel, my illustrious Lord.

WALLENSTEIN: Now listen.—But do not repeat what I
Shall tell you now in confidence.

       *(laying his hand on his shoulder, with a certain
        solemnity)*

                       The times'
Fulfillment is upon us, Burgomaster.
The high shall fall, the lowly shall arise.—
But keep this to yourself! The Spanish dual
Dominion is upon the wane, a new
Order of things is coming in.—You saw
Those three moons in the sky just recently?   2610

THE BURGOMASTER: With horror.

WALLENSTEIN: And two of the three were twisted
Awry and then transformed into the shape
Of gory daggers. Only one of them,
The middle one, retained its shining brilliance.

THE BURGOMASTER: We took it as referring to the Turks.

WALLENSTEIN: The Turks! Two empires will go down in blood,
I tell you, in the East and in the West.
There will be left the Lutheran faith alone.

       (He catches sight of the other two.)

There was some lively firing on our left
Last evening as we were approaching here.   2620
Did you here in the fortress notice it?
GORDON: Why yes, we heard it quite distinctly, General.
The wind brought up the sound straight from the South.
BUTTLER: It seemed to come from Neustadt or from Weiden.
WALLENSTEIN: That is the road by which the Swedes are coming.
What is the garrison's strength?
GORDON: A hundred-eighty
Able men. The rest are invalids.
WALLENSTEIN: How many more are in the Jochimsthal?
GORDON: I sent two hundred arquebusiers down
To bolster up the posts against the Swedes.   2630
WALLENSTEIN: I praise your foresight. Building is in progress
On earthworks too, I noticed at my entry.
GORDON: Because the Palatine is threatening us
So closely I had two more bastions built.
WALLENSTEIN: You are exact about your Emperor's service.
I am quite satisfied with you, Lieutenant.
    (to Buttler)
Withdraw contingents in the Jochimsthal
And others that oppose the enemy.
    (to Gordon)
Into your loyal hands, then, Commandant,
I now commit my wife and child and sister.   2640
For I shall not stay here. I merely am
Awaiting word to quit this fortress at
The earliest moment with all regiments.

(Enter Count Terzky.)

TERZKY: Here's welcome news indeed! And joyful tidings!
WALLENSTEIN: What do you bring?
TERZKY: A battle has been fought
Near Neustadt and the Swedes came out the victors.
WALLENSTEIN: What's that you say? Where did you get this news?
TERZKY: A farmer brought it up from Tirschenreit.

He said that it began just after sundown;
From Tachau a detachment of Imperials   2650
Made an incursion in the Swedish camp,
The firing lasted for two hours, and
A thousand of the Emperor's men were killed,
Their Colonel with them; that was all he knew.

WALLENSTEIN: How came Imperial troops to be near Neustadt?
Altringer—he would have to have grown wings—
Was sixty miles from there yet yesterday,
And Gallas' troops were gathering in Frau'nberg
And are not yet assembled. Could it be
That Suys dared to move so far ahead?   2660
That cannot be.

(Illo is seen approaching.)

TERZKY: We'll soon find out about it,
For here comes Illo full of joy and haste.

(Enter Illo.)

ILLO *(to Wallenstein):*
A courier is here and wants to see you.

TERZKY: The victory has been confirmed then? Speak!

WALLENSTEIN: What does he bring? Where does he come from?

ILLO: From
The Palatine, and I can tell what news
He brings: The Swedes are five miles distant now.
Near Neustadt Piccolomini made an
Attack against them with his cavalry,
A frightful slaughter then ensued, but in   2670
The end the weight of numbers finally
Prevailed, and all the Pappenheimers fell,
Including Max who led them, on that field.

WALLENSTEIN: Where is the messenger? Bring me to him.

*(He starts to go. Just at that moment Fräulein
    Neubrunn rushes into the room; several
    servants run through the room following her.)*

NEUBRUNN: Help! Help!

ILLO AND TERZKY: What's this?
NEUBRUNN: The Lady!
WALLENSTEIN AND TERZKY: Does she know?
NEUBRUNN: She's dying!

(She rushes out. Wallenstein and Terzky
follow her.)

GORDON *(in astonishment):*
                            What did that scene signify?
BUTTLER: The man is lost with whom she was in love,
  It was this Piccolomini who perished.
GORDON: Unhappy lady!
BUTTLER: You heard the news this Illo brought: the Swedes 2680
  Victoriously are coming on.
GORDON: I heard it.
BUTTLER: They number twelve full regiments; five more
  Are in the neighborhood to shield the Duke,
  While we have only my one regiment,
  And here a bare two hundred men are stationed.
GORDON: That's so.
BUTTLER: No prisoner of state can possibly
  Be guarded with so small a compliment.
GORDON: I realize.
BUTTLER: That host would soon disarm our little force   2690
  And set him free.
GORDON: That is a thing to fear.
BUTTLER *(after a pause):*
  Hear me then. I must guarantee the outcome.
  And I must answer with my head for his.
  I must make good my word, cost what it may,
  And if the living man can not be guarded,
  We must make certain of the dead one.
GORDON: Do I conceive your thought? Just God! You could—
BUTTLER: He must not live.
GORDON: You could do that?
BUTTLER: You *or* I. He has seen his final morning.
GORDON: You mean to murder him?

BUTTLER: That is my purpose.   2700

GORDON: Who trusted your good faith?

BUTTLER: His evil Fate!

GORDON: The General's sacred person?

BUTTLER: That he *was!*

GORDON: The thing he was no crime will wipe away.
    Without a verdict?

BUTTLER: Execution stands
    In place of verdict.

GORDON: That would be no justice,
    But murder. Justice hears the guiltiest.

BUTTLER: His guilt is clear, the Emperor has passed judgment,
    And we are only carrying out his will.

GORDON: We need not rush to carry out the sentence.
    A word may be retrieved, a life may not.   2710

BUTTLER: The quickest service pleases monarchs most.

GORDON: To hangman's service hastes no noble man.

BUTTLER: No man of spirit pales before bold action.

GORDON: Spirit will risk its life but not its conscience.

BUTTLER: What? Shall he go scot-free to light anew
    The inextinguishable fires of war?

GORDON: Go take him prisoner, but do not kill him,
    Do not forestall with rashness Mercy's Angel.

BUTTLER: Had not the Emperor's army been defeated
    I would have willingly left him alive.   2720

GORDON: Why did I open up the fortress to him!

BUTTLER: It is his Fate, and not this place, that kills him.

GORDON: Upon these walls I would have died defending
    The Emperor's castle in a knightly fashion.

BUTTLER: Meanwhile a thousand worthy men have perished!

GORDON: In line of duty.—That befits a man.
    But Nature put its curse upon black murder.

BUTTLER *(bringing forth a paper):*
    Here is the edict bidding us to seize him.
    It is addressed as much to you as me. Now will
    You bear the consequences if, through fault of ours,   2730
    He gets away to join the enemy?

GORDON: My God, I stand here powerless.

BUTTLER: Assume the consequences! Take it on
Yourself! Come what come may, on your head be it!

GORDON: O God in Heaven!

BUTTLER: Do you know some other
Way to fulfill the Emperor's will? Speak out!
For I would overthrow him, not destroy him.

GORDON: I clearly see, as you do, what must be.
But yet my heart beats with a different pulse.

BUTTLER: This Illo and this Terzky likewise must   2740
Not live when once the Duke has fallen.

GORDON: O, I have no regrets on their account.
Their evil hearts impelled *them,* not the force
Of stars. They were the ones who strewed the seeds
Of wicked passion in his tranquil bosom,
Who with their damnable officiousness
Fleshed up disaster's fruit in him.—May evil
Reward for evil service overtake them!

BUTTLER: They shall precede him also in their deaths.
All that is prearranged. We planned to take them   2750
Alive this evening in the pleasures of
Their banqueting and hold them in the castle.
It will be quicker so. I shall now go
At once and give the necessary orders.

(Enter Illo and Terzky.)

TERZKY: Well now, things will be different soon! Tomorrow
The Swedes arrive, twelve thousand doughty fighters.
Then on, straight to Vienna! Hey, cheer up,
Old man. Don't look so sour at such good news!

ILLO: Now it will be for us to dictate laws
And take revenge on all the filthy scoundrels   2760
Who have deserted us. One has already
Paid for his crime, this Piccolomini.
May it go thus with all who wish us ill!
How hard this blow will hit the old man's head!
He has been struggling all his life to raise

His family's grade of Count to Princely rank,
And now he buries the only son he had.
BUTTLER: Yet it's a shame about that youthful hero.
The Duke too took it hard, that was quite plain.
ILLO: Listen, old friend. That's just the thing I never   2770
Did like about our chief. It was my sole
Complaint. He always would prefer these Latins.
And even now, I swear it by my soul,
He'd see us all dead ten times over if
He could thereby call back his friend to life.
TERZKY: Be still, be still now! Leave the dead in peace.
Today we shall see who outdrinks the other.
Your regiment is playing host to us.
And we shall make a Mardi Gras of it.
Let night be day for once, and with full glasses   2780
We'll wait the coming of the Swedish vanguard.
ILLO: Yes, let us be of right good cheer today,
Because ahead of us hot days await.
This sword shall not have any rest until
It has bathed to its fill in Austrian blood.
GORDON: For shame! What kind of talk is that, Lord Marshal!
Why should you rage against your Emperor so?—
BUTTLER: Do not expect too much from this first triumph.
Recall how fast the wheel of Fortune turns,
The Emperor still is very powerful.   2790
ILLO: The Emperor has his soldiers, but no General,
For this King Ferdinand of Hungary
Does not know warfare.—Gallas? Has no luck,
And always was a ruiner of armies.—
As for that snake Octavio, he can deal
A sly wound in the heel quite well, but not
Stand up to Friedland in an open fight.
TERZKY: We cannot lose, believe me. Fortune will not
Desert the Duke. It's known that Austria
Can triumph only under Wallenstein.   2800
ILLO: The Duke will very soon have a great army
Collected, everybody will come thronging

And streaming toward the old fame of his banners.
I see the days of old returning now,
With him once more the great man that he was.
Those who have left him now, how they will find
That they have slammed the door on their own noses!
He will bestow estates on friends of his
And pay imperially for loyal service
Performed. And we stand closest in his favor.   2810
   (to Gordon)
You too will be remembered then. He'll pull you
Out of this hole, and let your loyalty
Shine in some other, more exalted post.
GORDON: I am content, I do not want to climb
So high. Where great height is, there is great depth.
ILLO: You have no further matters to arrange here.
The Swedes will occupy the fort tomorrow.
Come, Terzky. It is near to supper time.
What do you say? Let's light the city up
In honor of the Swedes, and who does not   2820
Comply, will be a Spaniard and a traitor.
TERZKY: No, none of that. The Duke would not approve.
ILLO: What! We're the masters here, and no one shall
Profess the Emperor where we have control.—
Good night, Gordon. I now commend the fort
A last time to your care. Despatch patrols.
You might, for safety, change the password too.
At ten you bring the Duke himself the keys,
Then you are finished with your warder's office.
The Swedes will occupy the fort tomorrow.   2830
TERZKY *(to Buttler, in parting)*:
You will come to the castle?
BUTTLER: In good time.

    (Exeunt Illo and Terzky.)

GORDON *(watching them out of sight)*:
Unhappy men! How unsuspectingly
They rush into the net of outspread death

In their blind drunkenness with victory!—
I feel no pity for them, though. This Illo,
The insolent and overweening villain,
He wants to wallow in his Emperor's blood!

BUTTLER: Do as he ordered you. Despatch patrols,
Look to the fortress's security.
Once they have gone upstairs I'll lock the tower   2840
Lest some noise of the deed get to the city.

GORDON (with anxiety):
O not so fast! First tell me—

BUTTLER: You heard what
He said: The coming day is for the Swedes;
The night alone is ours yet. They are swift,
But we shall be yet swifter still.—Farewell.

GORDON: Your look betokens nothing good to me.
O promise me—

BUTTLER: The sun's light has gone down,
An evening dark with destiny descends.—
Their self-deception makes them sure. Their star
Of evil puts them helpless in our hands,   2850
And in the midst of drunken dreams of fortune
Sharp steel shall suddenly cut off their lives.
A great arithmetician was this Duke
His life long; he could reckon anything;
And human beings he could place and move
Like pieces on a chessboard for his ends.
He had no qualms at playing with the dice
Of other people's honor and good name.
He reckoned on and on, yet in the end
His calculations after all have erred.   2860
He has involved his own life in the game
Like one of old who perished in his circles.

GORDON: O do not call his sins to memory now!
Recall his greatness and his graciousness,
Recall the winning features of his heart
And all the noble actions of his life,
And, like an angel pleading and imploring

For mercy, let them check the upraised sword.

BUTTLER: It is too late. For I must feel no pity
    Tonight. I must have none but bloody thoughts.   2870
       (taking Gordon's hand.)
    Gordon! It is not hate—I do not love
    The Duke and have no cause to do so—but
    My hate does not make me his murderer.
    It is his evil Fate. Ill-luck impels me,
    The hostile concentration of events.
    Men think they act of their own free accord,
    In vain. They are mere toys of blind compulsion
    Which of their own elections swiftly makes
    Grim ineluctabilities. How would
    It help him if some voice within my heart   2880
    Spoke for him?—I must kill him anyway.

GORDON: O if your heart speaks warning, heed its impulse.
    The heart is God's own voice; the work of man
    Is artful calculation's sly contriving.
    What good can thrive for you from deeds of blood?
    O nothing good has ever sprung from blood.
    Are they to set your ladder up to greatness?
    Do not believe it.—Murder can sometimes
    Please kings, but murderers have never pleased them.

BUTLER: You do not know. Don't ask. Why must the Swedes 2890
    Have won and now be coming on so fast!
    I meant to leave him to the Emperor's mercy,
    I do not seek his blood. No, he could live.
    And yet I must redeem my word of honor.
    And he must die, or else—hear what I say!—
    I am dishonored if the Duke escapes us.

GORDON: To rescue such a man—

BUTTLER *(quickly):*   What's that?

GORDON: Is worth a sacrifice.—Be generous!
    The heart respects a man if judgment does not.

BUTTLER *(coldly and proudly):*
    He is of high degree, this Duke.—While I,   2900
    You mean to say, am just a little person.

What is it to the world, you think, if one
Of low degree finds honor or dishonor
So long as those of princely rank are saved?—
Each man assigns his own worth to himself.
How high I rate myself depends on me.
No man is so exalted on this earth
That I despise myself when placed beside him.
It is man's *will* that makes him great or small;
Since I am true to mine, he shall not live.   2910
GORDON: O I am trying to persuade a stone!
    You are not human-born of human creatures.
    I cannot hinder you, but may some god
    Effect his rescue from your frightful hand.   [2914]

(Exeunt.)

SCENE 2

A room in the apartments of the Duchess.
Thekla is seated in a chair, pale, her eyes closed. The Duchess
and Fräulein von Neubrunn are occupied with her. Wallenstein
and Countess Terzky are talking.

WALLENSTEIN: How did she come to learn of this so fast?
COUNTESS TERZKY: She seems to have divined catastrophe.
    The rumor of a battle terrified her,
    In which a Colonel of Imperials perished.
    I sensed it right away. She flew to meet
    The Swedish courier and quickly, by   2920
    Her questions, drew his secret out of him.
    Too late we missed her, hurried after her;
    She had already fainted in his arms.
WALLENSTEIN: Completely unprepared she met the blow!
    Poor child.—How is she? Is she coming to?

      (as he turns to the Duchess)

THE DUCHESS: Her eyes are opening.

COUNTESS TERZKY: She is alive!
THEKLA *(gazing about)*:
  Where am I?
WALLENSTEIN *(going over to her and raising her up with his
  arms)*:
                    Wake to consciousness now, Thekla.
  Be my strong daughter! See your loving mother,
  And see your father's arms supporting you.
THEKLA *(standing upright)*:
  Where is he? Has he gone already?
THE DUCHESS: Who, my daughter?   2930
THEKLA: He who pronounced those dismal words—
THE DUCHESS: O do not think of that, my child! Avert
  Your thoughts from that sad image.
WALLENSTEIN: Let her sorrow
  Express itself. Allow her to lament.
  And mingle your tears now with hers, for she
  Has lived through the experience of great grief;
  She will survive it none the less, for my
  Own Thekla has her father's dauntless heart.
THEKLA: I am not ill. I have the strength to stand.
  Why is my mother weeping? Have I frightened   2940
  Her? It is past. I am myself again.

          *(She has stood up and is searching the room
              with her eyes.)*

  Where is he? Let them not conceal him from me.
  I have sufficient strength, I wish to hear him.
THE DUCHESS: No, Thekla, no! This bringer of ill tidings
  Shall never step before your eyes again.
THEKLA: Father—
WALLENSTEIN: Beloved child!
THEKLA: I am not weak.
  I shall recover presently still more.
  I beg you, grant me one request.
WALLENSTEIN: Ask it.
THEKLA: Grant your permission for this stranger to

Be called so that I may with privacy   2950
Hear his report and ask him questions.
THE DUCHESS: Never!
COUNTESS TEZKY: No, that is ill-advised. Do not consent.
WALLENSTEIN: Why do you wish to speak with him, my
    daughter?
THEKLA: I shall be calmer, knowing everything.
    I do not like to be deceived. My mother
    Is only sparing me. I do not wish that.
    The worst already has been said, I can
    Hear nothing yet more dreadful.
COUNTESS TERZKY AND THE DUCHESS (to Wallenstein):
                              Do not do it.
THEKLA: My horror took me by surprise, my heart
    Betrayed me in the presence of this stranger.   2960
    He was a witness of my weakness, yes,
    I fell into his arms.—I am ashamed.
    I must restore myself in his opinion
    And I must see him of necessity
    Lest this strange man should wrongly think of me.
WALLENSTEIN: I feel she is quite right—and am inclined
    To grant her this request. Go summon him.

            (Fräulein Neubrunn goes out.)

THE DUCHESS: But I, your mother, shall be present then.
THEKLA: I would prefer to speak with him alone.
    I shall conduct myself more calmly so.   2970
WALLENSTEIN (to the Duchess):
    Let it be done. Let her deal with this man
    Alone. For there are griefs where human beings
    Can only help themselves. Strong hearts prefer
    Reliance on their inner strength alone.
    She must derive her strength from her own heart
    And not from others to survive this blow.
    She is my doughty girl, whom I would have
    You treat as heroine and not as woman.

            (He starts to go.)

COUNTESS TERZKY (*detaining him*):
  Where are you going? I heard Terzky say
  You plan departure for tomorrow morning   2980
  But leave us here behind.
WALLENSTEIN: Yes, you remain
  Committed to the ward of trusty men.
COUNTESS TERZKY: O take us with you, Brother. Do no leave us
  Amid this dismal solitude to wait
  With anxious spirits for the final outcome.
  The present trouble may be borne with ease,
  But it is grimly magnified by doubt
  And harrowed waiting for one far away.
WALLENSTEIN: But who talks of disaster? Mend your speech.
  I have quite different hopes in view.   2990
COUNTESS TERZKY: Then take us with you. Do not leave us here
  Amid this place of dreary memories.
  Within these walls my heart is heavy-pressed,
  They breathe the breath of deathly vaults upon me.
  I cannot tell you how the place repels me.
  Take us away! Come, Sister, beg him too
  To take us with him! Help me, dearest Niece!
WALLENSTEIN: I'll change the evil omens of the place.
  Let it be where my dearest ones were guarded.

          (*Reenter Neubrunn.*)

NEUBRUNN: The Swedish Lord!
WALLENSTEIN: Leave her alone with him.   3000
THE DUCHESS (*to Thekla*):
  How pale you turn. You cannot possibly
  Speak with him, Child. Come with your mother now.
THEKLA: In that case Neubrunn may attend me then.

          (*The Duchess and the Countess leave.*)
          (*Enter the Swedish Captain.*)

THE CAPTAIN (*approaching respectfully*):
  Princess—I—must ask forgiveness for
  My rash and reckless words.—How could I have—

THEKLA *(with lofty dignity)*:
  You have beheld me in the midst of grief.
  Ill-fortuned accident transformed you from
  A stranger to my sudden confidant.
THE CAPTAIN: I fear that you now hate the sight of me
  Because my tongue pronounced those words of grief.   3010
THEKLA: The fault was mine. I wrested them from you
  Myself. You were no more than my Fate's voice.
  My fright cut short the tale you had begun.
  Therefore I beg you to continue now.
THE CAPTAIN *(dubiously)*:
  Princess, it will but start your grief afresh.
THEKLA: I am prepared for that.—I shall be calm.
  How did the battle start? Complete your story.
THE CAPTAIN: We had our posts, suspecting no attack,
  Near Neustadt in our camp of weak entrenchments,
  When toward the evening from the forest side   3020
  There rose a cloud of dust. Our fleeing vanguard
  Rushed into camp with cries: The enemy
  Had come. We had just time to throw ourselves
  Upon our horses when the Pappenheimers
  In full career of steeds spurred to the gallop
  Came bursting through the barriers upon us.
  The ditch that circumscribed the camp was likewise
  Swarmed swiftly over by those storming hosts.
  But recklessly their valor had outled them
  Far out beyond the rest; the infantry   3030
  Lagged far behind; the Pappenheimers only
  Had boldly followed their bold leader.
    *(Thelka stirs. The Captain pauses for a moment
    until she gives him a sign to continue.)*
  Head on and from the flanks we struck at them
  With all the forces of our cavalry
  And forced them backwards to the ditch, where then
  The infantry, arrayed in haste, formed up
  A hedge of pikes that bristled starkly at them.
  Advance they could not, nor could they retreat,

Wedged as they were into that deadly clamp.
The Rhinegrave shouted to their leader then   3040
To yield himself with honor in fair fight,
But Colonel Piccolomini—
          (Thekla sways, grasps a chair.)
                    We knew him
By token of his helmet-plume and his
Long hair—it had come down from rapid riding—
He beckons toward the ditch. Himself the foremost,
He spurs his noble steed to leap across it.
The regiment comes rushing in his wake—
But—then it happened. Pierced upon a pike
His horse rears back in frenzy, hurls its rider
Afar, and over him the violence   3050
Of steeds rides on, rebellious to the reins.

          *(Thekla, who has followed the last words with
          all the signs of growing anguish, begins to
          tremble violently; she starts to fall; Fräulein
          Neubrunn hastens to her and takes her into
          her arms.)*

NEUBRUNN: My dear young Lady—
THE CAPTAIN *(moved)*:   I had best withdraw.
THEKLA: No, it is over.—Go on to the end.
THE CAPTAIN: When the troops beheld their leader fallen, then
     A fierce and furious despair came on them.
     Now no man gives survival further thought,
     They fight like raging tigers; our men too
     Are roused to fury by their fierce resistance,
     So that conclusion of the battle did not
     Ensue until the last man had been killed.   3060
THEKLA *(with trembling voice)*:
     And where—where is—You have not told me all.
THE CAPTAIN *(after a pause)*:
     We buried him this morning. He was borne
     By twelve youths of the noblest families.
     The entire army filed behind his bier.

A laurel decked his coffin, and thereto
The Rhinegrave added his own victor's sword.
Nor did his fate lack tears, for there are many
Of us who knew his generosity
And friendliness of manners, and his death
Affected everyone. The Rhinegrave would   3070
Have gladly rescued him, but he himself
Forestalled that; people say he wished to die.

NEUBRUNN (*deeply moved, to Thekla, who has covered her face*):
My dear young Lady—Mistress, lift your eyes!
O why did you insist on hearing this?

THEKLA: Where is his grave?

THE CAPTAIN: He is entombed near Neustadt
Within a monastery church until
Word from his father shall have been received.

THEKLA: What is the monastery called?

THE CAPTAIN: St. Catherine's.

THEKLA: How far is that from here?

THE CAPTAIN: Some seven miles.

THEKLA: What road leads there?

THE CAPTAIN: The road to Tirschenreit 3080
And Falkenberg and passes through our fore-posts.

THEKLA: And who controls them?

THE CAPTAIN: Colonel Seckendorf.

THEKLA (*steps up to the table and takes a ring out of the jewel casket*):
You have beheld me in my hour of grief
And shown a human heart to me.—Accept this ring
    (*as she gives him the ring*)
As a memento of this hour.—Leave me.

THE CAPTAIN (*in dismay*):
Princess—

> (*Thekla gestures silently to him to go and walks
> away from him. The Captain hesitates and
> starts to speak. Fräulein Neubrunn repeats
> the gesture. He leaves.*)

THEKLA *(falling upon Neubrunn's neck):*
  Good Neubrunn, show me now the love which you
  Have always vowed to me and act as my
  True friend and my companion on a journey.—
  We must be gone this very night.
NEUBRUNN: Be gone? But where?   3090
THEKLA: Where? There is only *one* place in the world!
  The place where he is buried in his tomb.
NEUBRUNN: Dear Lady, what can you accomplish there?
THEKLA: Why I should go, poor creature? You would not
  Ask that if you had ever been in love.
  There, there, is all that still remains of him.
  That single spot is all of earth for me.
  O do not hinder me! Come and make ready
  And let us think of means for our escape.
NEUBRUNN: Have you reflected on your father's anger?   3100
THEKLA: I fear no human being's anger now.
NEUBRUNN: The world's contempt! The evil tongue of gossip!
THEKLA: I go to seek a man who is no more.
  Do I then flee into his arms?—Great God,
  I flee but to the tomb of my Beloved.
NEUBRUNN: And we alone, two weak and helpless women?
THEKLA: We shall take weapons and my arm shall guard you.
NEUBRUNN: In darkness of the night?
THEKLA: Night will conceal us.
NEUBRUNN: In this harsh night of storm?
THEKLA: How soft a bed
  Was granted him beneath his horses' hooves?   3110
NEUBRUNN: And all those guard posts of the enemy!
  They will not let us pass.
THEKLA: O they are human.
  Misfortune passes free through all the earth.
NEUBRUNN: So far a journey—
THEKLA: Does the pilgrim count
  The miles that bring him to the shrine of grace?
NEUBRUNN: Will it be possible to leave this city?
THEKLA: Gold will unclose the gates for us. Just go!

NEUBRUNN: If we are recognized?
THEKLA: No one will look
  For Friedland's daughter in a fugitive.
NEUBRUNN: Where shall we find the horses for our flight?   3120
THEKLA: My equerry will get them. Go and call him.
NEUBRUNN: But will he dare without his master's knowledge?
THEKLA: He will. But go now! Hesitate no longer.
NEUBRUNN: O, and what will become of your poor mother
  When you have disappeared?
THEKLA (pondering and staring sorrowfully into space):
                          O my poor mother.
NEUBRUNN: She has already suffered much, your mother,
  Must she be stricken with this final blow?
THEKLA: I cannot spare her that.—But go now, go!
NEUBRUNN: But ponder well the thing that you are doing.
THEKLA: What there was to be pondered has been pondered.
NEUBRUNN: Once we are there, what will become of you?   [3130
THEKLA: Once there, some god will then inspire my soul.
NEUBRUNN: Your heart is full of turmoil now, dear Lady,
  And that is not the way that leads to peace.
THEKLA: To deep peace, such as he has also found.—
  O hurry, go! Waste no more words! I feel
  Myself drawn irresistibly—I do not
  Know what to call it—onward to his grave.
  Once there, I shall feel lighter instantly.
  The bond of sorrow that chokes up my heart   3140
  Will be released.—My tears will flow. O go,
  We could long since have been upon our way.
  For I shall find no peace until I have
  Escaped these walls—they crumble in upon me—
  A darkling power thrusts me forth from here
  And drives me hence.—What kind of feeling is this?
  Now all the spaces of this house are filled to thronging
  With pale and insubstantial ghostly shapes—
  I have no room—More, ever more of them!
  The hideous host of them compels me—me,   3150
  The living one—to go forth from these walls!

NEUBRUNN: You fill me, Lady, with a dread and anguish
So that I do not dare myself to stay here.
I go at once to summon Rosenberg.

(Exit Neubrunn.)

THEKLA: His spirit calls to me. These are the host
Of loyal men who died avenging him.
They level accusation of ignoble
Delay against me. *They* did not desert him
In death, who was the leader of their lives—
Those rough hearts did so much, and *I* should live! —   3160
   No! For me too that laurel wreath was twined
That decked his funeral bier. What is life led
Without love's radiance? I have resigned
And cast it off, now that its soul has fled.
O when I found you, love, who now are dead,
Life was a thing of worth. In splendor lay
Before me new and golden day,
I dreamed two hours of beauty heaven-shed.
   Beside the entrance of the world you stood
Where I had walked in cloistered reticence;   3170
A thousand suns shone on it; kind and good,
You seemed an angel stationed there who should
Conduct me out of fabled childhood thence
And sweep me to life's peak of excellence.
My first emotion was joy of the skies,
Upon your heart first fell my eyes.

   *(She falls to brooding, then starts up with signs
      of horror.)*

   And then comes Fate.—Brutal and cold
It snatches my Belovèd's gracious mold
And under the hooves of horses has him hurled.—
Such is the lot of Beauty in the world.   3180

   (Reenter Neubrunn with the equerry.)

NEUBRUNN: My Lady, here he is, and he will do it.
THEKLA: Will you get horses for us, Rosenberg?

THE EQUERRY: Yes, I will get them.

THEKLA: Will you go with us?

THE EQUERRY: My Lady, to the ends of earth.

THEKLA: But you
Cannot come back then to the Duke.

THE EQUERRY: I will
Remain with you.

THEKLA: I will reward you and
Commend you to another master. Can you
Conduct us undiscovered from this fortress?

THE EQUERRY: I can.

THEKLA: When can I leave?

THE EQUERRY: This very hour—
Where do you wish to go?

THEKLA: To—Tell him, Neubrunn.   3190

NEUBRUNN: To Neustadt.

THE EQUERRY: Good. I shall attend to it.

(Exit the Equerry.)

NEUBRUNN: Alas, here comes your mother, Lady.

THEKLA: Heavens!

(Enter the Duchess.)

THE DUCHESS: Now he has gone, I find you more composed.

THEKLA: I am composed now, Mother.—Let me go
And presently find sleep. Let Neubrunn stay with me.
I need to rest.

THE DUCHESS: And you shall do that, Thekla.
I go with reassurance, for I can
Comfort your father.

THEKLA: Good night then, dear Mother.

*(She falls upon her neck and embraces her with
great emotion.)*

THE DUCHESS: You are not wholly calm, my Daughter, yet.
Why, you are trembling greatly, and your heart   3200
Is beating audibly on mine.

THEKLA: Sleep soon
Will comfort it.—Good night, beloved Mother.   [3202]

*(As she withdraws from her mother's arms
the curtain falls.)*

ACT V

Buttler's room.
Buttler and Major Geraldin.

BUTTLER: You will pick out twelve stout dragoons and arm them
  With pikes, for no shots must be fired.—You will
  Conceal them near the dining hall, and when
  They come to serve dessert you will rush in
  And shout: Who here's a good Imperial?—I
  Will overturn the table.—You will throw
  Yourselves against those two and cut them down.
  The tower will be under guard and bolted   3210
  So that no word of this will reach the Duke.
  Go now.—You sent for Captain Deveroux
  And for Macdonald?
GERALDIN: They will come directly.

(Exit Geraldin.)

BUTTLER: Postponement is not to be risked. The very
  Inhabitants are for him. I don't know
  What madness has possessed this entire city.
  They see this Duke as some great Prince of Peace,
  Some founder of another golden age.
  The Council has allotted arms; some hundred
  Have volunteered already to stand guard   3220
  Around him. Hence we must be quick to action.
  Foes threaten from outside and from within.

(Enter Captains Deveroux and Macdonald.)

MACDONALD: We're at your orders, Sir.
DEVEROUX: What is the password?

BUTTLER: Long live the Emperor!

MACDONALD AND DEVEROUX *(startled)*:   What!

BUTTLER: Hail Austria!

DEVEROUX: But did we not swear loyalty to Friedland?

MACDONALD: Were we not brought here as protectors for him?

BUTTLER: We shield a traitor and the Empire's foe?

DEVEROUX: Why yes, you swore us into service to him.

MACDONALD: And you have followed him up here to Eger.

BUTTLER: I did so to destroy him the more surely.   3230

DEVEROUX: You *did!*

MACDONALD: Well, that's a different matter!

BUTTLER *(to Deveroux)*:   Wretch!
   Do you desert so lightly flag and duty?

DEVEROUX: The Devil, Sir! I followed your example.
   If *he's* a rogue, thought I, you can be too.

MACDONALD: We do not think, Sir. Thinking's your affair!
   You are the General, you give the commands,
   We follow you, to Hell if necessary.

BUTTLER *(mollified)*:
   Good, then! We understand each other.

MACDONALD: Yes,
   I think so.

DEVEROUX: We are soldiers of Fortuna.
   Whoever bids the highest, gets us.

MACDONALD: Right!   3240

BUTTLER: And now you shall stay honorable soldiers.

DEVEROUX: We like to be.

BUTTLER: And make your fortunes at it.

MACDONALD: That's even better.

BUTTLER: Listen.

MACDONALD AND DEVEROUX: We are listening.

BUTTLER: It is the Emperor's will and proclamation
   That Friedland should be seized dead or alive.

DEVEROUX: The edict reads that way.

MACDONALD: Dead or alive.

BUTTLER: And opulent reward awaits the man
   In lands and money who performs the deed.

DEVEROUX: It sounds good. Word from down there always does
    Sound good. We've heard this sort of thing before.   3250
    Some golden chain of favor maybe, or
    Some sway-backed horse, some paper, or the like.—
    The Duke pays better.
MACDONALD: Yes, he is terrific.
BUTTLER: But he is through. His lucky star has fallen.
MACDONALD: Are you so sure?
BUTTLER: I tell you he is through.
DEVEROUX: His luck is finished?
BUTTLER: Finished and for good.
    He is as poor as we.
MACDONALD: As poor as we?
DEVEROUX: Macdonald, it is time for us to leave him!
BUTTLER: Twenty thousand have already left him.
    We must go further, Countryman. In short—   3260
    We've got to kill him.
MACDONALD AND DEVEROUX: Kill him?
BUTTLER: I said: Kill him.—
    And I have chosen you to do it.
MACDONALD AND DEVEROUX: Us?
BUTTLER: You, Captain Deveroux and you, Macdonald.
DEVEROUX (after a pause):
    Choose someone else then.
MACDONALD: Yes, choose someone else.
BUTTLER (to Deveroux):
    You filthy coward, does that scare you? Why,
    Your thirty souls are on you as it is—
DEVEROUX: But lay hands on the General—think of it!
MACDONALD: To whom we swore an oath of loyalty!
BUTTLER: The oath is null and void from his bad faith.
DEVEROUX: No, General! Listen. I think that's too beastly. 3270
MACDONALD: That's right! We have a conscience after all.
DEVEROUX: If only it were not the chief who had
    Command of us so long, and our respect.
BUTTLER: Is that the rub?
DEVEROUX: Yes! Anybody else!

I'll run my sword into my own son's vitals
If that is what the Emperor's service needs.—
But we are soldiers, and to murder our
Commander would be sin and blasphemy
For which no monk could give us absolution.
BUTTLER: I am your Pope, I give you absolution.   3280
Make up your minds.
DEVEROUX *(stands in a quandary):* It is no use.
MACDONALD: No, it's
No use.
BUTTLER: Then go—and—send me Pestalutz.
DEVEROUX *(startled):* Send Pestalutz—Hm . . .
MACDONALD: What do you want with him?
BUTTLER: If you disdain it, there are plenty who—
DEVEROUX: No, if he must be killed, we may as well
Put in for that reward as someone else.—
What do you think, Macdonald?
MACDONALD: Yes, if he
Has got to die, and if there's no help for it,
I wouldn't leave it up to Pestalutz.
DEVEROUX *(after some reflection):*
When must he die?
BUTTLER: Tonight, this very night.   3290
The Swedes will be before the gates by morning.
DEVEROUX: You'll back me for the consequences, General?
BUTTLER: I'll back up everything.
DEVEROUX: Is it the Emperor's
Clear-cut and outright will? There are examples
Of murder loved and murderers destroyed.
BUTTLER: The edict says: alive or dead. Alive,
You see yourselves, is quite impossible.
DEVEROUX: Well, dead, then. Dead—but how do we get at him?
The city is a-swarm with Terzky troops.
MACDONALD: And there is Terzky yet besides, and Illo—   3300
BUTTLER: We shall of course start with the two of them.
DEVEROUX: They too must die?
BUTTLER: They first.

MACDONALD: Say, Deveroux,
   This is becoming quite a bloody evening.
DEVEROUX: You have a man for that job? Let me do it.
BUTTLER: It is assigned to Major Geraldin.
   Today is Mardi Gras, and at the castle
   A banquet will be held. There they will be
   Attacked while at the table and cut down.—
   Lessley and Pestalutz are in the plot—
DEVEROUX: Listen, General, you can't care too much.   3310
   Listen—Let me swap with Geraldin.
BUTTLER: The Duke presents a lesser danger.
DEVEROUX: Danger?
   Now what the Devil do you take me for?
   It is the Duke's eye, not his sword, I fear.
BUTTLER: How can his eye harm you?
DEVEROUX: By all the devils!
   You know me, and you know I am no coward.
   But look, it is not yet a week ago
   The Duke advanced me twenty golden sovereigns
   For this warm coat that I am wearing now—
   And if he sees me standing with the pike   3320
   Above him there, and then looks at my coat—
   You see—well—Devil take me! I'm no coward.
BUTTLER: The Duke gave you this warm coat that you wear,
   And you, poor fool, on that account, would scruple
   About the running through him with your sword.
   Another coat that keeps a man far warmer
   The Emperor gave to him, the princely mantle,
   And for what thanks? For treason and rebellion.
DEVEROUX: That's so. The Devil take all grateful men!
   I'll—kill him off.
BUTTLER: If you must soothe your conscience   3330
   Then you have only to remove your coat,
   And you can do it briskly and with cheer.
MACDONALD: There is another thing to be considered—
BUTTLER: What else, Macdonald, is to be considered?
MACDONALD: What good are arms and armor against him?

For he can not be wounded. He is charmed.

BUTTLER (*with a start*):
What can he—

MACDONALD: Neither thrust of sword nor bullet!
He's proof, he's frozen by the devil's magic,
You cannot penetrate his flesh, I tell you.

DEVEROUX: Yes, there was one in Ingolstadt just like him,   3340
With skin as hard as steel, and in the end
They had to beat him down with rifle-butts.

MACDONALD: I'll tell you what I'll do!

DEVEROUX: What's that?

MACDONALD: I know
A friar in the monastery here,
A Dominican and countryman of ours,
He'll dip my sword and pike in holy water
And speak a mighty blessing over them
That guarantees to help against all spells.

BUTTLER: Do that, Macdonald. But now go and pick
Some twenty, thirty sturdy lads out of   3350
The regiment and swear them to the Emperor.
And when it strikes eleven—when the watch
Has passed first rounds—lead them in silence to
The house.—I won't be far away myself.

DEVEROUX: How will we get in past the bodyguard
That mounts its watch inside the inner courtyard?

BUTTLER: I have explored the layout of the place.
I'll introduce you through a postern gate
Which is defended only by one man.
My rank and office give me access to   3360
The Duke at any hour. I will precede you
And with a sudden dagger thrust into
The guardsman's throat I'll pave the way for you.

DEVEROUX: And once we get upstairs, how do we reach
The sleeping quarters of the Duke without
The servants waking and giving the alarm?
For an imposing escort came with him.

BUTTLER: The servants are all quartered in the right wing.

He dislikes noise and lives alone up in the left one.
DEVEROUX: Macdonald, I just wish this thing were over.— 3370
    The Devil knows I have the queerest feeling.
MACDONALD: I feel the same. He's far too high a person.
    We will be taken for a pair of scoundrels.
BUTTLER: In honor, wealth, and splendor you can laugh
    At people's judgments and at people's gossip.
DEVEROUX: If only we can be so sure of honor.
BUTTLER: Dismiss your fears. You rescue crown and empire
    For Ferdinand. He will not stint rewards.
DEVEROUX: He really means to overthrow the Emperor?
BUTTLER: He does! And rob him of his life and crown! 3380
DEVEROUX: Then he would perish by the hangman's hand
    If we sent him alive on to Vienna?
BUTTLER: He could not possibly avoid that fate.
DEVEROUX: Come on, Macdonald! He shall wind up as
    A General, honorably at soldiers' hands. [3385]

(Exeunt.)

SCENE 2

A room opening into a gallery that extends far to the rear.
Wallenstein is seated at a table. The Swedish Captain is standing
in front of him.

WALLENSTEIN: My greetings to your master. I too share
    In his good fortune, and if you do not
    See me displaying quite as much delight
    As these victorious tidings might deserve,
    Believe me, it is not lack of good will. 3390
    For our success is henceforth one. Farewell!
    Accept my thanks for all your pains. The fortress
    Shall open for you when you come tomorrow.
        (Exit the Swedish Captain.)
      (Wallenstein sits in profound thought staring

straight ahead, his head resting on his hand.
Enter the Countess Terzky, who stands for some
time unnoticed by him. At last he makes a
sudden movement, catches sight of her, and
quickly gets hold of himself.)
You come from her? Has she recovered? How is she?

COUNTESS TERZKY: My sister tells me she is calmer now
Since speaking with him.—She has gone to bed.

WALLENSTEIN: Her grief will grow more gentle. She will weep.

COUNTESS TERZKY: You are not quite yourself, my Brother,
   either.
I had expected you would be more cheerful
Just after victory. Keep strong! Support us!   3400
You are our light, you are the sun to us.

WALLENSTEIN: Be calm. I am quite well.—Where is your
   husband?

COUNTESS: They've gone down to a banquet, he and Illo.

WALLENSTEIN (*gets up and walks a few steps through the room*):
It is the depth of night.—Go to your room.

COUNTESS TERZKY: O do not bid me go, let me stay with you.

WALLENSTEIN (*who has stepped to the window*):
There is a busy movement in the heavens.
The tower flag is whipped with wind, the clouds
Sweep swiftly past, the sickle of the moon
Wavers, and formless light darts through the darkness.—
No star is visible. That dull gleam yonder,   3410
The only one, is out of Cassiopeia,
And over there stands Jupiter—but now
The blackness of the stormy sky conceals him.

   (*He falls to brooding and stares fixedly out of*
   the window.)

COUNTESS TERZKY (*looking sadly at him, takes him by the hand*):
So pensive?

WALLENSTEIN: I think I would be glad if I could see him.
It is the star that shines upon my life,
The sight has often given wondrous strength.

(A pause.)

COUNTESS TERZKY: You will see him again.

WALLENSTEIN *(has again fallen into profound abstraction. He musters cheerfulness and quickly turns to the Countess):*
See him again?—O never, never.

COUNTESS TERZKY: What?

WALLENSTEIN: He's gone—He's turned to dust.

COUNTESS TERZKY: Whom do you mean? 3420

WALLENSTEIN: He is the happy one. He has concluded.
For him there is no future any more,
Fate spins no further snares for him—his life
Lies spread out gleaming and without a fold
And no dark stain is left on it. For him
No hour strikes announcing new misfortune.
He is beyond desire and fear, and subject
No longer to the guile of fickle planets.—
He is well off! But who knows what the next
Hour brings to us beshrouded in black veils! 3430

COUNTESS TERZKY: You speak of Piccolomini. How did
He die? The courier had just left you when
I came.

(Wallenstein motions her to be silent.)
O do not look back to the past.
Let us look forward into brighter days.
Rejoice in victory, forget its cost.
Today is not the day you lost your friend;
For you he died when he deserted you.

WALLENSTEIN: I shall survive this blow, I realize.
What can man not survive? With highest things
As with the least, he learns to do without. 3440
The mighty hours triumph over him.
And yet I sense what I have lost in him.
The flower has now vanished from my life,
And cold and drab I see it lie before me.
For he stood next to me like my own youth,
He made reality a dream to me,
Around the mean significance of things

He shed the golden fragrance of the dawn.—
Within the fire of his affection's warmth
Stood forth, so that I was myself astonished,   3450
The flat and tedious shapes of daily life.—
Whatever I may further strive and reach,
The Beautiful has gone, not to return.
A friend is Fortune's crown, who by his feeling
Created it, who, sharing, makes it greater.

COUNTESS TERZKY: Do not lose hope in your own strength.
    Your heart
Is rich enough to animate itself.
You love and praise in him the virtues which
You sowed in him yourself, and fostered in him.

WALLENSTEIN (walking to the door):
    Who troubles us so late at night? It is   3460
The Commandant. He brings the fortress keys.
Leave us and go now, Sister. It is midnight.

COUNTESS TERZKY: My heart is heavy leaving you today
    And restless fear besets me.

WALLENSTEIN: Fear! Of what?

COUNTESS TERZKY: You might depart in haste during the night
    And we would never find you when we woke.

WALLENSTEIN: Imagination!

COUNTESS TERZKY: O my soul has long
    Been tortured by these gloomy premonitions,
    And if I fight them down awake, they fall
    Upon my troubled heart in sombre dreams.—   3470
    Last night I dreamed I saw you sitting with
    Your former spouse at table, richly dressed.

WALLENSTEIN: That was a dream of hopeful premonition.
    That marriage was the founding of my fortune.

COUNTESS TERZKY: Today I dreamed that I was searching for you
    Within your room.—As I stepped in, it was
    Your room no longer but the monastery
    At Gitschin which you founded and where you
    Have said it is your wish to lie in death.

WALLENSTEIN: Your mind was simply occupied with that.   3480

COUNTESS TERZKY: What? You do not believe a voice of
    warning
    Speaks to us with prevision in our dreams?
WALLENSTEIN: Such voices do exist—There is no doubt.
    But I should not term them the warning voices
    Which but proclaim the Unavoidable.
    Just as the image of the sun is painted
    In mist before it rises, so do spirits
    Of mighty destinies precede their coming,
    And the next morrow walks amid today.
    It always used to make me wonder, what   3490
    Is read about the death of that fourth Henry.
    The king had sensed the spectre of the dagger
    Long in his heart before the murderer
    Ravaillac armed himself with it. Repose
    Fled from him, he was haunted in his Louvre
    And driven to the open air; the bells
    At his wife's coronation tolled as for
    A funeral; his ear fore-heard the footfalls
    That sought for him throughout the streets of Paris.
COUNTESS TERZKY: And does your inner voice give you no
    prompting?   3500
WALLENSTEIN: None. Be assured.
COUNTESS TERZKY (lost in sombre brooding):
                         And then another time
    As I pursued in haste, you ran ahead
    Of me down a long corridor, through rooms
    Of which there was no end—Doors clashed and slammed—
    Breathless I followed on, yet could not reach you—
    Then suddenly I felt myself seized from
    Behind by some cold hand, and it was you,
    You kissed me, and upon us then it seemed
    As if a scarlet covering was laid—
WALLENSTEIN: That was the scarlet carpet of my room.   3510
COUNTESS TERZKY (looking at him):
    If it should come to that—If you, who now
    Stand here before me full of life, were to—

(She falls weeping upon his bosom.)

WALLENSTEIN: The Emperor's edict worries you. Mere letters
Can deal no wounds. And he will not find hands.

COUNTESS TERZKY: But should he find them, my resolve is fixed.
I carry with me that which will console me.

(Exit the Countess Terzky.)
(Enter Gordon.)

WALLENSTEIN: The town is quiet now?

GORDON: The town is quiet.

WALLENSTEIN: I hear a jubilant music and the castle
Is bright with lights. Who are the festive ones?

GORDON: There is a banquet being given at   3520
The castle for Count Terzky and the Marshal.

WALLENSTEIN: It's for the victory.—This generation
Can not enjoy itself except at table.

(He rings. A servant enters.)

Assist me to undress. I wish to sleep.

(He picks up the keys.)

We are secured now from all enemies,
Enclosed here as we are with proven friends.
Unless I am misled entirely, such
A face as this

(looking at Gordon)

                    is no deceiver's mask.

(The servant has removed his cloak, gorget, and sash.)

Watch out! What fell there?

THE SERVANT: Your golden chain has come apart.

WALLENSTEIN: Ah, well,   3530
It had held long enough. Give it to me.

(as he gazes at the chain)

This was the first mark of the Emperor's favor.
As Archduke he bestowed it on me during
The Friaul war, and I have worn it till
Today from habit—or from superstition
If you prefer. As long as I still wore it
In faith about my neck it was to be

My talisman and link to me forever
That fleeting fortune whose first sign it was.—
So be it.—New luck must henceforth begin   3540
For me, for this spell's force is spent.
> (*The servant withdraws with the garments.*
> *Wallenstein rises, walks across the room, and*
> *finally stops pensively in front of Gordon.*)

How the old times come closer to me now.
I see myself amid the court of Burgau
Again, where we were pages once together.
We often had our quarrels. You meant well,
And used to like to play the moral preacher.
You used to lecture me for my immoderate striving
For lofty things, my trust in daring dreams,
And you would praise the golden middle course.—
Ah yes, your wisdom has ill stood the test,   3550
It has reduced you early to a man
Worn out, and, if with my more generous stars
I did not intervene now, it would leave you
To be extinguished in your lowly corner.

GORDON: Lord Duke, with easy mind the humble fisherman
Ties up his little skiff in the safe port
When he beholds great ships go down in storm.

WALLENSTEIN: Are you in port already, aged man?
Not I. My unabated spirit drives me
Still fresh and fine along the sea of life,   3560
And I call Hope my goddess still; my mind
Is still a youth, and as I now compare
Myself with you, yes, then I would make bold
To boast and say that over my brown hair
The rapid years have passed to no avail.
> (*He paces the room with long strides and stops*
> *on the opposite side of Gordon.*)

Who still calls Fortune false? She has been true
To me. She raised me from the ranks of men
With love and bore me up through life's degrees
With god-like arms of strength devoid of effort.

My ways of destiny show nothing common,   3570
Nor do the furrows of my hand. Who would
Presume to read my life by human lights?
It seemed of late that I had fallen far,
But I shall rise again, and soon high tide
Will follow swelling on this present ebb.—
GORDON: And yet I do recall a time-worn saying:
Praise not the day before the evening falls.
I would not build up hope upon long-lasting luck,
It is misfortune to which Hope is sent.
Fear should attend the heads of happy men.   3580
The scales of Destiny are never stable.
WALLENSTEIN (smiling):
I hear again the younger Gordon speaking.—
I realize that earthly things revolve
And change. The evil gods demand their toll.
The pagan ancients understood that clearly.
On that account they used to choose misfortune
Of their free will to placate jealous gods,
And human sacrifices bled for Typhon.
        (after a pause, solemnly and more quietly.)
I too have offered sacrifice to him.—
My dearest friend is dead—through fault of mine.   3590
No turn of luck can equal in delight
What this blow has occasioned me in pain.—
Fate's jealousy is sated, life for life
It took, and toward that pure beloved head
The lightning bolt has been diverted which
Was to have struck me down and shattered me.
            (Enter Seni.)
Is that not Seni coming? And as if
In terror? What brings you so late, Baptista?
SENI: Alarm for your sake, Highness.
WALLENSTEIN: What's the matter?
SENI: Flee, Highness, flee before the daybreak! Do not put 3600
Trust in these Swedes!
WALLENSTEIN: Now what makes you think that?

SENI *(his voice rising)*:
  Put no trust in these Swedes!
WALLENSTEIN: What is it then?
SENI: Do not await the coming of the Swedes!
  Disaster from false friends hangs over you,
  The signs are horrible, and closely, closely
  The nets of ruin are spread out around you.
WALLENSTEIN: Baptista, you are dreaming, fear deludes you.
SENI: O do not think that empty fear deceives me.
  Come, read it for yourself among the planets:
  Disaster from false friends hangs over you.   3610
WALLENSTEIN: My whole misfortune rises from false friends.
  This guidance should have come a little sooner,
  I need no stars by now to tell me this.
SENI: O come and see! Find out with your own eyes.
  A ghastly sign is in the House of Life,
  An enemy close by, a fiend lurks there
  Behind your own star's rays.—O heed my warning!
  Do not commit yourself unto these heathens
  Who now wage warfare on our Holy Church.
WALLENSTEIN *(smiling)*:
  Is *that* the prompter of your oracle?   3620
  Ah yes, I do recall—This Swedish pact
  Could not help but displease you.—Go to bed,
  Baptista. I fear no such signs as these.
GORDON *(who, terribly shaken by this conversation, turns to
    Wallenstein)*:
  My gracious Lord, may I say something? Good
  Advice will often fall from humble lips.
WALLENSTEIN: Speak freely.
GORDON: Lord Duke, what if it were no empty phantom
  Of fear, what if God's providence were using
  This voice to save you by a miracle!
WALLENSTEIN: You both speak as if in delirium.   3630
  How can mischance come to me from the Swedes?
  They sought this pact, it is to their advantage.
GORDON: But what if the arrival of these Swedes

Were just the thing that lends catastrophe
The wings to reach your overtrusting head?—
      (throwing himself on his knees before him)
There is still time, my Lord—
SENI *(kneeling):*   O hear him, hear him!
WALLENSTEIN: Time, and for what? Get up—Get up, I wish it.
GORDON *(rising):*
The Rhinegrave is as yet far off. Just give
The orders and this fort will close before him.
If he wants to besiege us, let him try it.   3640
But this much I will say: he will be lost,
And with him all his men, outside these walls
Before our spirit's valor is worn down.
He will find out what a heroic band
Can do, inspired by its heroic leader
Who means in earnest to make good his error.
The Emperor will be touched and reconciled,
For his heart gladly turns to clemency,
And Friedland, coming back a penitent,
Will stand far higher in his Emperor's favor   3650
Than ever stood the one who never fell.
WALLENSTEIN *(observes him with unpleasant surprise and
      astonishment and is silent for a while, displaying an
      intense inner emotion):*
Gordon—your warmth of zeal has led you far.
A boyhood friend may take some liberties.—
But, Gordon, blood has flowed. The Emperor never
Can pardon me. And even if he could,
I could not tolerate to be forgiven.
If I had known before what was to happen,
That it would cost the dearest of my friends,
And if my heart had spoken as it speaks now,
May be I would have changed my mind—may be   3660
I wouldn't.—What is left to lose? This has
Begun too seriously to end in naught.
So let things take their course! *(as he steps to the window)*
See, all is dark now.—In the castle too

It is quite still.—Hold light there, chamberlain.

> (*The chamberlain meanwhile has entered softly
> and stood at a distance with visible concern
> at the conversation. He now comes forward,
> greatly excited, and throws himself at the
> Duke's feet.*)

You too? But I quite understand why you
Should wish my peace were settled with the Emperor.
Poor man! He has a small estate down in
Carinthia and fears they'll take it from him
Because he is with me. But am I then   3670
So poor I cannot compensate my servants?
Well, I shall not force anyone. If you
Feel Fortune has abandoned me, then leave me.
A final time today you may undress me
And then go over to your Emperor's side.—
Good night, Gordon.
I wish to go and sleep a long, long sleep.
The strain of these last days has been extreme.
See to it they do not wake me too soon.

> (*He goes out. The chamberlain holds the
> light. Seni follows. Gordon remains standing
> in the darkness, watching the Duke until he
> has disappeared at the remote end of the
> gallery. Then he gives vent to his grief in
> gestures and leans sorrowfully against a
> pillar.*)

BUTTLER (*offstage*):
Stand quiet here until I give the sign.   3680
GORDON (*with a start*):
It's he. He's bringing up the murderers.
BUTTLER: The lights are out and all are deep in sleep.
GORDON: What shall I do? Attempt to rescue him?
Shall I stir up the house, arouse the guards?
BUTTLER (*appearing at the rear*):
Light shines here from the corridor. It leads

On toward the chamber of the Duke.

GORDON: But won't I
Be breaking my oath to the Emperor? Then,
If he escapes and gives the foe fresh strength,
Won't I have all the consequences on
My head?

BUTTLER *(coming somewhat nearer)*:
            Be still! Hark! Who is speaking there?   3690

GORDON: Better I leave it up to Heaven. Who
Am I to venture such great matters? If
He dies, why, *I* will not have murdered him;
His rescue would, however, be *my* doing
And I would have to take the consequences.

BUTTLER *(stepping up)*:
I know that voice.

GORDON: Buttler.

BUTTLER: Why, it is Gordon.
What are you doing? Did the Duke dismiss you
So late?

GORDON: You have your hand wrapped in a bandage?

BUTTLER: Yes, it is hurt. That Illo fought just like
A madman till we finally brought him down—   3700

GORDON *(shuddering)*:
Then they are dead?

BUTTLER: The matter is accomplished.
Is he in bed?

GORDON: Oh, Buttler!

BUTTLER: *Is* he? Tell me!
The action cannot be concealed for long.

GORDON: He is not bound to perish. Not through you!
Your hand is wounded, Heaven does not wish it.

BUTTLER: *My* hand is not required.

GORDON: The guilty ones
Are dead. For Justice' cause sufficient has
Been done. Appease her with this sacrifice!

        (The chamberlain comes down the corridor

with his finger on his lips bidding silence.)

He sleeps. O do not murder holy sleep.

BUTTLER: No, he shall die awake.

(He starts to go.)

GORDON: Alas, his heart is still   3710
Involved with earthly matters, he is not
Prepared to step before his God.

BUTTLER: Well, God
Is merciful.

(He starts to go.)

GORDON *(holding him back)*:
          Allow him this one night.

BUTTLER: One moment more and we may be betrayed.

(He starts to go.)

GORDON *(holding him back)*:
          A single hour!

BUTTLER: Let me go! What good
Would that short time be to him?

GORDON: O, time is
A wonder-working god. Within a single hour
Run many thousand grains of sand, and thoughts
Of human beings move as swift as they.
A single hour! *Your* heart may be changed,   3720
Or *his* heart may be changed—some news may come—
Some fresh event conferring happiness
May fall from heaven bringing sudden rescue,—
O what may not an hour do?

BUTTLER: You make me realize
How precious minutes are.

(He stamps his foot.)
*(Enter Macdonald and Deveroux armed
with halberds.)*

GORDON *(throwing himself between them and Buttler)*:
                    No, monster, no!

You shall go in there over my dead body,
I shall not live to see this monstrous deed.
BUTTLER *(thrusting him aside)*:
You feeble-witted dotard!

(Trumpets are heard in the distance.)

MACDONALD AND DEVEROUX: Swedish trumpets!
The Swedes have come to Eger! We must hurry.
GORDON: God save us!
BUTTLER: To your post now, Commandant!   3730

*(Gordon hurries out. The chamberlain comes
rushing in.)*

CHAMBERLAIN: Who makes noise here? Be still, the Duke is
sleeping.
DEVEROUX *(in a loud, terrible voice)*:
A friend! Now is the time for noise!
CHAMBERLAIN *(setting up a cry)*:   Help! Murder!
BUTTLER: Down with him!
CHAMBERLAIN *(pierced by Deveroux's weapon, falls at the entrance
to the gallery)*:
                    Jesus and Mary!
BUTTLER: Break down the doors!

*(They step over the corpse and go down the
corridor. Offstage two doors in succession are
heard being smashed in.—Muffled voices—
Sound of weapons—then suddenly profound
silence.)*
(Enter Countess Terzky with a candle.)

COUNTESS TERZKY: Her chamber is deserted, she can nowhere
Be found. And Fräulein Neubrunn too is missing
Who was to stay with her.—Can she have fled?
But where can she have gone? We must make haste
To follow after her, rouse everyone!
How will the Duke receive this fearful news?—
If only now my husband would return from   3740
The banquet! Is the Duke awake, I wonder?

It seemed to me I heard the sound of voices
And footsteps. I will listen at the door
Hark! What was that? They're running up the stairs.

(*Enter Gordon running and out of breath.*)

GORDON: I was mistaken—It is not the Swedes.
You must proceed no further—Buttler—God!
Where is he?
                    (*as he catches sight of the Countess*)
                    Countess, tell me where—
COUNTESS TERZKY: Have you come from the castle? Where is my
husband?
GORDON (*in horror*):
Your husband—Do not ask me that! Go in—

(*He starts to go.*)

COUNTESS TERZKY (*detaining him*):
O not before you have revealed to me—   3750
GORDON (*urgently*):
The entire world depends upon this moment!
In Heaven's name, go in, go in!—While we
Are talking—God in Heaven—
                    (*shouting*)   Buttler! Buttler!
COUNTESS TERZKY: But he is at the castle with my husband.

(*Buttler steps forth from the gallery.*)

GORDON (*catching sight of him*):
I was mistaken—It is not the Swedes—
It's the Imperials who have broken in—
The Lieutenant General sends me, he will be here
Himself directly—You should go no further—
BUTTLER: He comes too late.
GORDON (*throws himself against the wall*):
                    O God! O God of Mercy!
COUNTESS TERZKY (*with a presentiment of the truth*):
What is too late? Who will be here directly?   3760
Octavio has broken into Eger?
We are betrayed! We are betrayed! Where is

The Duke?

> *(She hurries toward the corridor. Enter Seni
> from the gallery with all the signs of horror.)*

SENI: O bloody deed! O deed of monstrous horror!

COUNTESS TERZKY: What
Has happened, Seni?

> *(Enter a page.)*

THE PAGE: O this pitiable sight!

> *(Enter servants with torches.)*

COUNTESS TERZKY: What is it? In God's name!

SENI: Do you still ask?
In there the Duke lies murdered, and your husband
Has been stabbed at the castle.

> *(The Countess stands as though frozen.)*
> *(Enter a chamber lady in haste.)*

THE CHAMBER LADY: Help! Help! The Duchess!

> *(Enter the Burgomaster full of horror.)*

THE BURGOMASTER: What a cry of grief
Is rousing up the sleepers of this house?   3770

GORDON: A curse has fallen on your house forever!
The Duke lies murdered in this house of yours.

THE BURGOMASTER: O God forbid!

> *(He rushes out.)*

FIRST SERVANT: Flee! Flee! Before they murder
Us   all!

SECOND SERVANT *(carrying silver objects)*:
Out this way! There the lower passageways are guarded.

CRIES OFFSTAGE: Make way for the Lieutenant General!

> *(At these words the Countess rouses from her
> inaction, gets control of herself, and goes
> swiftly out.)*

The gate there! Man the gate! Hold back the mob!

*(Enter Octavio Piccolomini with his retinue.
Deveroux and Macdonald emerge from the
background at once with halberds. Wallenstein's corpse, wrapped in a scarlet carpet, is
carried across the rear of the stage.)*

OCTAVIO *(entering swiftly)*:
Impossible! It cannot be! Buttler!
Gordon! I can't believe it. Tell me No!

GORDON *(without answering, gestures towards the rear. Octavio
looks and stands in horror)*:

DEVEROUX *(to Buttler)*:
Here is the Golden Fleece, the princely sword.

MACDONALD: Is it your will that chancery—

BUTTLER *(pointing to Octavio)*:   Here stands   3780
The only man to issue orders here.

*(Deveroux and Macdonald retire respectfully.
Everyone disperses silently until only Buttler.
Octavio, and Gordon remain on stage.)*

OCTAVIO *(turning to Buttler)*:
Was this your purpose, Buttler, when we parted?
O God of Righteousness, I raise my hand on this!
I am not guilty of this monstrous deed.

BUTTLER: Your hand remains entirely clean. You have
Made use of mine instead.

OCTAVIO: Infamous villain!
Why did you have to make this misuse of
Our master's orders and put blood and horror
Of murder on our Emperor's sacred name?

BUTTLER *(coolly)*:
I only carried out the Emperor's verdict.   3790

OCTAVIO: O curse of kings, which to their words imparts
A frightful force of life, which to their swift
And transient thoughts will link immediately
The fixed, irrevocable deed! Must it
Have been obeyed so soon? Could you not grant
A time for mercy to the man of mercy?

The angel of mankind is time.—To join
The sudden execution to the sentence
Befits the changeless Deity alone.
BUTTLER: Why do you rail at me? What is my crime?   3800
I have performed a noble action here,
Delivering the Empire from a dreaded
Opponent and I lay claim to reward.
The only differentiation is
Between your deed and mine: where you had whetted
The arrow, I despatched it. You sowed blood
And stand aghast beholding blood sprung up.
I always knew what I was doing, hence
Success can neither frighten nor surprise me.
Have you some further errand to assign me?   3810
This very instant I am leaving for
Vienna. I shall lay my bleeding sword
Before the Emperor's throne and claim the praise
Which swift, punctilious obedience may
Demand of judges who are truly just.

(Exit Buttler.)
(Enter the Countess Terzky, pale and haggard.
Her speech is slow and faint, without passion.)

OCTAVIO *(going toward her)*:
O Countess Terzky, did it have to come
To this? These are the consequences of
Unhappy deeds.
COUNTESS TERZKY: These are your actions' fruits.—
The Duke is dead, my husband too; the Duchess
Lies in death's throes; my niece has disappeared.   3820
This house of splendor and magnificence
Stands desolate, and out through all the doors
The menials, terrified, are rushing forth.
I am the last one here, and I have closed it.
Here I deliver you the keys.
OCTAVIO *(with profound sorrow)*:   O Countess,
My house is desolate as well.

COUNTESS TERZKY: Who yet
  Must perish? Who must be mistreated yet?
  The Duke is dead, the Emperor's vengeance can
  Be satisfied. I beg you, spare the old retainers
  So that the love and loyalty of faithful   3830
  Persons will not be reckoned as a crime.
  My brother was surprised too fast by Fate,
  He was not able to consider them.
OCTAVIO: O, no mistreatment, Countess! And no vengeance!
  The heavy guilt is heavily atoned,
  The Emperor is appeased, and from the father
  Nothing passes to the daughter but
  His fame and worth. The Empress honors your
  Misfortune, opens her maternal arms
  To you in sympathy. No more of fear   3840
  Therefore! Take confidence, commit yourself
  To the Imperial mercy.
COUNTESS TERZKY (with a glance toward heaven):
                    I commit
  Myself unto a greater Master's mercy.—
  Where shall the ducal corpse be laid to rest?
  At Gitschin, in the cloister he himself
  Once founded, rests the Countess Wallenstein.
  Beside her, who created his first fortunes,
  He wished some day, from gratitude, to sleep.
  I beg you to permit him to rest there.
  Let me entreat like favor for my husband's   3850
  Remains. The Emperor has possession of
  Our castles. Let us only be permitted
  A grave beside the graves of our forefathers.
OCTAVIO: How pale you grow—You're trembling, Countess.—
  What
  Interpretation shall I give your words?
COUNTESS TERZKY (summons her last strength and speaks with
      vivacity and nobility):
  You think too highly of me to imagine that
  I would survive the downfall of my house.

We did not feel ourselves to be too lowly
To reach our hands out toward a royal crown.—
But that was not to be.—And yet our thoughts are royal,   3860
And we esteem a free, courageous death
More worthy than a life deprived of honor.—
The poison I have . . .

OCTAVIO: Save her! Help!
COUNTESS TERZKY: It is too late.
My fate in a few minutes' time will be
Fulfilled.

(She walks away.)

GORDON: O house of murder and of horror!

*(Enter a courier with a letter. Gordon steps
up to him.)*

What is it? This is the Imperial seal.

*(He has read the name on it and hands the letter
to Octavio with a reproachful glance.)*

It's for *Prince* Piccolomini.   [3867]

*(Octavio is startled and casts his eyes
sorrowfully toward heaven.)*

THE END